# THE
# PRAIRIE
# WORLD

# THE
# PRAIRIE
# WORLD

## David F. Costello

WITH PHOTOGRAPHS BY THE AUTHOR

UNIVERSITY OF MINNESOTA PRESS
Minneapolis

**Library of Congress Cataloging in Publication Data**

Costello, David Francis, 1904–
  The prairie world.

  Bibliography: p.
  Includes index.
  1. Prairie ecology —Great Plains.   2.   Natural
history —Great Plains.   I.   Title.
QH104.5.G73C67   1980      574.5'2643'0978      80-10299
ISBN 0-8166-0938-1

# *Acknowledgments*

---

A LL THINGS cannot be included in a book of this kind on the prairie. Many people have made helpful suggestions about what should be included. As usual, when I started writing, my friends understood my preoccupation and left me alone with my labor when they would have preferred to visit, go fishing, or go traveling with me. I thank them. I am grateful in particular to my former Forest Service colleagues in grass research, W. M. Johnson, Gradon E. Klipple, and George T. Turner, who always were tolerant of my digressions to observe the antics, home lives, and ecological relations of birds, mammals, reptiles, and insects on the prairie. Donald B. Lawrence, University of Minnesota, was especially helpful in obtaining vegetation maps and historical information. Kathryn Flaherty of Portland, Oregon, gave me the benefit of her expert hand in drafting the map of the mid-continental prairie.

My greatest debt is for inspiration and knowledge obtained through travel, discussion, and correspondence over many years with four friends—dedicated students of the prairie—who are not here to see this book: F. W. Albertson, Fort Hays Kansas State College; F. E. Clements, Carnegie Institution of Washington; H. L. Shantz, U.S. Forest Service; and J. E. Weaver, University of Nebraska.

Grateful acknowledgment is made to Ross & Haines, Inc., Minneapolis, for permission to quote Geo. Catlin's description of a prairie fire, taken from his "Letters and Notes on the Manners, Customs, and Condition of the North American Indians"; and to *Nature Magazine*, which published some of my prairie observations, now written in slightly different style in these pages.

DAVID F. COSTELLO

*Portland, Oregon*

*To my teachers, who taught*
*even when they were not teaching*

# Contents

# *Introduction*

THIS BOOK IS ABOUT A LANDSCAPE that at first sight seems to consist only of earth and sky—the mid-continental prairie of North America. But the prairie is more than earth and sky. Out of its earth comes all the living plant material that nurtures innumerable animals, both mighty and humble. Out of its sky come wind, rain, and the climatic influences that make life possible, that shape the face of the land, and that set limits to the boundary of the prairie.

The prairie, at second sight, presents a remarkable diversity of environments—rolling grasslands, seemingly limitless level plains, bluffs, forested river bottoms, lakes, and ponds. In each of these environments, inseparably linked with the grassland about them, are a myriad of plants and animals, all acting and interacting with one another under the pressure of nonliving forces—soil, weather, geologic change—that have been active since the prairie began.

When one begins to understand its individual living creatures, the prairie becomes more than a place of colorful vistas or lonely beauty. It becomes a dynamic entity in which plants, mammals, birds, insects, fish, and minute unseen creatures are constantly struggling among themselves, and with one another, for existence. When one begins to see how the living things of the prairie have adjusted themselves to living together so their kinds can be perpetuated through generation after generation, then one comes to an appreciation of the complexity as well as the inner beauty of the prairie.

This is a book about relationships. If one thinks long enough about the one-celled plants in a prairie pond he may ultimately see their relationships with the eagle that circles in the sky above. It takes trillions of one-celled plants to support millions of microscopic animals in the pond; millions of minute animals to support thousands of minnows; hundreds of minnows to support dozens of larger fish; a few fish, frogs, and birds to support a mink, which the eagle catches in an unwary moment. This is just one of the prairie food chains. Others have fewer links: grass to rabbit to live coyote; dead coyote to scavenger insects to birds to hawks; grass to bison; bison to wolf; dead wolf to bacteria and insects. The interlocking of all these chains, involving population shifts in both producer and consumer organisms, results in the ever-changing web of life on the prairie.

The patterns taken by living and nonliving things and their individual contributions to the web of life are what make the prairie fascinating in its sameness and in its diversity. If one considers these things thoughtfully, he comes to the realization that nothing is insignificant in nature. The mere presence of anything, living or nonliving, seems to be sufficient justification for its existence. Its presence answers the question so often asked by my friends about a grasshopper, a toad, a tuft of tumblegrass, a snake, a hawk, or a worm: "What good is it?" I answer: "It is good in that it plays a part in the web of life." If it were not there, some other creature would tend to be there. And, if a great many creatures were not there, and some others were there, then the place would not be the same. The prairie would not be the prairie, just as the prairie is not the prairie where man has removed many plants with his grazing animals, and has destroyed nearly all plants and animals by covering the land with his crops of wheat and corn, his highways, and his cities.

This is a book about one of the great heritages of man, the grassland on which we have built a civilization and from the soil of which we feed ourselves and a large number of other people in the world. It is concerned with the prairie past and present. There is still much prairie to be seen. For those who cannot go to see the prairie itself, the book perhaps will give an insight into its vastness, complexity, unity, and variety of plant and animal life. For those who can go, it may help them to see for themselves what a magnificent grassland can produce.

# THE
# PRAIRIE
# WORLD

*The beauty of grass on the windswept prairie is unforgettable. Under favorable rainfall grasses exhibit marvelous productivity.*

# 1

## *The Grassland Sea*

YEARS AGO, WHEN I WAS A BOY and the prairie was still there, I went regularly to see a quartzite boulder that stood high above the grasses in a farm pasture that belonged to my Uncle John, who lived south of Tecumseh, Nebraska. I liked to climb on this boulder and feel its warmth stored from the heat of the summer sun. It fascinated me because it was the only boulder on the landscape. It was higher than my head, long enough to fill a wagon box, and so heavy no one ever thought of moving it. It was quite the largest rock I had ever seen.

In my boyhood simplicity I never wondered why it was there, if it came from any other place, or even if it had to come from somewhere. But the speculations of my elders about this rock were more interesting than fairy tales. Some said it was a meteor from outer space. Others insisted that frost had heaved it from the ground. One farmer, who always could see arrowheads better than the rest of us, believed that Indians had placed it there to cover the grave of a great chief. No one related it to Pleistocene geology or to the great ice sheets that once flowed down from the pole to cover almost half of the North American continent.

In those days I never wondered about the history or the true nature of the prairie around this boulder. But the "devil's darning needles" produced each year by the needlegrasses made excellent darts for throwing at people's clothing. I discovered early how the awns, or bristles, became twisted when dry and how they squirmed and un-curled when I breathed on them. Years later, I learned that this mecha-nism literally plants these grass seeds by screwing them into the ground as the weather changes from wet to dry and back to wet again. I also learned that needlegrasses have been around for some millions of years, their fossil seeds having been found in rocks of the Tertiary period of geological time.

There were other grasses near my boulder. I used to brush the "ticklegrasses" on my dog's nose to make him sneeze. Blue grama, one of the most widely distributed of the prairie grasses, intrigued me because its inflorescences looked like little flags. On sandy areas the big bluestems reached higher than my head, especially in autumn, when their seed stalks, branched at the top, resembled turkey feet. And always in early autumn the place was showy with yellow sunflowers and purple asters.

I knew another prairie that had abundant wildlife. Its upper edge was bordered by bur oaks and hickories. Its sides halfway down the slope were fringed with green ash and a shrubby mixture of hazel, dogwood, sumac, chokecherries, and wild plums. A great host of insects and insect-eating birds lived in this shrubby border. Skunks, opossums, rabbits, squirrels, mice, pocket gophers, and woodchucks found food and shelter in this prairie-forest edge according to their needs.

At the foot of the slope, where the prairie merged with red elm and basswood trees a deep spring of cold, gin-clear water gave birth to a full-fledged tinkling brook that gathered volume from other springs as it wandered down to the floodplain of the Missouri River. Carp used to come up from the big river to spawn in the lower reaches of this brook in such numbers they filled the stream bed from bank to bank. My boyhood friends and I found it great sport to sit in some of the deeper pools until the carp jostled themselves into our overalls. Then grasping the cloth around our ankles we would scramble up the bank, our pant legs bulging with water, and release our holds to see who could cascade the largest number of fish onto the ground. It was exciting business because the fish tickled as they squirmed and flapped against our bare skins.

Many creatures visited the spring. Mink and muskrat tracks in the soft mud were generally present. Track patterns along the brook showed clearly where raccoons had felt with their hands in crayfish funnels for morsels of food. My grandfather told me he once saw a whitetail deer drink at this spring in the year 1880. On humid summer afternoons when the thunderheads were building it was fun to chase the water striders across a cloud reflected in the spring before taking a refreshing drink.

*The windmill, a symbol of the prairie, pumps a never-ending supply of water for thirsty cattle.*

I did not realize then that the water in this spring flowed from sub-terranean channels under the prairie. Nor did I realize how the prairie maintained the spring, the brook, and the habitat for a multitude of birds, insects, and mammals. Then a farmer broke the sod in 1918 and planted the field to corn. In 1930, the brook became an intermittent stream; it ceased to flow in late July that year. In 1934, the year of the great drought, the spring died and the brook never flowed again.

As I grew older and wanderlust took me from home I learned that my own little prairies were merely small examples of a larger grassland that stretched beyond horizons unimagined in my youth. In the beginning, the great mid-continental prairie extended westward from the forest of broad-leaved trees in what is now Pennsylvania and Ohio to the Rocky Mountains and southward from southern Canada to the Gulf of Mexico. Other grasslands similar to the great central prairie and the high plains grasslands existed under the arid climate of northern New Mexico, Arizona, and southwestern Texas. The Palouse grasslands, thick with bunchgrasses, occurred in Oregon and Washington east of the Cascade Mountains. When the explorers came to the Great Valley in California they found magnificent grasslands dominated by purple needlegrass (*Stipa pulchra*). Together these grasslands made up the prairie formation, the most extensive natural vegetation type on the North American continent.

The great prairie in the center of the continent had many geographic variations and flourished under different climates. Its botanical composition varied from place to place as did its indigenous mammals, reptiles, birds, and insects. But its universal characteristic was the dominance of grasses. Even though the prairie supported a wealth of showy broad-leaved herbs and shrubs, the vegetation offered no obstruction to vision. Its endless vistas were relieved by slopes, hills, ravines, ponds, lakes, streams, and rivers. Trees and shrubs grew along the watercourses and under the protecting escarpments and ridges developed by geologic uplift, erosion, and deposition by wind and water through the ages.

The large mammals—bison, pronghorn, deer, and elk—contributed to the physiognomy of the landscape by their presence in enormous numbers and by their grazing effects on the vegetation. Because of the high visibility on the prairie, animal adaptations and habits were adjusted accordingly. The prairie dogs, the ground squirrels, and their enemies, the coyotes, foxes, hawks, and eagles, possessed keen eyesight as an essential part of their survival equipment.

Before the coming of white men, the prairie was not empty of human life. Man was present during Pleistocene time and for ten thousand years or more lived under various forms of primitive culture. The natural state of the prairie found by the first Europeans was the condition brought about by the interrelations of climate, soil, plants, animals, and men who had come from Asia thousands of years before.

This prairie in the natural state was the grassland that covered one-third of the continent in the early morning of October 12, 1492, a date which marks the beginning of one of the greatest changes in history. The three ships of Columbus, sailing westward, had encountered migrating birds that set him on the course toward a new land. Some of these birds previously had made the trip northward in the spring over the vast, uncharted prairies of the mid-continent and now were winging down the eastern coast to the West Indies or across the Gulf of Mexico to another unknown continent. They had been doing this for millennia, since man had not disturbed their environment or hunted them to near extinction, as they would be hunted in the years to come.

On the uncharted prairies of the new continent there were only the Indians and the physical and biological elements that periodically destroyed parts of the living environment and then interacted to make them whole again. The scars made by drought, flood, wind erosion, overgrazing by game animals, fire, the searing heat of summer, and the blinding blizzards of winter made temporary wounds on the face of a landscape too large for the whole panorama of the grassland to be destroyed.

The prairie was a great productive land that absorbed generation after generation of Red Men, who did not conquer the sod, the marshes, or the sandy wastes by toil. They had no need to destroy the prairie. They lived lives of violence and insecurity but not of poverty, since the lordly bison and the stately antelope were always available with their meat for food and their skins for shelter and clothing.

The prairie contained no forms of civilization or marks of culture as Europeans had known them for centuries. The only arenas were the fighting grounds of the buffalo, where mighty bulls battled for the privilege of selecting their harems. The only theatres were the booming grounds of the prairie grouse, where the gaudy males strutted on their earthen stages to catch the fancy of somber females. The only temples were the grotesque carvings of water and wind in the badlands. The only poetry, of spirit or form, was the poetry of grass in motion, buffeted by the wind. The only music was the music of bird song. The only warnings from the spirit world were the flickering lightning and the crash of thunder from the towering fortresses of cumulus clouds.

For many years after Columbus landed in the New World there were no records concerning the nature of the original prairie. Even reports of intrepid marches to the west, by Narváez and Cabeza de Vaca in 1528–36, De Soto in 1539–42, Coronado in 1540–42, Vérendrye and sons in 1742, and Lewis and Clark in 1804–1805, left much to be desired concerning the detailed nature of the prairies and their plant and animal inhabitants. Biological records written by the early travelers generally were poor because scientific knowledge was not far advanced and plant families of the New World were strange even to scientists. Descriptions of the plants awaited the attention of botanists who lived in Europe or who came to America and gave the first competent accounts of the forest and grassland vegetation.

Many of the plants were described by early observers such as the botanist André Michaux, and by J. M. Peck (1834) and H. L. Ellsworth (1837). In 1845, C. W. Short told how the prairies increased in magnitude west of the Wabash River, and noted that the scenery was pleasing to the eye. F. Gerhard (1857) found the undulating prairies of Illinois charming in summer and magnificent in winter. Other writers found the prairies striking in appearance, exhilarating in extent, graceful in outline, and of infinite diversity in their profusion of light, color, and

*Small oak woodlands, extending from Oklahoma far into Texas, alternate with strips of prairie.*

changing aspects brought on by the weather and the advance of the seasons.

Daniel Boone in his explorations of Kentucky rejoiced in the "elbow room" of the wilderness, which was not all forest. Many parts of that country were level or only moderately hilly and covered with open prairie made delightful by carpets of grass and flowers. Buffalo and elk grazed there in such abundance that one hunter counted a thousand animals in the vicinity of one salt lick.

Explorers along the Ohio River as early as 1774 noted the abundance of wild game, particularly turkeys, in the woods and intermingled grasslands. Reverend Timothy Flint, a frontier preacher, stated that the middle western prairies were diminutive replicas of the larger western ones. Many other travelers noted the beauty of the prairies east of the Mississippi and remarked that the only clumps of wood were those along the river bottoms and on moist ravines on the hillsides.

In Illinois the first white settlers saw prairies fringing the wooded bottoms where the rivers periodically overflowed and fertilized their floodplains with rich black soil. Many of the unforested bottomlands were swampy and covered with "rip gut" grass that grew ten feet tall so that men became lost on the labyrinthine trails made by game animals.

Where the original village of Chicago stood on the west shore of Lake Michigan there was much level prairie. When I first attended the University of Chicago I was amazed to learn that the campus was built on what was once a prairie swamp. But civilization had since covered the land for many miles north, west, and south of the campus. Many years ago we botanical students found it necessary to go to the vicinity of Ashburn, Illinois, to study relatively undisturbed prairies.

The prairies west of Chicago contained all the familiar grasses I had known in Nebraska beyond the Missouri River. On my first ecological excursion to these prairies with Dr. Henry C. Cowles I encountered other plants I had known in southern Nebraska but had been unable to name in my boyhood. The black-eyed Susan (*Rudbeckia hirta*), which I recently saw by the millions in Oklahoma, was there. So were the blazing star (*Liatris spicata*), many-flowered aster (*Aster multiflorus*), compass-plant (*Silphium laciniatum*), and the ironweed (*Vernonia fasciculata*), which for some reason I have always associated with butterflies. There I first saw *Eryngium yuccaefolium*, which belongs to the carrot family. Its rigid, leathery yuccalike leaves and its white or blue flowers in dense bracted heads attracted me because they are so unlike the usual umbel-type inflorescence characteristic of most herbs in the carrot family. Its common name, rattlesnake master, implanted it in my memory, and since then I have always associated snakes with *Eryngium*.

There still remain on the Illinois landscape many tracts of relatively undisturbed prairie. The majority of these prairies have never been plowed, probably because they occur on loess bluffs, mounds, and steep slopes of glacial drift. The vegetation of sixty-one of these so-called *hill prairies*, a term originally used by Dr. Arthur G. Vestal of the University of Illinois, has been described by Robert A. Evers. Many of the important grasses of these prairies are the same species that were seen, but not described, by the early travelers on the western prairies and plains.

The German explorer F. A. Wislizenus, on his way west in 1839, crossed the tall-grass prairie without naming a single one of its grasses. John C. Frémont, who marched by way of the Santa Fe Trail and then the Oregon Trail in 1842, seemed to be more impressed by showy herbs and shrubs than by the grasses which supported millions of buffalo. He specifically mentioned the false indigo, the sunflowers, and the sagebrush that usurped the place of grasses in Wyoming. On his second expedition in 1843–44 he was impressed by the sight of Kansas Indian women digging prairie potatoes (*Psoralea esculenta*). He also mentioned red three-awn (*Aristida longiseta*), that grew in western Kansas, but did not list the major grasses that covered the prairie for hundreds of miles. Like other explorers he recorded his first sighting of prairie dogs and buffalo.

When the emigrants began to flood the trails of the early explorers they saw an unnatural prairie. They stuck to the trails and followed the river bottoms and missed the endless upland grasslands. Much of the overgrazing they encountered had been done by livestock moving along the trails. In 1849, when Major Osborne Cross led a regiment from Fort Leavenworth to Oregon, four thousand wagons and fifty thousand animals bound for California already had gone ahead of his dragoons on the south side of the Platte River.

Many conflicting descriptions of the prairie were written, depending on the year, the season, and the locality. Some writers spoke of the grasslands as deserts. Others wrote of the freshness of spring, when the whole plain was covered with the sky-blue flowers of spiderwort (*Tradescantia virginiana*) and the light red of phlox (*Phlox aristata*) woven into a vast carpet of green. Many travelers who had been

*Constant winds have caused massive transportation of soil since prehistoric times. Destruction of grass cover by grazing animals results in this type of erosion in the Nebraska sandhills.*

[ 9 ]

familiar with the eastern prairies intermingled with forests took the tall grasses for granted. Others mentioned the timber of hickory, oak, walnut, elm, cottonwood, and ash, while travelers on the high plains in late summer noted the short grass, hard soil, cacti, and scarcity of wood and concluded that the country was uninhabitable and never would be settled.

The constant undulations of the terrain immediately west of the Missouri and the waving of tall grasses in the wind reminded many travelers of the waves of the ocean. Lieutenant J. W. Abert, who traveled out of Fort Leavenworth in 1845, saw the rolling prairie as a series of gentle curves, one swell melting into another. He noted that the whole country was verdant with the rank growth of tall grasses. He observed the relation of the pocket gopher to the tall grasses and the prairie dogs to the short grasses. In western Kansas he noted abandoned buffalo wallows and stated that even the bleached bones left upon the plains by the hunters had long since moldered away.

The early travelers said little about the climate of the prairie, although they recorded the difficulties brought on by drought, blizzards, and floods. They did not relate extremes and deficiencies of rainfall to kinds of vegetation; nor did they have a basis for mapping climatic zones, although they knew that in general the prairie varied from humid to semiarid as they traveled westward. Only in recent decades have climatologists devised indexes of temperature-precipitation-evaporation and other factors to explain the relation of climate and weather to the problems of biology. But, out on the prairie, the wind and the sky tell more of the beauty, the fury, and the silence than all the thermometers, barometers, and weather gauges put together.

On the vast open grasslands you can look into the sky, feel the wind, and know hours ahead what the weather will be. In the years I spent with my research colleagues on the prairies we made our own wind scales. A strong breeze of twenty-five to thirty miles per hour tossed the horned larks in the air while the hawks still rode out the wind. If the temperature dropped to forty degrees, and the wind blew forty miles an hour, we added a heavy coat, put on our hunting caps and pulled the flaps over our ears.

Our windmills turned their faces from the wind and shut off when the wind blew at twenty to twenty-five miles per hour. In autumn the Russian thistles ran freely before the wind at thirty miles per hour and pushed down fences by concerted action at seventy miles per hour.

At forty to fifty miles per hour dust clouds streamed off fields like smoke from vast stationary fires. At wind speeds above that, the whole landscape turned yellow with the soil-laden air. At sixty to seventy miles per hour the hum of our telephone wires rose to a screaming cadence and boards jumped along the ground. At seventy to one hundred miles per hour, when the Chinook blew, tin roofs from cow sheds sailed into the sky, twisting and turning like kites with broken strings. The Chinook lifted ducks from their acre-sized rafts on frozen lakes and made them fly backward until they could tack into the wind and return to huddling spots behind protective ice ridges.

The prairie winds touched our senses in many ways. The winds made different sounds on grass, on buildings, on wire, and on sand. In protected creek bottoms we could hear it roar, whistle, and rumble above, while near at hand its fingers scarcely plucked at our sleeves. On dry spring days it tasted sweet from the flower fields, or gritty from the sandhills, or salty from the alkali flats. It rippled the prairie, or it made giant grass billows that rolled down over the hills. It made the eagles and buzzards constantly adjust their airfoils to maintain a steady course in the sky. When the breeze was strong the curlews and killdeers called the loudest. Then the cattle and horses, unlike the bison that faced into the storm, turned their tails and drifted with the wind.

The caprice of the wind is evident everywhere on the prairie. The wind plants the seeds of grasses and forbs by its vagaries near the ground. It cleans the sand out of creek bottoms in summer and fills them with snow in winter. It cuts off seedling trees with sandblasts, stirs up wind devils on hot summer days, and breeds violent tornadoes that leave devastation in their paths.

In summer, on the western prairie, the wind is persistent but moderate and steady, mostly from the northwest. Its direction may partly explain why the harvester ants have their doorways mostly on the southeast sides of their mounds. With the evening calm the air settles in layers with different temperatures, which we discerned by climbing our highest windmill.

In summer evenings we often dumbfounded strangers by making our windmill pump water in utter calm. By leaving the pump rod connected and the mill in gear, we worked the pump handle and got the fan started. With diligent pumping we made the fan go faster and faster until it created a turbulence that locally disturbed the fine balance between the air temperature layers. A breeze then started up and frequently the mill ran for several minutes, long enough to pump us a drink of water. Gradually the disturbance subsided and all was calm again.

We now know much more about wind and other climatic factors on the prairie than the early travelers ever dreamed about. Temperature, moisture, and solar radiation are essential features of any habitat, and in combination with minerals in the soil they determine to a large extent the community life, the distribution, and the abundance of plants and animals in any given locality. The ecology of the prairie, of course, is more complex than the mere interaction of plants and animals to climate and their local environment. In subsequent chapters we shall examine the dynamic nature of the prairie and the adaptations of its organisms by noting some of their life histories, structures, and physiological responses to the grassland habitat. Many of the close relations of organisms have been in process of development for a long time; some of them are bound up with the origin of the prairie itself.

The forming of the prairie is obscured in the mists of time. Like all things on earth it can be traced back to the Archeozoic, beginning some 3.6 billion years ago; indirect evidence indicates the existence of living things in that era. Primitive plants and animals increased in complexity through the one billion years of the Proterozoic Era while the earth was being reworked by tremendous volcanoes, extensive erosion, and repeated glaciations.

During the age of ancient life in the following Paleozoic Era, which lasted for some 365 million years, lands were submerged and rose again from the seas, and mountains were formed. In this same era land plants appeared, and fishes, reptiles, and insects began the long process of diversification that ended in the extinction of some and the production of others which were the ancestors of our modern plants and animals.

Strange animals and plants appeared in the Mesozoic Era, which lasted for about 165 million years. In this era continents were exposed, inland seas and swamps were prevalent, and in the Cretaceous Period near the end of the Mesozoic Era the Andes, Alps, Himalayas, and Rocky Mountains were formed. Seed ferns and ancient gymnosperms, relatives of our conifer trees, became extinct. Seed-bearing plants, both broad-leaved and grasslike, became common. Dinosaurs and toothed birds reached their peak and then became extinct.

The real beginning of the prairie occurred in the Cenozoic, the last of the great geological eras, known as the age of mammals. In the Tertiary Period, the beginning of which dates back about 60 million

*Mixed prairie grasses blanket a vast expanse of land in the Great Plains and provide food for numerous herds of cattle such as these Herefords.*

years, geologic conditions became favorable for much plant and animal life as we now know it. No continental seas existed, the climate became much warmer, and conditions for living things remained favorable until the four glaciations of the Ice Age extinguished many species of plants and most of the great mammals.

In the Miocene and Pliocene epochs, which covered a period of some 25 million years, mountains rose in western North America and created a continental climate favorable to grasslands. Ancient forests declined, grasslands became widespread, flowering plants evolved, and elephants, horses, and camels almost like our modern species flourished on the ancient prairies.

The Pleistocene, which began about one million years ago, was a time of continuous change. There were four major ice advances and retreats. The interglacial periods appear to have been warmer than the present. In the northern portion of the continent this waxing and waning of the glacial ice displaced the floras and faunas and greatly changed their areas of distribution. The fossil evidence indicates, however, that most plants of the modern prairie were present during Pleistocene time, although certain species have migrated from other regions during postglacial time.

It is possible to see evidence of this history of the prairie if you know where and how to look. East of Gillette, Wyoming, you can stand among the grasses, look into the deep pit of an open coal mine, and see the mechanical shovels loading trucks that carry the coal to the steam power plant across U.S. Highway 16. Here, radiant energy stored in the Paleozoic swamps more than 300 million years ago is being converted into modern electrical energy. The thought occurs to you that this place was not always prairie. Since the great forests of seed ferns and conifers grew in that ancient swamp the restless earth has passed through periods of mountain uplift, erosion, deposition of sediments by wind and water, hardening of the rocks, volcanic activity, and more erosion and mountain uplifts.

You can see more history if you stand on the hogbacks north of Denver, Colorado, at the western shoreline of the prairie sea, and observe the strata dipping eastward under Colorado, Kansas, and Nebraska. Behind you are the Rocky Mountains, still being stripped of their material, which is being deposited by erosion far out on the plains and prairies.

You can contemplate the power of the wind as a force in nature if you explore the billowing prairie on the sandhills of western Nebraska. In early Pleistocene time, a million years ago, the post-Pliocene valleys were filled with sands and gravels capped with silts. After the continental glaciation, the windblown dust known as loess was blown up from alluvial flats, and from the sandhill region, and carried by the prevailing winds over Nebraska and into Iowa and Missouri.

The loess mantle, which now bears some of the prairie remnants, is 150 feet or more in depth in some localities. Its topography and its various types of vegetation are products of the texture and permeability of the clayey subsoil developed from this windblown material. The springs that flow from the valley sides now water livestock, as they once watered countless generations of buffalo. They are discharged because the water cannot sink through the hardened earliest layers of loess.

You can learn much of the prehistory of the prairie by study of the islands in the grassland sea. The Wichita Mountains, for example, in western Oklahoma were formed some 300 million years ago, long after the land had been uplifted from the early Paleozoic seas. The tremendous uplift was accompanied by large faults and folds. This upheaval exposed lavas and sediments of sandstone that were overlain by limestone. Subsequent erosion stripped off much of the mountains, which once were higher than the present ones, and deposited their materials in the intervening flats where we now find the modern prairie.

The origin of the vegetation of the modern prairie has been the subject of much speculation by scientists. The prairie's vegetational history has been developed from interpretations of the living distributional patterns of plants and their associations, supplemented by fragmentary fossil records. Henry Allen Gleason in deciphering the origin of the midwestern prairie stressed the dynamics of vegetation. He noted that the history of vegetation is a history of repeated migrations of many kinds of plants arriving in a region from many directions, persisting there for a time, and then disappearing under the stress of environmental change.

The mingling of species of different origins and the persistence of relics of earlier migrations results in a fascinating botanical crossword puzzle for anyone interested in the dynamics of vegetation. The seasons, plant associations, mammals, and other animal life of the prairie will be discussed in later chapters to show how the prairie biome, or community of living things on the grassland, exemplifies the complex of all of nature's processes.

*Harbinger of spring on the prairie, purple townsendias appear in March. The flowers, on stems only an inch in height, nestle among dried blue-grama leaves that grew in the previous summer.*

# 2

## *The Prairie Year*

IF YOU LOOK OFF TO THE HILLS on a tranquil summer day, the green of the prairie seems like a vast ocean, dominated by grass in such dense stands that only the mosaic of cloud shadows breaks the endless serenity of the view. But it is not that way all through the year. On a winter night, with the blizzard blasting out of the northwest, it is a place of cold white death for warm-blooded creatures that find neither food nor shelter. But the storms come and go, with mild periods between, and suddenly it is early spring. Then the first showy plants begin their orderly succession of blooming among the perennially present grasses.

The somber tone of winter is broken when we see the first pasque-flower in the eastern prairie, the first dog's-tooth violet in the central prairie, or the purple townsendia on the Western plains. This miracle of new growth generally is in harmony with local climatic conditions. The prairie as a whole exhibits a wider range of floral grouping than any other area on the continent. We know that grasses are always there, and that they burst from the earth, grow, flower, and produce fruit in their own good time. But it is the forbs, or broad-leaved herbs, with their showy flowers, that cause the colorful seasonal changes in appearance of the prairie. They come and go in orderly progression through the growing period of the year.

The prairie presents four conspicuous aspects, in addition to the somber one of winter. The earliest aspect is the prevernal one that precedes the actual coming of spring. Although the grasses have scarcely started growth the prairie cat's-foot and the windflowers appear in bloom. In April the vernal, or spring aspect, is initiated by greening of new growth over the whole of the grassland. Then many showy plants of short stature burst into view before they are out-stripped by the lengthening stems and leaves of grasses.

When I examine the prairie closely at this time I also see the first green shoots of plants that will bloom in summer and autumn. They will have much competition with other plants, but eventually they will surmount the grasses and come into their full glory in the season appointed for the summit of their growth and fruition.

The summer, or estival, aspect begins in May, after the spring flowers have dried or have been overtopped by the bluestems and other grasses, which now cover the landscape with luxuriant growth. Then the prairie produces a charming variety of forb and shrub societies in which legumes, roses, coneflowers, and larkspurs make a varicolored pattern against the green background of grass leaves. The pattern is kaleidoscopic in that new elements are added almost weekly as old ones produce seeds and become senescent.

Then, while summer is at its height, as early as mid-July, the grass cover itself undergoes a change. The summer-blooming grasses begin to open their flowers in preparation for pollination and eventual matur-ity and fruition. At the same time some of the first yellow and golden flowers of autumn forbs appear. Soon the variety increases and the prairie becomes varicolored with ironweeds, gentians, asters, sun-flowers, goldenrods, the silvery canescent leaves of herbaceous sages, and the bright grays and greens of the prairie shoestring and other vigorous shrubs.

In September and October the yellows, whites, and purples of tall plants of the aster family combine with the fruiting fields of grasses in a landscape riotous with color and astounding in the profusion of animal and bird life that remains, even though the summer bird residents have abandoned their homes and left on their annual southward journeys.

The fruition of the prairie plants and the early frosts of autumn initiate the senescence and death of their aerial parts and foreshadow the retreat of the vegetable fires into the roots and underground buds of the perennial prairie plants. Dissemination of seeds from dried fruit pods goes on apace, aided by the wind and by animals that also must change their habitations in order to endure the winter ahead. In this shifting of seasonal activities, many of the smaller forms—mice, toads, insects, worms, spiders—find shelter and home beneath the blanket of vegetation that gradually falls to the ground, providing cover for creatures that move and for others that hibernate until the miracle of spring comes again.

The prairie is so vast that no plant species starts growth in the spring or blooms in summer everywhere at the same time. Many plants start growth in February on the southern prairie. The same species may not begin growth until May on the northern prairie. Thus, if one were to travel slowly over a period of three months from southern Texas to Montana he could see buffalo grass just beginning to bloom at each stage in his journey. Plants also start growth and come into bloom earlier at low altitudes than at high altitudes. Thus the traveler who moves hundreds of miles in a few days must be aware of the effects of altitude and geographical location on the seasonal aspects of the prairie if he is to appreciate the time of appearance of plant or animal friends he may encounter in such widely separated places as the lowlands of Iowa, the mesas of New Mexico, or the plains of Saskatchewan.

Insects, migrating birds, reptiles, and other creatures of the prairie also have their annual routines that coincide with the advance of the seasons. Many people who live in one place have found it interesting and instructive to keep records of the dates of first appearance of everything from bees to robins to flowers. Such records, kept over a period of years, give one an insight into the built-in periodicity possessed by most living things. In combination with weather records, one also becomes aware of factors that cause slight changes in the periodicity of specific kinds of plants and animals from year to year.

Most of us who are lucky enough to live in one place for a number of years think of natural flowering plants in terms of the calendar. Violets bloom in May, sunflowers in July, and goldenrods in September. Even the inconspicuous plants live and flower according to the seasons. Years ago I found a dwarf gray willow (*Salix tristis*), sometimes called the sad willow, growing in the cemetery where my father is buried beneath the prairie sod. Its small narrow leaves with rolled margins and the grayish matted woolly hairs on their undersides make it unmistakable. I first saw it in early May when most of the small globular catkins had fallen. They are always present if I visit the cemetery in early April, and I am pleased to see this miniature willow, born to the dryness and sunshine of the prairie, flourishing in season with the other vernal species that grow among the bluestem grasses.

The awakening of the prevernal plants of the prairie begins early.

*In periods of heavy spring rainfall evening primrose flowers cover the mixed prairie like new-fallen snow. Partially closed in the daytime, the white petals blossom forth on the evening air.*

On the plains of eastern Colorado I used to look for the rose-purple or pinkish rays of *Townsendia grandiflora* in the last days of March, when the western wheatgrass leaves were three inches high in the swales. Sometimes the star lilies (*Leucocrinum montanum*) appeared even before the first greenness of grass could be seen. Farther east and north, the pasqueflower (*Anemone patens*) produced its lavender cast on the sandy uplands soon after snowmelt.

All the prevernal bloomers are of short stature; some are rosette formers like dandelions, and most are short-lived. Food for early growth has been stored in corms, tubers, and roots produced in the previous season. The fire of life, smoldering during the dormant season of the previous summer and winter, bursts into the flame of rapid growth, often before spring is assured. But the prevernal plants must complete their growth cycles before taller herbs and the dominant grasses compete with them for light and moisture.

In an interesting study of the flowering dates of prairie plants of Wisconsin, J. E. Butler observed that the height of plants increases as the flowering date occurs later in the growing season. May bloomers averaged thirteen centimeters in height. In June the average height was twenty-three centimeters; in July, thirty-two centimeters; in August, forty-one centimeters; and in September, forty-six centimeters. Most of the prevernal, or very early spring bloomers, such as pussytoes (*Antennaria neglecta*), rock cress (*Arabis lyrata*), prairie buttercup (*Ranunculus fascicularis*), and pasqueflower, produce basal rosettes of leaves with flower stalks rising from the centers.

Many of the prevernal plants of the prairie grow as isolated individuals and one must search for them among the dried leaves and flower stalks of last year's grasses. Threadleaf sedge (*Carex filifolia*) and other dry land sedges frequently grow in small inconspicuous tufts, although on bare areas they sometimes produce tiny green carpets which are tinted yellow by their staminate flowers.

I always associate the true advent of spring and its vernal aspect with the croaking of frogs and the rapid growth of early-season grasses. Spring-flowering grasses include buffalo grass (*Buchloë dactyloides*), poverty oat grass (*Danthonia spicata*), Indian ricegrass (*Oryzopsis hymenoides*), witchgrass (*Panicum capillare*), and sand dropseed (*Sporobolus cryptandrus*). Present with these are the new green shoots of other grasses which will bloom later and produce the profusion of summer and autumn foliage. For a time in spring, however, the rapid growth of radiant flowering plants outstrips the growth of grasses and produces a variegated carpet of entrancing beauty.

If you want to go north with the spring on the prairie you should take your field guides to birds, mammals, insects, and wild flowers, and start early. Some of the migrant birds will be starting their northward journeys. The grazing mammals will be looking for the tonic of green things to eat. The harvester ants will be repairing their mounds and the first generations of insects will be hatching and seeking their favorite plant or animal foods. And the prairie will be in the process of redecoration with the new colors of multitudes of forbs and shrubs.

In Texas and Oklahoma many herbaceous perennials break their dormancy in February and March. Then the prairie soon becomes gay with the blues, whites, and yellows of sedges, anemones, bluets (*Houstonia minima*), johnny-jump-ups (*Viola kitaibeliana*), Nuttall onions (*Allium nuttallii*), and bigleaf pussytoes (*Antennaria plantaginifolia*). By April tumblegrass (*Schedonnardus paniculatus*), violet wood sorrel (*Oxalis violacea*), yellow tansy mustard (*Descurainia pinnata*) and greenthread (*Thelesperma trifidum*) have bloomed along with a multitude of other forbs and grasses.

In the central prairies of Nebraska and South Dakota, wild strawberries, prairie phlox, and Canada anemone are in bloom in late April. Much farther north in the Canadian mixed prairie the vernal aspect reaches its height in early May. The April bloomers are still there, including ground plum (*Astragalus crassicarpus*) and prairie bean (*Thermopsis rhombifolia*). The later species of the vernal aspect include puccoon (*Lithospermum linearifolium*), beard-tongue (*Penstemon nitidus*), and chickweed (*Cerastium campestre*).

Late spring on the high plains marks the advent of a vernal flora entirely different from that of the tall-grass prairie. In drought years, and on overgrazed land, the prickly pears reach their peak of flowering with striking pink and yellow blossoms set against a background of fleshy green stems studded with gray spines. If overgrazing has been long and severe, blue grama (*Bouteloua gracilis*), western wheatgrass (*Agropyron smithii*), and sand dropseed remain in the protection of the cactus clumps and produce flower heads after the cactus petals have fallen and the spiny fruits have formed.

Among the grasses, the woolly Indian wheat (*Plantago purshii*) sometimes floods the landscape with silvery gray. After the great drought of 1934 to 1939, the rains came in 1940 and the woolly inflorescences of this little annual plant covered the short-grass country for miles on end. Intermingled with these were tufts of six-weeks fescue (*Festuca octoflora*). On a single square yard of ground I counted 11,253 plants belonging to these two species.

In periods of normal rainfall the mixed prairies of the high plains are adorned in late spring with a wealth of evening primroses, purple larkspurs, locoweeds with white, pink, or red flowers, dwarf lupines, and the decorative spikes of purple penstemons. Even before the indigo flowers of the lupines appear in late June, the silvery foliage of silky sophora (*Sophora sericea*) and of fringed sagebrush (*Artemisia frigida*) give character to the landscape which later will be spattered with butterweed (*Senecio crocatus*) and broom snakeweed (*Gutierrezia sarothrae*).

The varying moods of the prairie are influenced by the yearly variation in height and appearance of prairie perennials, which live in the same spot year after year. Some of the individual clumps of grasses, and many of the perennial forbs, live for as long as fifty years. A clump of coneflowers (*Ratibida columnifera*) that I visited periodically for seventeen years illustrated how the growth of an individual plant varies from year to year. I found it at the edge of the bullrushes near a spring we had fenced to exclude cattle. It attracted my attention since it was the uncommon variety *pulcherrima*, with brown-purple ligules.

In the exceedingly dry year of 1939 it produced only a few short stems with deformed leaves. In the following years it produced from five to fourteen flower stalks, which varied in height from eleven to twenty-six inches. In 1952, our cattle broke through the fence and grazed it to the ground before the blossoms appeared. Then I moved to another state and did not visit the spot again until the early summer of 1966. There was my plant, with three flower stalks. I do not know what vicissitudes it endured during the fourteen years of my absence, but it dramatically illustrated the longevity of herbaceous perennials and taught me much about the ever-fluctuating aspects of the prairie.

The summer aspect of the unspoiled prairie is one of profusion of species and variegated patterns. Although the grasses are predominant, the rolling hills are decorated with showy daisies, purple legumes, and white and purple prairie clovers. In Kansas the black-eyed Susan occurs in solid stands along roadsides. The tall autumnal forbs which will reach far above the grasses for the waning sunshine of September and early October are in evidence but not yet in flower.

If you look closely in June and July you will see that the prairie is characterized by a multiple layer of species, arranged one above the other. The rosettes of prairie buttercup (*Ranunculus fascicularis*) and rock cress (*Arabis lyrata*) still remain. Bird's-foot violets (*Viola pedata*) and shooting-stars (*Dodecatheon meadia*), which earlier studded the moist hillsides with blankets of pink and white, are hidden among the grasses and no longer are in flower. Each week brings new elements of greater height and striking color into the sea of grass. New forbs blossom with such prodigality that one must visit favorite spots again and again to view the endless parade of color. Dry seasons sometimes cause an overlapping or telescoping of seasonal aspects so that autumnal species may bloom in June before the vernal species have vanished and while the summer aspect is in full sway. Some plants bloom for long periods and persist through all the seasonal aspects of the entire growing season.

Autumn begins early in the far northern reaches of the prairie. In late July on the Canadian and Minnesota prairies the blossoms of hairy goldaster (*Chrysopsis villosa*), blanketflower (*Gaillardia aristata*), gumweed (*Grindelia perennis*), blazing star (*Liatris punctata*), and the strange "leafless" skeleton plant (*Lygodesmia juncea*) are conspicuous among the flaglike inflorescences of blue grama and the feathery stalks of plains muhly (*Muhlenbergia cuspidata*). Soon after, yellow societies of goldenrods, snakeweeds, and sunflowers appear. By mid-August the various species of sagebrush are in bloom and add their gray and silvery tones to the landscape along with the whites and blues of asters. In this northern zone all plants must hurry to complete their cycles before frost brings about their universal senescence.

On the dry prairies of Minnesota and Wisconsin the colorful mouse-eared aster (*Aster sericeus*) makes a striking appearance with its display of amethyst-violet flowers against a background of silver-green leaves. Here also are the clustered stems of the downy gentian (*Gentiana puberula*) with their chalicelike flowers that rival the blue of heaven itself. And in violent contrast the flaming orange umbels of butterfly weed (*Asclepias tuberosa*), blooming late in the year, add to the magic of the autumn flora.

If you follow autumn on the prairie southward into Oklahoma and Texas you will see that dormancy of the grasses creeps southward at an ever slower pace, but nearly always in advance of the killing frosts. All plant life in the southern prairie does not retreat underground in late fall. While silver beardgrass (*Andropogon saccharoides*), switchgrass, love grass, and western ragweed are entering winter dormancy, willow trees along the watercourses still have a few green leaves. On the uplands the green of common mesquite and coralberry is still conspicuous. And the fresh green winter rosettes of hairy pinweed (*Lechea villosa*), slender verbena (*Verbena halei*), and low poppy mallow (*Callirrhoë involucrata*) may be observed along with the newly germinated Texas bluegrass (*Poa arachnifera*), six-weeks fescue (*Festuca octoflora*), and woolly Indian wheat (*Plantago purshii*).

When winter comes to the prairie, vegetal growth virtually ceases aboveground. But winter is not a season of death for all plants. Only the annuals, which variously complete their life cycles in different seasons, actually die. Their demise follows a universal senescence which ends the existence of countless millions of plants of each species, just as all individuals in a field of wheat simultaneously dry and die at their appointed time. In a sense, even the annuals do not die; their fallen seeds contain the germ of life which will renew their growth in another year.

The perennial vegetation, of course, still lives when winter comes. The standing cover of grasses and forbs gradually returns to earth through transfer of food substances to buds, underground bulbs, corms, stems, and roots. Much of this translocation of manufactured plant food takes place in summer and autumn so that the deteriorated leaves and stems at autumn's end have given much of their vital substance back to the dormant portions of plants that live underground in winter.

The desiccated leaves and stems that remain on the prairie have many uses in winter. As cured forage, they provide food for herbivorous animals, ranging in size from mice to bison, which in turn provide food for carnivores and scavengers—including birds—all of which make up the web of life. The sea of grass gradually returns to the earth under the buffeting of winter winds and the weight of snow. It forms a protective blanket that retards wind and water erosion and conserves soil moisture needed for regrowth of plants in spring.

Total deterioration of dried leaves and stems does not occur on the prairie in winter. The final dissolution of debris left from the previous summer is speeded by the warmth and moisture of spring and the increase of vital processes carried on by bacteria, fungi, worms, and other users of organic matter. Even when winter is past, the living grasses play an important role in the disposal of nonliving plant parts, since there is scientific evidence that organic substances in attached dried leaves and stems are transmitted by diffusion or related processes back to the growing parts of plants. Thus the prairie, in its renewal of growth in spring, uses some of the remaining substance of its winter protective cover to augment the nutrients previously stored in roots and buds. The remaining litter and debris of dead plants is used by microscopic organisms, insects, and other creatures in their own energy systems.

It must be apparent to anyone who observes nature closely that without energy transfers there could be no life and no system in the living environment. Energy is everywhere. Light and other radiations fall on the earth. When radiation is absorbed it produces heat, another kind of energy. The energy from light is used by plants in the manufacture of food in green leaves. This food is used by the plant for its own growth and by animals for their life processes. This transfer of food energy, when it moves through a series of organisms, constitutes the *food chain*.

Since plants are the primary producers in food chains—without plants there could be no animals—we can see how the progression of plant growth in accord with the seasons produces a multitude of variations in habitats and niches of the myriad insects, birds, reptiles, mammals, and other creatures that inhabit the prairie. Without knowledge of the habitats and niches of organisms we cannot truly understand the functioning of the prairie and its ecosystems.

The concept of the ecological niche should be made clear before we use the term with respect to birds, insects, and mammals which will be mentioned in the following pages and chapters. Charles Elton of England was one of the first ecologists to give it specific meaning. Eugene P. Odum in his *Fundamentals of Ecology* more recently has likened the *habitat* of an organism to its "address" and the niche to its business or "profession," which of course is its whole way of life.

Thus the habitat of the large predatory water beetle *Dytiscus* is the local area in a prairie pond where it lives. But its business of living includes swimming about to capture tadpoles, small fish, and insects for food; avoiding enemies, including its own voracious larvae, large fish, and wading birds; and mating with others of its kind. *Dytiscus* is at the end of the food chain for the animals it eats, but is itself in the food chain of the fish that eats it, which is eaten by the heron, which is eaten by the skunk or coyote or carrion beetles that roam the prairie.

There is a water bug, *Corixa*, which also lives in ponds but plays an entirely different ecological role, since it eats decaying vegetation instead of other insects, tadpoles, and small fish. Thus it is at the beginning of a food chain that ends with the same animals that eat *Dytiscus*. These two insects illustrate how different species can occupy essentially similar habitats but have different niches. By having different niches they do not endanger their own existence by competition for food, nesting space, or deleterious effect on their environment.

For birds, an amazing number of habitats exist in the prairie country. Each species, of course, has its own niche within its chosen habitat. Even in winter, large numbers of birds live on the prairie or in habitats associated with grasslands. The Christmas bird census, for example, which has been made each year since 1907 in the area from the foothills of the Rocky Mountains east to Sterling, Colorado, has recorded more than 150 species.

The census has shown that the wooded and shrubby borders of prairie streams and ponds nearly always have populations of red-shafted flickers, Lewis' woodpeckers, red-tailed hawks, crows, evening grosbeaks, Oregon juncos, and black-capped chickadees. Frequent inhab-

*Lush stands of black-eyed Susan appear in early summer on prairie soils disturbed by plowing, soil drifting, and excessive trampling by grazing animals. These yellow flowered plants cannot endure competition from grass.*

itants of open prairie waters and their vegetated borders are mallards, kingfishers, green-winged teal, baldpates, great blue herons, American goldeneyes, marsh wrens, and yellow-headed blackbirds. On the prairies are many ground-loving species, including the Lapland longspur, Alaskan longspur, horned lark, snow bunting, and western meadowlark.

Around the seasons birds are always in evidence on the prairie. And when I look closely I realize that their activities are activated not only by the weather, their food requirements, and the necessity of avoiding enemies, but by internal urges related to the length of days and the seasons of the year. When I read my notes, taken in different seasons, I see that I have unconsciously recorded some of these relationships between weather, habitat, and activities of birds in their niches. Here are some examples:

*February 5.* The weather has moderated—beautiful clear day. In the open spots and long fissures in the ice on Eaton's Lake the ducks are swimming with outstretched necks, dabbling all the way. They remind me of blood corpuscles seen under a microscope, following one another swiftly in single file in a capillary. In the more open water the ducks cohere in groups of ten to fifty and dabble in such close formation they make solid masses six to eight feet in diameter. The masses turn counterclockwise like wheels. Some of the masses break apart and the new wheels revolve rapidly and independently, like two Texas stars in square dancing. This is the love dance of the ducks. I know that ducks are not the only birds that engage in elaborate courtship antics or perform dances. The greater sandhill cranes stand in circles, prance up and down, throw sticks, dip their heads with upraised wings, bow, and jump into the air. Cranes are sociable birds and these performances may be training exercises for the young in the art of killing snakes, which are thrown like sticks, or in the use of their newly feathered wings. Since humans cannot think as cranes think, these "dances" seem mysterious to us. As to the ducks, their gregarious performance seems to be elicited by improving weather and by internal physiological changes that impel the selection of mates in preparation for the mating season. The dance provides opportunity for contact between many individual birds and a choice of mates, based on display ability that only a duck can understand.

*April 8.* The sky is filled with puffy clouds above the prairie near Cheyenne, Wyoming. Although the wind is strong, about thirty miles per hour from the northwest, birds are active everywhere. Horned larks are especially numerous, searching for food on the short-grass swards. Western meadowlarks are calling from the tops of fourwing saltbushes. Magpies are being buffeted by the wind. A red-shafted flicker is investigating the dead branches of a cottonwood. Three killdeer are paddling in the water of a stagnant pool where the algae are thick and green. In another pool a Wilson's snipe is probing the mud, belly deep. I toss a stone and he sticks his long bill in the mud and spreads a fanlike tail as would a miniature turkey gobbler. Then he flies a few feet and resumes his probing.

In spite of the wind, the birds are active since the weather of the previous week has been cold, wet, and unfavorable for food gathering. Now the puffy clouds indicate the coming of clear weather and the birds are actively searching for insects and calling to establish their future breeding territories. The magpies have already started their nests, and they are aloft searching for the meat of some animal that may have died during the night. I believe the Wilson's snipe spreads his tail at the disturbance of my stone as a warning to stay out of his territory. Another snipe invading his feeding area would elicit the same visual warning.

*May 9.* Weather is warm and clear today. The different birds are doing things according to their specific and individual needs. The cliff swallows are here again and already they are packing mud from the stock-watering tank to their nests under the eaves of our cookhouse. Nest construction is first-order business for them since they have no safe places to rest in until their homes are built. I flush a dozen mourning doves from the thickets of dried sunflowers as I go to open the corral gates. At this time of year the sunflower patches furnish the best supplies of seeds for the doves since the open grasslands have been thoroughly gleaned by the longspurs and juncos during the winter. While driving the cows to water, I see five long-billed curlews standing among the antelope that have wintered on the uplands. Could these be some of the same curlews I saw in January on the King Ranch in Texas?

*August 11.* The harvester ants have swarmed, since late morning, in countless millions and the air in early evening is filled with other flying insects. The nighthawks are booming now. All through the day they have rested on fence posts, facing into the wind like weather vanes, and have not attempted to catch the winged ants swarming about them. The grasshoppers have reached maturity and are prey for the sparrow hawks. A pair of these handsome little falcons hover motionless time after time for as long as twenty seconds; then they swoop into the grass, capture large grasshoppers, and hold them in their talons as expertly as squirrels hold nuts.

The swarming of the harvester ants, I know, is the culmination of a summer of colony development. The worker ants have gathered adequate seed supplies, and the well-fed males and queens with fully developed wings are ready for the mating flight. The nighthawks do not hunt them until evening since nighthawks are birds of the dusk and night. The falcons do much hovering now because the grasshoppers are especially abundant and easy to pinpoint from the air. At other times the sparrow hawks have to cruise over the prairie, like their larger relatives the marsh hawks and the eagles, in search of elusive prey. In thinking of all these varied bird activities, I realize that each specific undertaking is elicited by some less visible influence, such as the appearance of new insect or rodent crops, which in turn have resulted from periodic events in the lives of lesser and lesser creatures, all of which are likewise influenced by weather, enemies, and food supplies on the prairie.

Of all the animals of the prairie the insects seem to be attuned best to the seasonal march of the flora and its varied aspects. The ants are among the earliest to appear. Their food supply consists of seeds, the flesh of dead insects, and organic debris, and hence they are not dependent on early green foliage. The aphid-tending and honey-gathering ants become active when the aphids begin to excrete the honeydew the ants use for food. The native bees also are seasonal in abundance since many of them depend on pollen from certain species of plants.

The time of abundance for the innumerable insects of the prairie depends largely on their individual life patterns. The moths and butterflies pupate over the winter and hatch in the spring as adults. The May beetle, after a three-year period of root chewing as a grub, transforms into a pupa and finally emerges as an adult in the spring of the fourth year. Some of the cicadas take thirteen or seventeen years for this process.

Dragonflies hawking over the prairie for insect food are in their finest fettle in July. Grasshoppers reach their ascendancy in August, after numerous molts and much feeding during their instars, the periods between molts. The population explosion for aphids comes in late summer and early autumn, when they thrust their sucking spears into everything from wild roses to goldenrods.

As might be expected, insects on the prairie occupy almost every conceivable habitat. In ponds, slow-flowing streams, and stagnant water, one can easily find dragonfly larvae, mosquito larvae, and water beetles with bifocal eyes—the upper half for seeing in air, the lower half for seeing in water. The diving beetles *Dytiscus* and *Hydrophilus* pursue their tadpole and insect prey underwater. In turn, they are eaten by frogs, fish, and snakes.

In the soil are mole crickets and seventeen-year cicadas with forelegs enlarged into digging shovels. Beneath the litter of dead vegetation are innumerable insects that live on roots, vegetable debris, minute crustaceans, and other insects. On and in the soil are ground beetles, solitary bees, and fierce hunting wasps searching for spiders to stock their larders. These wasps dig holes in soft earth, where they lay eggs on the spider which serves as food for the developing larva.

This wasp always leaves its prey near the hole while it inspects the burrow to see that all is well. I have amused myself many times by moving the prey while the wasp was belowground. Invariably she searches, finds the spider, places it near the opening, and again inspects the burrow. The French entomologist Fabre once induced a wasp to make forty of these inspections. I tried this recently on a wasp in western Oklahoma. After the third trip she outwitted me by placing the spider in a kangaroo-rat hole until her inspection was complete.

Many insects of the prairie lay their eggs in fresh dung. Some insects that spend much time in the air parasitize other insects or pester grazing mammals. Flies that prey on pronghorn antelope have excellent vision and can see for considerable distances. The bison originally had a host of insect pests, including bot flies, warble flies, and "heel" flies that now pester our domestic livestock on the prairies.

The insects associated with plants, of course, are legion. Some of these chew leaves. Others suck juices from leaves and stems. Still others eat pollen. And a great many live on roots during at least parts of their life cycles and are seldom seen unless one digs to find them.

Many of the grasshoppers are nonselective and eat almost any plant available. Other insects, such as the monarch butterflies, commonly associate with milkweeds; blister beetles frequent snakeweed flowers; and cactus-boring insects, found on the Great Plains, live only in the stems of prickly pears. The female pronuba moth is so specialized she can pollinate only the flowers of the yucca. She lays her eggs in the seed capsules that can develop only after pollination. The larvae rarely consume all the seeds and so the yucca is able to perpetuate itself.

Even the amateur collector soon becomes aware of the unlimited variety of insect habitats in the grasslands. The sophisticated collector, like some of our more experienced bird watchers, learns to recognize the different kinds of katydids, grasshoppers, tree crickets, common crickets, and cicadas by their sounds. If one excavates the burrows of digger wasps he may find many species of insects ordinarily difficult to find. These wasps store metallic wood borer beetles, snout beetles, leaf-hoppers, flies, and native bees in their burrows.

With careful searching one may find representatives of most of the orders of insects in prairie habitats. Springtails live under decaying vegetation. Stoneflies, mayflies, damselflies, and caddiceflies rest on rocks, reeds, cattails, and shrubs near streams and ponds. Praying mantids, walking sticks, grasshoppers, spittle bugs, and innumerable other insects are found on the leaves of grasses and forbs. Beetles are so common they may be found almost anywhere: under rocks, in burrows, on plants, under dung, under animal carcasses, in pools of water, and in the air while flying at night. Bugs may be found almost anywhere that vegetation grows.

Butterflies, skippers, and moths are numerous on the prairie. The larvae of the families in the order Lepidoptera are so diverse in their habits and choice of habitats that careful study is necessary before one can identify even a few of these immature insects. Adult butterflies are day fliers and can be found wherever the prairie forbs are in bloom. Moths are night-flying insects and can be collected on flowers and where electric lights attract them in large numbers. Flies, ants, bees, and wasps are so numerous that it is impossible to cite all of their diverse habitats, which include everything from the soil to green plants to living animals.

The diversity of insect habitats becomes even more astounding when one remembers that different stages in the life cycles of insects are usually spent in surroundings other than those occupied by the adults. The eggs of grasshoppers remain in the ground over winter. The cater-pillars of butterflies eat the leaves of plants different from those visited by the adults that sip nectar from flowers. The grubs of hornets live in underground paper nests, while the omnivorous workers hunt for meat, nectar, and the juice of ripe fruits in the world of sunshine above. In making their paper they also search for plant fibers and weathered wood for building material, an occupation that extends their niche be-yond that of most insects in nature.

The season of reproduction for most mammals coincides with the growth seasons of grasses, forbs, and shrubs. The summer profusion of plant growth and the protective cover of luxuriant plant societies allows prey species to reproduce and build up their numbers. The breeding stock thus produced must be sufficient to allow for losses to predators and still maintain a supply of animal life to perpetuate the species in the following year. How the mammals do this provides an

*Prairie snow protects mice and other small creatures that live in grass tunnels below the soil, but usually leaves the seeds of herbs and grasses available for winter birds. The author is examining seeds left by meadow mice.*

inexhaustible source of fascinating study material for anyone interested in natural things.

Until white men came, the bison survived because of their gregariousness, size, strength, and migrational ability. The jackrabbits still survive because of their durability, speed, and inclination to live in spots where visibility of enemies is high. The kangaroo rats survive because they dig labyrinthine tunnels in the sand and because they have many structural specializations.

Muskrats build marsh lodges of cattails and rushes plastered with mud and also they build shoreline houses in the banks of streams and rivers. They survive since their vegetable food usually is plentiful; a mile of overgrown streambank may support dozens of muskrats, and a few mink which prey on them.

The nests of mice are made of vegetable fibers, leaves, and bird down and are suspended among grass stems, or hidden beneath stones or in vegetable debris. Mice survive because they produce many litters in a season and because their chosen plant, insect, and other animal food is nearly always abundant.

Much mammal activity in the prairie is carried on underground. Some of the burrowing creatures go about their food-gathering business in full sunlight, and use their burrows at night for sleeping. Many rodents build several burrows, which offer avenues of escape from predators. The ground squirrels, for example, are great tillers of the soil and their digging activities create seedbeds where annual and weedy plants can grow. The sunflowers, thistles, peppergrasses, pigweeds, and goosefoots which occupy these disturbed areas furnish hiding space and green vegetable food for the ground squirrels. The seeds also feed harvester ants, birds, and mice and other rodents.

The round of the year on the prairie, with its varied plant associations and aspects, is marked by a myriad of seasonal niches for other animals. In preparation for the winter sleep, innumerable creatures retire to the subterranean recesses of the soil for shelter or hibernation. Toads dig into sandy areas while frogs submerge themselves in the muddy bottoms of ponds. Racers, rattlesnakes, and other crawling creatures secrete themselves in prairie-dog holes, badger burrows, or in rocky crevices along the escarpments of the prairie.

Centipedes, spiders, ground beetles, and scores of other lowly creatures seek refuge in the bases of thick grass tufts or in the sheltering earth itself. Some endure frost and are not harmed by desiccation. Grasshopper eggs, for example, remain within an inch or two beneath the soil surface. The little *Lasius niger* ants live beneath stones, while the larger harvester ants (*Pogonomyrmex occidentalis*) live six to ten feet down, below the frost line. May beetle larvae burrow to depths of forty inches or more among the grass roots.

Few of the prairie mammals are natural hibernators. The bears, which once roamed the prairies, do not go into continuous lethargy and, with sufficient provocation, they can be aroused from their sleep. When their cubs are born in late winter the females undoubtedly display a certain wakefulness and they also change positions of their bodies during the winter sleep.

Hibernating animals do not enter their lethargic period merely as a response to cold. Woodchucks and jumping mice grow drowsy even when the weather is mild. A chipmunk I once kept in our house where the temperature never dropped below 65 degrees F. finally hibernated in early November. Household noises did not disturb him. He continued to sleep even when he was lifted from his nest and passed from hand to hand. Beneath his nest in a wooden box he had stored more than three pounds of seeds we had given him in September and October. When he awakened in the following spring he ate from his hoarded seeds.

Woodchucks and western thirteen-lined ground squirrels do not store food in their burrows. Instead, they store fat in their bodies to provide the necessary energy for their low rates of metabolism during the dormant period. As the amount of fat increases the animals remain closer to home and show an increasing tendency to drowsiness. In their dens they gradually sink deeper into sleep, their temperatures drop, and finally their bodies are motionless, except for their very slow breathing.

Skunks and raccoons go into partial hibernation in northern localities. If the weather is mild they may be abroad all winter. Only during severe weather and in periods of great food scarcity do they den up in burrows, caves, or other dark places where they are secure against extreme cold. When the weather moderates, and food is again obtainable, they emerge from their sleeping quarters and actively explore the countryside at night. Even deep snow does not bother the skunk if weather conditions otherwise are favorable.

Warmth in early spring wakens some hibernators, but it is not the only cause of their rapid return to activity. Woodchucks stir out of dormancy in late March when cold weather still pervades the land. In the high western mountains I have seen hundreds of marmots and ground squirrels running over the snow-covered meadows at elevations of ten thousand feet. In order to reach the open they had to burrow up through more than ten feet of snow.

Undoubtedly the rapid awakening of hibernating animals is triggered in part by built-in periodicities that return them to active lives in preparation for the mating season and the profusion of food that once more becomes available as the drabness of winter merges into the greenness of spring.

*Isolated patches of grass in Eastern forests herald the beginning of the prairie. Grassland openings gradually become larger and more numerous as one travels westward until the forests give way to the prairie.*

# 3

# The Prairie Ocean
# and Its Shoreline

AS THE EARLY EXPLORERS and European settlers pushed westward from the New England coast they encountered interminable
forests of pine, oak, and chestnut. South of Lake Erie they entered
forests of magnificent hard maple and smooth-barked beech trees. In
what is now Ohio they skirted great swamps and came upon small
grassland openings in the forest. Some of the low-lying grasslands were
mixtures of lush grasses, taller than a man's head, with islands of cattails
and sedges in the wetter spots. The grasslands on dry upland slopes dis-
played a great variety of tall grasses and showy forbs. These isolated
patches of grassland, completely surrounded by forest, were the east-
ernmost outliers of the prairie that once covered one third of the North
American continent.

As travelers pushed westward the grassland openings became larger
and more numerous. In what is now Indiana and Illinois the prairie was
more or less continuous on the uplands, while the forests formed strips
along the streams and rivers. West of Illinois the prairie became dominant and covered much of western Minnesota, Wisconsin, Iowa, and
Missouri. Here the forest belts narrowed until they occurred mainly
along stream courses and on river bottoms.

West of the Missouri River the forests continued for many miles beside the rivers and streams. But above the streams lay the seemingly boundless prairie that ended only at the foot of the Rocky Mountains.

Many travelers noted the gradual change in the prairie flora as they moved westward from the wetter eastern grasslands. Tall grasses were dominant where precipitation was thirty-five inches or more. These grasses also dominated the bottomlands along western streams and in sandhill areas where water did not run off or evaporate rapidly in summer. But on the uplands of Iowa, eastern Nebraska, and Kansas, grasses of lesser stature intermingled with the tall grasses to form a transition zone that extended more than two hundred miles west of the Missouri River.

Beyond this broad zone stretched a drier grassland that covered even more territory than did the true prairie. Here, grasses of medium height (mid-grasses), such as western wheatgrass, and short grasses, such as blue grama and buffalo grass, formed a two-story association now recognized by most ecologists as mixed prairie. The mixed prairie occupied the land known as the Great Plains.

On maps published in recent years three principal grassland types are shown for the mid-continental prairie: tall-grass prairie, mixed-grass prairie, and short-grass prairie. Some ecologists consider the mixed-grass prairie to be a broad transition zone in which the tall grasses of the true prairie mingle with the short grasses of the Great Plains' physiographic province. This broad transition zone extends from Saskatchewan through the Dakotas, central Nebraska, Kansas, and Oklahoma into northern Texas.

Other ecologists believe there is no essential distinction between the prairie and the plains. Both are characterized by a dominant cover of perennial grasses developed in harmony with climate and a former population of grazing animals. They believe that the short-grass community of the Great Plains is the result of overgrazing. We know definitely that the mid-grasses can be reduced in size and number, or even eliminated in local areas, if they are abused by too many livestock. Undoubtedly the buffalo periodically overgrazed large areas of the semi-arid plains in former times.

The presence and persistence of mid-grasses throughout the plains area has been demonstrated in recent years. When these grasslands are moderately grazed the mid-grasses become conspicuous, especially during cycles of high rainfall. The mid-grasses are excluded by climate only in the arid Southwest, where the mixed prairie borders the desert plains.

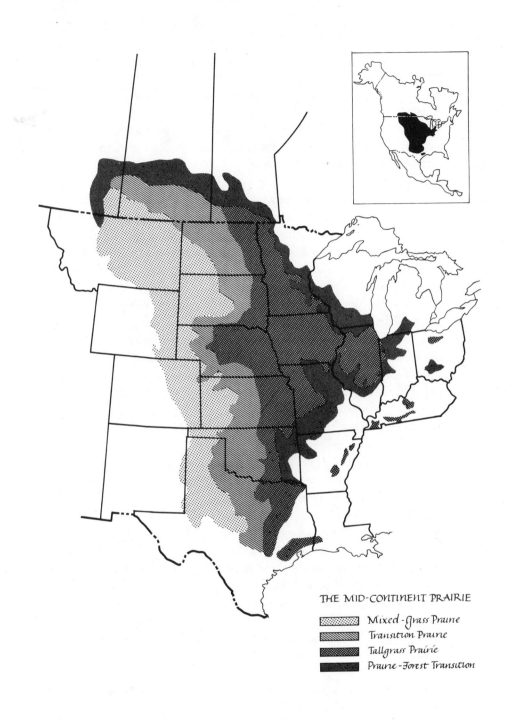

THE MID-CONTINENT PRAIRIE

- Mixed-Grass Prairie
- Transition Prairie
- Tallgrass Prairie
- Prairie-Forest Transition

The short-grass vegetation of the plains is distinctive because of the preponderance of sod-forming grasses, which grow beneath the taller grasses. In drought periods, the continuous presence of blue grama and buffalo grass accounts for 70 to 95 percent of the vegetation and its predominantly swardlike appearance. The bison maintained millions of acres of the plains grassland in a sod condition just as cattle maintain a bluegrass pasture in lawnlike condition, by close grazing. The bison, the prairie dogs, and other grazing mammals, however, never completely killed out the mid-grasses.

In all of the North American prairie there were no more luxuriant stands of vegetation than those dominated by prairie cordgrass, which covered hundreds of square miles of bottomlands along the rivers and their tributaries throughout the tall-grass prairie region. This coarse, woody-stemmed grass, also known as sloughgrass, grew taller than a horse's back and produced shade so dense that other plants were virtually excluded from its presence.

I knew the sloughgrass as a boy on our eastern Nebraska farm. My father called it "rip gut" grass because the sawtooth margins of the four-foot-long coarse leaves could cut bare arms and hands like razor blades. He regularly cut sloughgrass for hay, and the intertwined stems and leaves clung so closely together in the stack that only a strong man could lift a pitchforkful. When the stacked hay settled it had to be cut with a hay saw.

In earlier times sloughgrass was used by the Indians as a thatching for their permanent lodges, which then were covered with earth. The pioneers also used this grass for covering haystacks and cribs of corn. Immigrants in Minnesota burned sloughgrass hay for their only fuel throughout the year. Winchell and Upham wrote in 1884:

Large wisps of this are twisted, doubled, and tied by hand, being thus brought into compact and convenient form for putting into the stove. One or two of these twisted bunches are supplied every five or ten minutes, and they maintain a hot fire as serviceable as that of wood or coal. The amount of hay thus used in a year for heating in an ordinary room is from eight to twelve tons. An hour's time is sufficient for twisting up a winter day's supply of this fuel.

Fire usually did not destroy the sloughgrass, since the thick, much-branched woody rhizomes were in moist soil and the coarse roots extended ten feet or more into the earth. Although the seeds germinated readily and produced plants with flower stalks within two or three years, the rhizomes, or underground stems, usually renewed growth of the stand each spring.

The fabulous production of sloughgrass may be implied from George Catlin's description of prairie fires near Fort Leavenworth. He wrote:

There are many of these meadows on the Missouri, the Platte, and the Arkansas, of many miles in breadth, which are perfectly level, with a waving grass, so high, that we are obliged to stand erect in our stirrups in order to look over its waving tops, as we are riding through it. The fire in these . . . travels at an immense and frightful rate, and often destroys, on their fleetest horses, parties of Indians, who are so unlucky as to be overtaken by it; not that it travels as fast as a horse at full speed, but that the high grass is filled with wild pea-vines and other impediments, which render it necessary for the rider to guide his horse in the zig-zag paths of the deers and buffaloes, retarding his progress, until he is overtaken by the dense column of smoke that is swept before the fire—alarming the horse, which stops and stands terrified and immutable, till the burning grass which is wafted in the wind, falls about him, kindling up in a moment a thousand new fires, which are instantly wrapped in the swelling flood of smoke that is moving on like a black thunder-cloud, rolling on the earth, with its lightning's glare, and its thunder rumbling as it goes.

On drier land at the edges of slough zones, switchgrass and nodding wild rye (*Elymus canadensis*) thrived. These stands of grass were so dense they excluded most other grasses and all but the tallest forbs. This zone was intermediate between the waterlogged sloughgrass and the big bluestem prairies on well-drained lowlands and lower slopes of hills.

Big bluestem communities originally covered thousands of square miles in the eastern prairie region. These communities occurred over much of Illinois, Iowa, and parts of Minnesota and Missouri. They were dominant on the broad lowland valleys of the Red River, the Missouri, the Platte, and the Arkansas. But westward, other important grasses, particularly little bluestem, needlegrasses, Indian grass, and prairie dropseed occurred with increasing frequency.

On the upland prairies of Oklahoma, Kansas, Nebraska, and South Dakota, little bluestem ranged far westward into the mixed prairie, which continued onward to the Rocky Mountains. This great upland grass country was decimated by innumerable cattle following the destruction of the bison. It was over this prairie that the Texas cowboys pushed the cattle northward through heat, dust, Indians, rustlers, and armed homesteaders. The book *Prospector, Cowhand, and Sodbuster,* edited by Robert G. Ferris, states:

> In the peak year 1871, cowhands probably drove 700,000 Texas cattle to Kansas railheads, and between 1866 and 1885 millions of head moved to the railheads and northern ranges. In the level and open country droves were seldom out of sight of other herds. From a hilltop in Nebraska, one cowboy saw 7 herds to the rear of his own and 8 in front, while the dust of 13 more could be observed across the North Platte. . . . When a thunderstorm stampeded 11 trail herds, including about 30,000 Longhorns, which were waiting to cross the Red River at Doan's Store in 1882, it took 120 cowboys 10 days to unscramble the cattle, reassemble the herds, and get them moving again.

These vast cattle herds moved over productive upland prairies in which five grasses were important: little bluestem, porcupine grass (*Stipa spartea*), June grass, side-oats grama (*Bouteloua curtipendula*), and prairie dropseed. Of these, little bluestem had the widest range and was especially abundant southward through Kansas and Oklahoma. It grew in bunches along with other grasses and forbs that flourished between the clumps. On rich moist soils, big bluestem mingled with little bluestem, especially in the Flint Hills of Kansas.

Prairie communities characterized by needlegrasses once dominated thousands of square miles in the northern parts of the prairie. In the Dakotas, these grasses grew in association with the bluestems, June grass, and side-oats grama. When the tall, flexible stems of needlegrass were mature they reached a height of three to five feet and presented a magnificent sight as they bent in waves that ran with the wind. When the seeds with the long awns were disseminated, the bleached stalks and leaves remained to give the prairie a snow-covered appearance when viewed from afar.

Other prairie communities were dominated by prairie dropseed, a bunchgrass adapted to dry uplands. The long leaves of this grass, and

*On the western edges of the prairie, the junipers come down from the foothills of the Rockies to meet the grasslands of the plains.*

of its relatives, tall dropseed (*Sporobolus asper*) and sand dropseed, are flexible and curve gracefully downward in summer. In winter they bleach white and become conspicuous among the tans, grays, and purples of western wheatgrass, hairy grama (*Bouteloua hirsuta*), and purple love grass (*Eragrostis spectabilis*).

Many forbs still are widely distributed in the upland communities of the true prairie. Silver-leaf psoralea (*Psoralea argophila*), a common legume on well-drained soils, is found in all the upland prairie types, especially in places where little bluestem grows. After the small blue flowers of late spring have vanished it still can be easily recognized by its conspicuous silvery foliage. Late in summer its stems break off squarely at the ground level and the dried plants become tumbleweeds. One unacquainted with the prairie in autumn might believe that psoralea plants never grew there.

The large racemes of cream-colored flowers of the white wild indigo (*Baptisia leucantha*), which later give rise to inflated seedpods, are always attractive amid the upland prairie grasses. The shape of this legume makes one think of a miniature oak tree. The six-foot flower stalks rise high above the widely spread branches and leaves. Its relative, the large-bracted wild indigo (*B. leucophaea*), has sap which becomes dark purple on exposure to air, hence the name "false indigo." I have never been able to press and dry satisfactory specimens of this species for my herbarium. The leaves and stems always turn black.

Most people observe and are attracted by the flower heads of white prairie clover (*Petalostemum candidum*) and purple prairie clover (*P. purpureum*) which rise above the surrounding grasses. The deep

*Blue grama is the commonest and most nutritious short grass on the western prairie. Bison subsisted largely on blue grama and buffalo grass.*

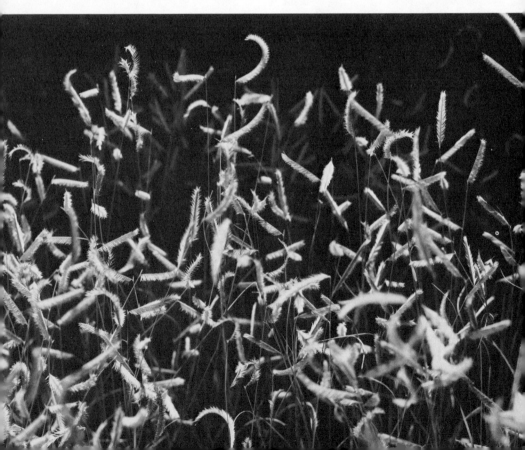

taproots are perennial. If you know where they are, you can return year after year to see the new stems and the beautiful blossoms in season. Even more conspicuous, but not so abundant, are the white larkspurs (*Delphinium virescens*) that stand high above the general level of the prairie.

The brilliant orange-red bouquets of butterfly weeds are among the most brilliant flowers in America. These bushy plants attract many interesting insect visitors, including monarch butterflies and the large bumblebees which are strong enough to pull free from the pollen traps that catch their legs. In similar habitats are purple coneflowers (*Echinacea pallida*). Each stem of these showy composites supports a head with purple rays that last for several weeks. The black central cones remain until late autumn, reminders of the myriads of flowers that contributed beauty to the prairie in midsummer.

According to the physiographers, the vast area between the central lowlands and the Rocky Mountains and between the Rio Grande River in Texas and the delta of the Mackenzie River in Canada is the Great Plains. Much of this enormous expanse of land is covered with mixed prairie.

The eastern edge of this greatest of grasslands on the North American continent is marked by no distinct physiographic boundary. Geographers and ecologists have marked it by the ninety-seventh meridian, and by the line of twenty-inch rainfall, which occurs in general at an altitude of fifteen hundred feet or about halfway across the states of Nebraska, Kansas, and Oklahoma. Ecologists think of this boundary as a broad transition zone between the true prairie and the short-grass prairie.

If you follow the highways westward across the Dakotas, Nebraska, or Kansas you will hardly be aware that the mixed prairie on the great plain stretching ahead rises about 10 feet per mile. At the foot of the Rocky Mountains it reaches an average elevation of 5,500 feet. In Wyoming it rises to 7,000 feet. The whole vast area originally was lifted from the Cretaceous Sea. After the Rocky Mountains were uplifted some fifty million years ago, their eroded materials were carried eastward by rivers and streams and deposited in an alluvial fan that covered thousands of square miles.

In the following ages the streams went through repeated cycles of cutting, depositing, and eroding so that the original structural slope became much modified. As a result the modern traveler now sees on the Great Plains topographic features that include plateaus, badlands with fantastic erosional forms, sandhills, buttes, escarpments, mesas, canyons, rolling hills, endless plains, and eastward-flowing rivers with terraces and sandy bottomlands. These varied features afford many habitats for grassland vegetation and adapted animals.

Big bluestem, so common in the lowland areas of the true prairie, extends far westward in the valleys and ravines of the Great Plains. In these favorable habitats, deeper soil moisture, protection from desiccating winds, and accumulated runoff from summer rains create favorable environments for moisture-loving species. Associated with big bluestem are other grasses which require soil moisture throughout the growing season: Indian grass, switchgrass, and Canada wild rye.

On stream terraces and moist slopes other western grass associates of big bluestem include silver beardgrass, western wheatgrass, and sand dropseed. Showy forbs commonly present are stiff goldenrod (*Solidago rigida*), Baldwin's ironweed (*Vernonia baldwini*), and false boneset (*Kuhnia eupatorioides*). The short grasses on the higher and drier slopes normally do not thrive under the dense tall foliage of the big bluestem stands. But drought periods of several years so reduce the vigor of the tall grasses that their habitat is invaded by blue grama, buffalo grass and many forbs from the drier upland prairie.

Throughout the prairie from east to west, little bluestem grows in places that are not overgrazed. In Indiana, Illinois, and Iowa it occupies the driest upland sites on bluffs and along the fringes of timber. On sandy knolls and the edges of rocky escarpments east of the Rocky Mountains the reddish-brown bunches persist where grazing animals have not depleted the prairie. But the true home of little bluestem is the mid-grass region extending south from central Nebraska across central Kansas and western Oklahoma to the Canadian River.

Little bluestem prairie is colorful at all seasons since it contains a great many showy forbs. Little bluestem itself presents various aspects. On moist soils it forms a continuous sod and the whole area has the appearance of a grain field. On the drier soils of steep hillsides and rocky outcrops, and on heavily grazed areas, it forms bunches a half foot or more in diameter and two to four feet high.

In early spring the grass stand is light green when you look with the wind, and dark green when you look toward the wind. In summer the grasses take on a reddish-brown hue and by autumn they show purple and copper tints which contrast with the red, gray, white, and silvery tones of tall dropseed, switchgrass, squirreltail (*Hordeum jubatum*), and Indian grass.

Fresh banks cut with road graders through the prairie always are instructive because they reveal much of the root growth and moisture conditions in the various prairie communities. With close attention to the soil exposed by modern road construction one can examine many miles of the prairie "underground" with a minimum of digging.

In the little bluestem community the soils are lighter in color than those of the tall-grass prairies. The layer of carbonate accumulation lies two to four feet deep. This indicates that the normal penetration of rainfall ranges from fifteen to thirty inches, depending on geographic location.

Growth of the grasses in little bluestem stands usually diminishes in midsummer when the vegetation passes into a drought-rest condition. But many forbs are present when moisture conditions are favorable. In the understory, skullcap (*Scutellaria resinosa*), whitlow-wort (*Paronychia jamesii*), few-flowered psoralea (*Psoralea tenuiflora*), and purple coneflower occur along with blue grama and tall dropseed. Tooth-leaved primrose (*Oenothera serrulata*), western wallflower (*Erysimum asperum*), and gayfeather (*Liatris punctata*) occasionally are abundant. Less frequent are the prairie rose (*Rosa suffulta*), slender indigo bush (*Dalea enneandra*), and woolly loco (*Astragalus mollissimus*), made conspicuous by its silvery canescent leaves and purple blossoms.

When the local topography is variable, the little bluestem community occupies an intermediate position between the tall-grass communities in the moist lowlands and the short-grass communities on the dry uplands. In a larger geographic sense it is also intermediate between the tall-grass prairies of the East and the short-grass communities of the West.

In the semiarid short-grass country of the high plains blue grama and buffalo grass are dominant and nearly omnipresent. The dense sod formed by these grasses, and their low stature, explain the origin of the name "short grass." Although these two species produce the bulk of the vegetation over thousands of square miles they are accompanied by many other grasses, particularly such mid-grasses as western wheatgrass, June grass, side-oats grama, three-awns, needlegrasses, and various dry-land sedges.

The presence of mid-grasses throughout the Great Plains explains the inclusion of short-grass communities in the major category, mixed prairie, by modern ecologists. The mixture of mid- and short grasses is almost universally present, although the taller species may not be apparent during long periods of drought or of heavy grazing. The mixed prairies of the Great Plains were the true home of the buffalo. These mighty beasts, grazing in herds of thousands and millions, maintained the prairie in a short-grass condition in which the matlike growth was the most conspicuous feature of the landscape.

When the buffalo migrated and gave the prairie a chance to recover, the short-grass country became a veritable flower garden, especially during wet cycles. Innumerable forbs and grasses appeared in and above the layer of short grasses. When the rains came, after a year or more of drought, the ground often was white with woolly Indian wheat, which produced as many as ten thousand plants per square yard. Six-weeks fescue occasionally was superabundant. In early spring it made a green carpet which soon turned into a yellowish-brown sward as the plants matured and died in early summer.

In mixed prairie on the Great Plains one may see many forbs that extend above the short-grass sod. Conspicuous among these are Rocky Mountain beeplant (*Cleome serrulata*), frequently found at the edges of cleared circles made by harvester ants; curlycup gumweed (*Grindelia squarrosa*), with sticky flower heads; wavyleaf thistle (*Cirsium undulatum*), avoided even by antelope; and the many-flowered aster.

Although we will never know in detail how the wild bison grazed the prairie it is instructive to note how cattle select various plants for their seasonal diets. Blue grama is the outstanding forage producer in spring and early summer. Buffalo grass is second in forage production but is little used before August 1, if a sufficient quantity of blue grama is available. The tops of needle-and-thread (*Stipa comata*) are used sparingly at first; but, as the season progresses, the stubble is regrazed if the supply of blue grama and buffalo grass becomes limited.

Scarlet globe mallow (*Sphaeralcea coccinea*) is taken readily by cattle during May, June, and July. By early summer, if 55 to 60 percent of the blue-grama foliage has been used, the stubble presents a "slicked-off" appearance. When the grasses are grazed this much, winter fat (*Eurotia lanata*) is trimmed back to the woody crowns. About 50 percent of the rubber rabbitbrush (*Chrysothamnus nauseosus*) plants show grazing. A very short, inconspicuous stubble is all that remains of needle-and-thread plants. If large numbers of buffalo grazed as cattle do, then we may conclude that the close-cropped vegetation seen by the earliest explorers was the result of buffalo overgrazing on what was called the Great American Desert.

The traveler who goes southward across the Great Plains from Sas-

*One of the tall grasses of the prairie, big bluestem grows to a height of six feet or more. Bluestem communities cover the true prairie and extend far westward into the Great Plains.*

katchewan to Mexico sees a land of much diversity of climate, topography, and vegetation. Buffalo used all of these millions of acres of grassland. And throughout this vast expanse swards of short grasses and mid-grasses are present. In Wyoming and Colorado, various cacti, especially plains prickly pear (*Opuntia polyacantha*), are present on the semiarid plains. The white spikes of yucca are abundant on sandy soils from the Rocky Mountains to the Mississippi River and southward into Mexico. In southern Colorado and southward other grasses such as galleta (*Hilaria jamesii*) grow in mixture with the gramas.

Topographic irregularities and soil factors in the Great Plains account for much of the diversity of plant associations and their species mixtures. The desert salt grass (*Distichlis stricta*) vegetation type, for example, is restricted to saline soils and is found along stream courses and in the beds of intermittent ponds. When the water table recedes during drought periods, squirreltail first invades and then is rapidly taken over by salt grass when the water table stabilizes at a high level. Livestock graze these areas; the salty vegetation undoubtedly was palatable to buffalo.

Many other vegetation types or subdivisions have been described by the numerous scientists who have studied the prairie. The individuality of these types comes from their physiognomy or general appearance, which is created by different combinations of grasses, forbs, and shrubs, and to some extent by the influence of the animals that inhabit these types. At the edge of the prairie these types blend with a remarkable diversity of forest, swamp, and desert communities which form the threshold of the great interior grassland.

In its unending variety the prairie border reminds one of the edge of the sea. Here are broad, flat marshes and estuaries where water-tolerant vegetation gradually merges with dry-land vegetation. There are bold promontories and headlands where the sea abuts on the land, permitting no encroachment of animal life or transition of plant forms from one habitat to another. Again, here are islands in the sea where land-dwelling plants and animals make their homes just as forest inclusions in the grassland permit the characteristic growth of trees with their own ground layers and adapted species of animals.

Whenever I cross the shoreline of the grassland sea I stop and eagerly examine a niche or two of this extraordinarily variable boundary to see what it harbors. Maybe it is a silphium, or compass-plant, presenting the edges of its leaves north and south, and I wonder, as did Aldo Leopold, "what a thousand acres of Silphiums looked like when they tickled the bellies of the buffalo. . . ." Maybe it is a colony of snow trillium (*Trillium nivale*), such as I once saw in eastern Iowa, growing among the prairie grasses at the edge of a rich woods. This dwarf trillium, only a few inches in height, and with three white petals on each flower, is so uncommon that one never forgets the pleasurable experience of seeing it in a new habitat.

Once when I crossed the prairie boundary between Mankato and St. Cloud, Minnesota, I paused to examine the shrubs at the edge of the deciduous forest known to the early settlers as the "Big Woods." The dogwoods, sumacs, and thorn apples were there. And twining over them was an old friend of my boyhood days, the wild yam-root (*Dioscorea villosa*), with its heart-shaped leaves and pale yellowish-green flowers in drooping panicles. Here was a plant accustomed to woods and prairie borders, using shrubs for support, living in full sunlight, and enduring periodic droughts with the aid of its matted rootstocks. It gave me a moment for thought about climatic, biotic, and physical factors involved in ecotones and transition zones.

The ecologists call the area of transition between vegetation types a tension zone or *ecotone*. In some instances the ecotone is characterized by gradual zonation from one type to another. The transition area between forest and prairie, however, usually is abrupt. But it may be characterized by shrub thickets which buffer the forest interior from the rigors of the grassland climate. But in contrast with the eastern forest-prairie edge, many of the western grassland-forest transitions begin with a savanna or parkland aspect where trees are isolated and the ground beneath is covered with grasses. Let us now travel around the borders of the grassland sea in order to bring the whole prairie into view.

Few people realize that in historical time there was a crescent-shaped prairie covering five thousand to six thousand square miles amidst the original forest in Kentucky. The early settlers there called it the "Big Barrens" because they believed the absence of trees indicated low productivity of the soil. The buffalo knew this prairie and made paths from the West that were followed later by the explorers. The area now is occupied with cultivated fields, pasture land, and forest vegetation, but the forest is new growth, not virgin forest.

The cause of the Barrens is open to speculation. The presence of the prairie in that part of Kentucky cannot be explained by average precipitation or its seasonal distribution in recent times when climatic conditions would have produced forest. But within recent centuries there may have been an extremely dry spell conducive to the growth of prairie. Soil and rock also probably were contributing factors, since the region of grassland coincides closely with an area of land derived from soluble limestones. Soil with this origin becomes dry in a short time. Once established, frequent fires set by Indians or by lightning would have maintained the prairie.

The occurrence of the prairie and isolated typical prairie communities as far south as Kentucky and Tennessee, as far east as northwestern Pennsylvania, and as far north as central Wisconsin and Michigan has led to many points of view as to its origin. This eastern extension, called the "Prairie Peninsula" by Edgar N. Transeau, has been interpreted by some as deciduous forest with trees absent because of former ecological conditions and kept open by human intervention. Others have held that the prairies grew on immature soils while the forests grew on mature soils. Still others believe the Prairie Peninsula was caused by fires set by Indians of recent and historic times attempting to enlarge their pastures or to capture game animals.

The true explanation of the eastern prairies probably rests on prehistoric factors; the causes of prairie formation probably go back thousands of years. Recent studies of opal isolated from Ohio soils lead to the conclusion that this plant-formed substance, biogenetic opal, was produced under a prairie vegetation. L. P. Wilding states that radiocarbon dating indicates an age of more than thirteen thousand years for this opal. Consequently, evaluation of the original prairie must include consideration of past climates. At least, we know that prairie bordered the eastern forests for thousands of years before the coming of white men.

The eastern prairie was bordered regularly by oak, oak-hickory, and oak-maple-linden, and these borders were often miles in width. In central Ohio there are scattered small areas now occupied by beech-maple on soil profiles that indicate prehistoric prairie sites. But in general the Prairie Peninsula originally was a mosaic of prairie and forest communities, between which the local transitions were narrow borders, at most a few rods in width.

Most of the prairie in Wisconsin has been placed under cultivation but much of the southwestern half of the state was prairie at the beginning of settlement in the 1830's. Many of the early accounts emphasize that the flatter prairies east of the Mississippi River were wet or swampy in spring. Since they have been drained in recent times for farming, the present growth of trees cannot be used as evidence that trees lived there one hundred years ago.

As we travel across western Wisconsin and into Minnesota we see the land where forests and grasslands originally alternated all the way to the international boundary. In 1880, forest covered the northeastern two-thirds of the state. The prairie, lying at the south and southwest, and reaching into the Red River Valley as far north as Lake Winnipeg, was abundant with tall grasses and bore a great variety of flowers, including asters, goldenrods, blazing star, prairie clover, roses, lilies, phlox, and fringed gentian.

The prairie edge in southern Minnesota was an oak savanna in which big bluestem and other grasses grew beneath the widely spaced trees. For many miles the margin of the prairie touched the maple-basswood forests. This band of deciduous forest grew between the coniferous forests of spruce and fir to the east and the prairie to the west. The transition from hardwood to coniferous forest was much more gradual than the transition to prairie. The change to open prairie, at the latitude of Itasca Park, is usually through "brush prairie," a mixture of scrubby growth of bur oak, American hazelnut (*Corylus americana*), and smooth sumac (*Rhus glabra*).

These brush transitions have always been favorite homes for many wildlife species. The prairie-shrub-tree combination provides food, shelter, nesting habitat, and observation perches for bobwhites, warblers, cardinals, catbirds, and song sparrows. The prairie itself gives sanctuary to ground-nesting species, including meadowlarks, pipits, and cottontails. Fox squirrels live in the treetops and forage among the grasses. Deer hide in the forests in the daytime and venture into the grasslands in late evening.

The forest-prairie margin west of Itasca Park coincides with the big moraines left by the retreating ice sheets of the Pleistocene. Westward, beyond this, oak and oak-aspen groves, aspen stands, shrub communities, marshes, wet prairie, moist prairie, and dry prairie communities are present, depending on topography and distribution of soils of different textures. Since W. Upham mapped the vegetation prior to 1884, woodland has increased and prairie has decreased in extent.

In Indian days fires were known to sweep through this area regularly. Intense fire kills both the aspen trees and their sprouts, which develop from roots that spread as much as one hundred feet from the trees into the adjoining grassland. Since settlement and cultivation have resulted in fire control, the aspen shoots now can grow into thickets from which new propagating roots push outward into the prairie. Before settlement, fires set by lightning and Indians burned the prairie without harm but kept the forests of oak and aspen from invading the grasslands in western Minnesota.

From Minnesota the northern border of the grassland extends far into Canada and is a broad transition zone of aspen-grass between the prairie and the northern conifer or boreal forest. From the Red River in Manitoba the prairie extends 750 miles westward to the Rocky Mountains and northward almost 300 miles to its most northern extremity in the vicinity of the Saskatchewan-Alberta boundary.

Aspen groves are associated with true prairie in Canada in the east and with mixed prairie in the west. The width of the aspen savanna varies from 50 to 150 miles. North of this lies the boreal forest in a belt up to 500 miles wide. Out of the lakes, swamps, muskegs, and tundra of this great northern wilderness come the hosts of migrating water-fowl which have streamed southward each autumn for thousands of years. Before the white men drained the ponds and plowed the land, the ducks, geese, and shorebirds on their way south found temporary sanctuary in the prairie waters and obtained food from the ripened grasses and other seed-bearing plants.

There is history along the western prairie border. Recently I came over Lolo Summit from the west in the Bitterroot Mountains, where the road drops down into Lolo Creek Valley in western Montana. The sign at the summit says that the Lewis and Clark party crossed this pass September 13, 1805. I was impelled to tarry a while to absorb some of the misty beauty of the forests in early morning. A walk through DeVoto Woods reminded me of the giant red cedars that once were so numerous along the lower Indian trails. Then, in the valley, nestled below the dominant mountains I saw Herefords grazing as the buffalo once grazed on the foothill prairies.

Here was the far western edge of the great central grassland. South of Willow Creek, near the place where the Madison, Jefferson, and Gallatin rivers unite to form the Missouri River, I visited a rancher friend. We drove over a winding road into the hills. Here we found old friends I had known for many years in the Dakotas and eastern Wyoming and Colorado: western wheatgrass, blue grama, needle-and-thread, fringed sagebrush, threadleaf sedge, and June grass. Growing with these were bluebunch wheatgrass (*Agropyron spicatum*) and Idaho fescue (*Festuca idahoensis*), characteristic of the far western prairies in Idaho and Washington.

The intermingling of these grasses of the great central prairie and the Palouse prairie illustrates the broad and gradual transition between grasslands that flourish in widely separated geographic areas. These transitions in the West commonly extend over many miles.

Savanna transitions, consisting of ponderosa pine and blue grama, needlegrasses, and western wheatgrass, can be seen in central Montana and in Wyoming east of the Big Horn Mountains and east of the

*Needle-and-thread, a common grass of medium stature, can be found in the mixed prairie. The sharp-pointed seeds are attached to a long bristle which twists and untwists with changes in humidity. This twisting helps screw the seed into the ground.*

Laramie Range. Westward from Miles City, Montana, you can see the transition from mixed prairie to sagebrush-wheatgrass. If you pass through the country near the battlefield where George Armstrong Custer and his cavalry troopers fought some four thousand Cheyenne and Sioux warriors, June 25, 1876, you will see the sagebrush-prairie mixture.

This gradual change from mixed prairie to sagebrush-wheatgrass extends westward for many miles in central Wyoming. As the country becomes more arid, blue grama and buffalo grass thin out and finally disappear. At this western edge of the prairie the grassland is more drought resistant than the forests on its eastern shore but less drought resistant than the Wyoming sagebrush or the desert grassland of New Mexico and Arizona.

In central Wyoming, the prairie plants are replaced by more semi-arid species because of lessened rainfall and later disappearance of frost in spring and earlier occurrence in autumn. Sagebrush lands were not burned as much in the past because there were fewer grass plants to sustain the fires. Since fires periodically thinned the grasses there were more legumes in the prairie. Mammal and bird life likewise was influenced by differences in food and shelter in these two great plant communities. Prairie chickens, for example, flourished on the prairie because their supply of grass seeds was dependable; sage grouse lived in the far west because they could subsist on sagebrush leaves and were not dependent on regular crops of grass.

The transition from grassland to pine forest is conspicuous along the mountain front from Cheyenne, Wyoming, to Colorado Springs. It is abrupt where mountain mahogany grows in pure stands on the east slopes of the hogbacks and foothills of the Front Range of the Rockies. Where altitude increases gradually along the river courses the grassland extends far into the mountains. In the open pine forests you can see blue grama intermingled with mountain muhly (*Muhlenbergia montana*) and Arizona fescue (*Festuca arizonica*) if you drive to Lookout Mountain, where Buffalo Bill is buried, or if you drive from Colorado Springs through Ute Pass to Cripple Creek or north to Deckers.

South of Colorado Springs the prairie borders the juniper woodland which extends far to the east along the Colorado–New Mexico boundary. Here, blue grama mingles with galleta, a grass characteristic of the semiarid lands to the south. In southern Colorado and northern New Mexico, near the mountains, temperature and drought become so extreme that blue grama is replaced by ring grass (*Muhlenbergia torreyi*). The landscape is made picturesque by cane cactus (*Opuntia arborescens*). On this inferior grazing land the woodrats make nests of dried horse pellets, which are placed in piles two feet high and five or six feet in diameter among the stems of skunkbush and other shrubs.

Farther south, in New Mexico and western Texas, the prairie blends into mesquite and desert grass savanna. Small trees and thorn bushes are scattered over the short-grass cover. Distribution of rainfall is somewhat similar to that in the desert region to the west. Prickly pear

(*Opuntia lindheimeri*) is abundant along with grasses such as curly mesquite (*Hilaria belangeri*), buffalo grass, and various species of three-awn grasses. This transition area forms a belt almost two hundred miles wide south of the Canadian River.

The southern boundary of the prairie lies in southern Texas and northeastern Mexico. This grassland originally was composed of northern and southern elements. Now it is characterized by subtropical shrubs that have invaded from Mexico. In eastern Texas it borders the pine and oak-hickory forests; on the north it merges into true prairie; on the northwest it passes into mixed prairie; and in the west it meets the desert plains grassland.

Along the Gulf of Mexico the coastal prairie lies in a narrow belt between the coniferous and hardwood forests. In this region of little drainage and high rainfall, thirty to fifty inches, there are few trees except for the transition between the prairies and the forest to the north. The moisture-loving vegetation consists mainly of rank-growing grasses such as smooth cordgrass (*Spartina alterniflora*) and seacoast bluestem (*Andropogon littoralis*). Various panic grasses (*Panicum*), the dropseed (*Sporobolus virginicus*), and the common reed (*Phragmites communis*) also are present.

Live oak mixes with post oak and blackjack oak in the northeastern coastal prairie. Elm, hickory, and sycamore trees are found on the moist bottomlands. Where the coastal prairie pushes southwestward toward the semidesert country, yuccas and agaves form savanna with grassland in the drier sites.

The coastal prairies and marshes afford unexcelled habitat for many birds from the northern prairies. Geese, ducks, herons, gulls, terns, and shorebirds are attracted to the many square miles of coastal waterways, swamps, and marshlands. In seasons of migration this area receives both eastern and western forms and is one of the notable places in the United States to see a large percentage of the avifauna of the continent.

With its flat silvery leaves, the lead plant, or "prairie shoestring," is one of the most conspicuous of the prairie shrubs. It grows in company with bluestem grasses.

# 4

## Plants of the Prairie

ONE DAY IN JULY, I was showing a group of land appraisers over our prairie pastures. One, with an inquisitive turn of mind, had borrowed my hand lens, and was busily turning it on insects, pebbles, and all manner of flowers, remarking on the astonishing variety and beauty of their colors. I had him try it on a Russian thistle flower, and he was more intrigued than ever. Like most people he had never looked at the inconspicuous flowers that characterize many of our weedy plants. Then I had him look at the flower of a grass plant.

The flower itself consisted of three yellowish-red stamens and a tiny hair-covered pistil, which I explained would ultimately produce the fruit or grass seed when it was mature. I doubt if this man had ever consciously realized that grasses have flowers, as do all plants that produce seeds. He certainly was unaware of the vast numbers of plants that produce flowers without sepals or colorful petals.

Although we found more than twenty different grasses growing in our pastures that day, only three kinds were in bloom. But these were sufficient to demonstrate to my friend that the flowers of all three had the same essential elements—stamens and pistils—and that each flower was subtended by a pair of tiny bracts, one of which is called the lemma and the other the palea. He also learned that grass flowers or florets are attached to a tiny branch or axis, from the base of which grow two papery bracts called glumes. These glumes form much of the chaff that is produced when wheat is threshed. All together the tiny axis, with its glumes and florets, with their stamens, pistils, and bracts, forms the spikelet which is the unit of the inflorescence of all grasses.

[59]

The spikelets of different grasses vary greatly in their size, color, number of florets, and arrangement on the main axis or stem of the grass plant. The whole group of spikelets, regardless of how they are arranged to form the flower or seed head, is called the inflorescence. Most frequently the inflorescence is a panicle, that is, a branched inflorescence in which the flowering units or spikelets occur on branches of the main axis. The tassel of maize, the spike of timothy, and the panicle of bluegrass are familiar inflorescences. The size, shape, and appearance of all these parts of inflorescences, together with the characteristics of leaves, stems, buds, and even the roots, are the characters by which grasses are distinguished one from another.

My friend and I, that July day, briefly considered how nicely nature has provided for the pollination of grasses and the scattering of seeds. Insects inadvertently pollinate some grasses, but most of the job is done by the wind, which seldom fails to blow on the prairie. And since grasses are mostly wind pollinated, they have no need for colorful petals to attract insects.

The seeds of grasses are shaken from their seed heads by the wind, are blown from place to place, and are buried by drifting sand or soil. Grass seeds also are provender for numberless animals such as mice, ground squirrels, harvester ants, quail, prairie chickens, and sparrows. But all seeds are not eaten. Rodents store them in caches, ants drop them in their travels, and large mammals transport them in their furry coats and trample them into the ground. These planted seeds are more likely to survive drought than are wind-sown seeds fallen on barren and unshaded ground.

Some grass seeds lose their viability after a few months in the soil. Others can begin growth after many years of storage. When the seed does germinate its first effort is to put down a primary or seminal root, using energy from its stored food. The young plant soon is dependent upon this primary root for water and nutrients from the soil. It must hurry into its growth cycle—three to five consecutive days with moist surface soil are necessary for its roots to penetrate sufficiently to become established.

If the grass is an annual it will reach maturity, produce seed, and die within a few weeks or months. If it is a perennial its full root and top development may not be reached until it is five years old, although it may produce seeds in its second year. In its tenth, or even its fiftieth year, it may still be living. Through the years it is cruelly subject to heaving of the soil by frosts, to long summer droughts, to competition

*Silky sophora is one of the many legumes that supply nitrogen to the soil. Appearing in the spring, its silvery foliage lends character and beauty to the landscape.*

for light and moisture from younger robust plants, to grazing by large animals, to chewing by grasshoppers and other insects, to burrowing by insect larvae, gophers and moles, and to invasion of its tissues by bacteria and rusts and other fungi. In its senescence, its vigor declines, its stems decrease in number, and its root system becomes shallow. In death it contributes its litter to the soil and its substance becomes available for use of other plants and animals.

In the early stages of germination of grass seeds the stored food is digested by enzymes. For a short time the embryo plant is dependent on its own reserves for production of the radicle, which grows downward to form the first root, and for production of the plumule which grows upward to form the stem and leaves. The plumule, or primary bud of the embryo, is protected by a sheath or seedling leaf called the coleoptile, which protects the tip of the tiny plant from abrasion as it pushes upward through the soil.

At this time the grass plant performs a minor miracle of adjustment to the depth at which its seed was planted. A growth hormone, auxin, which moves downward from the coleoptile tip, stimulates growth of that portion of the stem between the seed and the first node. This node is moved upward until the tip of the new plant breaks through the soil surface. Light then reduces the auxin production and the growth processes suddenly are reversed. Roots form at the first nodes at the same level, regardless of the varying depths at which the seeds were planted. The plumule begins to produce a stem with leaves that grow from its nodes. Elongation of the internodes increases the height of the green plant, which now has the ability to manufacture food from raw materials derived from the soil and the air.

If you examine a stem closely you will see that the leaves alternate in opposite directions from the stem, and only one leaf grows from a node. The leaf itself consists of two parts: the sheath which forms a tube around the stem, and is split for its full length; and the blade, which is wide and often flat but nearly always elongated. The portion of the leaf at the junction of the blade and sheath is called the collar.

The membranous or hairy structure where the base of the blade touches the stem is called the ligule. This structure, which varies greatly among different grasses, is useful in their identification. It keeps water from flowing inside the sheath where fungi might grow. Some grasses have appendages, one on either side of the base of the blade, known as auricles. The size and shape of these auricle tips that clasp the stem also are useful in the identification of genera and species of grasses.

As the grass plant continues its seasonal growth it produces new stems from buds that develop from old stem bases near the surface of the ground. When these new stems become numerous the grass forms a tuft which is characteristic of bunchgrasses such as little bluestem and Indian ricegrass. Other grasses produce runners or creeping stems which grow horizontally aboveground (stolons) or belowground (rhizomes). The sod of buffalo grass is formed by stolons which take root at the nodes. This and other forms of vegetative propagation enable grasses to persist for many years without seed formation.

Grasses have withstood grazing by herds of bison, elk, pronghorns, deer, prairie dogs, and other native animals. This miracle of persistence is possible because of another built-in provision for regrowth not found in broad-leaved herbs, shrubs, or trees. Each grass leaf grows from its base instead of its tip. When the tip part of the leaf is eaten, growth continues from below and the leaf reaches or surpasses its former size. This explains why we can mow our city lawns throughout the summer without killing the grass.

The wonders of grass plants, however, are not all aboveground. When we walk on the prairie few of us realize we are treading on soil that may contain more organic material in the form of living and dead roots than exists in all the vegetation aboveground. The roots of grasses are fibrous and their branches may be so abundant that a square yard of soil four inches deep may contain roots that would stretch for twenty miles if all were placed end to end.

Until recently little information was available on how long the roots of perennial grasses persist in the soil. A partial answer was obtained by J. E. Weaver and Ellen Zink by an ingenious experiment in which they banded the roots of prairie grasses with very thin pliable sheet tin and then examined them at the end of one, two, and three growing seasons. Survival on switchgrass and western wheatgrass, at the end of the second summer, was 100 and 42 percent, respectively. After three growing seasons, 81 percent of the roots on big bluestem survived, but none on nodding wild rye. Losses in all species were gradual, and after three growing seasons, survival of roots for other grasses was as follows: blue grama, 45 percent; side-oats grama, 14 percent; and little bluestem and porcupine grass, each 10 percent.

On the open prairie the rates of survival and death of grass roots undoubtedly differ from those in the laboratory since plants in nature live in more than a world of grasses. I remember a green island of big bluestem in a sandhill blowout that my students studied for one whole summer. The grass tussocks were two feet across, and in autumn the flower stalks with their "turkey-foot" racemes were seven feet high. The clumps were widely spaced, and although prairie forbs were present, many of the sandy interstices were bare.

In this place, kangaroo rats excavated their burrows beneath the grass clumps. A mother skunk and her five kittens used an abandoned badger hole for home. Lizards daily scuttled over the burning sand as did the exceptionally alert metallic green and bronze tiger beetles. Golden-orange velvet ants, which actually are parasitic wasps, also wandered through the grasses, ran over the barren areas, and dug holes near the grass clumps. When we excavated one of the tussocks and shook the stems and roots over a white sheet a veritable menagerie of animal life came into view: leafhoppers, crickets, katydids, ground beetles, ants, ambush bugs, ground-dwelling bees, harvestmen, spiders, root-eating grubs, and a walking stick. What other creatures had

*Cattails are common around the world. In prairie lakes and ponds they provide nesting sites for waterfowl and furnish food for insects that live in their seed clusters, stems, and roots.*

descended among the deeper roots to eat or sleep we did not know since we did not dig far into their underground world.

The list of prairie forbs could be expanded endlessly. On a single square mile of mixed prairie in eastern Colorado, I once identified 143 species of forbs. At the same time I found 22 species of grasses, 10 kinds of shrubs, and 4 kinds of trees. The variety is even greater in some of the eastern grasslands. Thus we cannot conceive of the prairie as being merely a vast expanse of grasses.

The broad-leaved herbs, or forbs, of course, are always present among the grasses on the prairie, and they add much to its beauty. From early spring until late autumn, their blooming adds variety to the landscape. Some are abundant. Some are rare. In early summer in the tall-grass prairie the familiar strawberry (*Fragaria virginiana*), the prairie phlox (*Phlox pilosa*), and the whorled milkweed (*Asclepias verticillata*) are nearly always present. In autumn, a bewildering variety of sunflowers, asters, and goldenrods burst into bloom. At this season the silvery leaves of the lead plant (*Amorpha canescens*) add further color to the landscape.

On the western plains other kinds of herbs grow in season among the shorter grasses. Some of the common showy ones are few-flowered psoralea, hairy goldaster, plains prickly pear, ball cactus (*Mammillaria vivipara*), prickly poppy (*Argemone intermedia*), western wallflower, curlycup gumweed, and scarlet globe mallow. This mallow is found almost everywhere on the western prairies. Its high protein content undoubtedly made it a valuable supplement in the diet of the buffalo. Like other members of the mallow family, including the hollyhock of our grandmothers' gardens, scarlet globe mallow flowers are interesting because their stamens are united by their filaments into a tube or column.

The forb aspect of the prairie is never the same. The combinations of the broad-leaved herbs are kaleidoscopic in their variety. From place to place, season to season, and year to year, the colorful mixtures and combinations of flowering herbs are influenced by permutations of weather, grazing, competition with grasses, and seed abundance.

During long drought cycles, which may last several years, millions of seeds of annual forbs lie dormant in the soil despite all the yearly gleanings of birds, ants, and mice. The deep-rooted perennial herbs retain the spark of life by putting forth a minimum of herbage, which sprouts from buds nourished by deep and permanent roots. Then when the rains come the prairie springs to life in a panoramic display that is a joy to behold.

On abandoned plowed lands, Russian-thistle seedlings sometimes grow so thickly their patches resemble green velvet rugs. By their very numbers they exhaust the moisture in the surface layers of the soil, quickly reach the wilting point, and die by the end of May. In contrast, the grama-three-awn prairies are blanketed with the snow-white flowers of evening primroses (*Oenothera albicaulis*), which have deeper root systems than the Russian thistles.

The remarkable stability of some perennial forbs is illustrated by the bush morning glory (*Ipomoea leptophylla*). The large hemispherical tops, covered by purple blossoms, are conspicuous since the plant frequently grows alone on bare sandy soils of the Great Plains. Several years ago I facetiously advised a student who wanted to press a specimen of this plant that he should include the roots, since roots sometimes aid in the identification of certain species. After several hours of hard digging he had a hole large enough to hold a cookstove, but still had not excavated the root system. Later, I learned that my student was not the first to lay his shovel aside and rest from such a labor. Under the direction of Lieutenant Abert in 1846 in Kansas north of the Arkansas valley, a soldier spent several hours trying to dig up a bush morning glory but finally abandoned the task because the ground was so hard. Abert stated that the Cheyenne Indians dug and ate these roots but he did not describe the tools used by the Indians.

The taproot of bush morning glory enlarges at a depth of six or eight inches to a diameter of twelve inches, and in some instances to eighteen to twenty-four inches. Then it gradually tapers to a diameter of an inch or two at a depth of three to five feet, where it breaks up into many branches. Some of these grow sideways and others penetrate to a depth of ten to fifteen feet. The enlarged portion of the root may weigh from ten to one hundred pounds.

Many other grassland forbs penetrate the soil ten feet or more. Some of these lessen competition by absorbing moisture far below the roots of grasses. Others avoid competition by producing superficial roots; few are entirely dependent on surface absorption, excepting the cacti, which store the subsurface moisture from light rainfall in their fleshy stems.

Forbs, shrubs, grasses, and animals not only avoid competition but nicely complement one another in their underground habits in the prairie. The grasses are good soil binders because of their fibrous roots.

*Roses grow in great numbers on the prairie and their thorny tangles
furnish protection from predators for rabbits, grouse, and other birds.
The fruits of the rose are eaten by birds, deer, antelope, and small
animals. When food is scarce, grazing animals eat rose leaves and
twigs.*

The legumes add nitrogen to the soil to the benefit of all plants. When
the deep roots of forbs die and decay they leave channels for the
passage of air and moisture. Ground squirrels, gophers, and badgers
burrow into the earth as do harvester ants and many dung-burying
insects. The once widely distributed prairie dogs also dug deeply and
transported large quantities of soil to the surface. This cooperative soil
tillage, in which animals and plants were involved for millennia, did not

destroy the soil. It contributed to the monumental fertility of the aboriginal prairie.

The story of the vegetation of the prairie would be incomplete if the shrubs, vines, and small trees were overlooked. All around the borders of the prairie, fringing thickets of shrubbery occur. Some of these make a zone only a few feet wide at the forest edge. Shrubs here and on the prairie often withstand droughts because of their deep root systems. Their persistence frequently is of benefit to grasses and forbs which grow in their shade while unsheltered plants wither and die. Grasses that send up their seed stalks among the shrub branches also are protected from grazing animals.

In the open prairie, shrubs have always been a part of the flora. One of the most abundant, conspicuous, and widely distributed shrubs is the lead plant or prairie shoestring (*Amorpha canescens*). The silvery foliage of this semiwoody plant blends with the bronze of the little bluestem, the shining yellow of the sunflower, and the brilliant orange of the "pleurisy root" or butterfly weed to form an intricate mosaic on the green background of other prairie plants. The leaflets of the lead plant, which is a legume, fold together to reduce water loss in times of drought. When it is heavily grazed it behaves like a forb and sends up succulent shoots from the woody base. It flourishes best in grasslands that have not been grazed for several years.

In the central prairies west of the Missouri River, shrubs are common on rugged uplands. On north-facing slopes, in ravines, and in places where water runs down from the slopes or windblown snow accumulates, shrubs are frequently intermixed with the tall grasses. Thickets of buckbrush (*Symphoricarpos occidentalis*) often grow so dense they shade out the grasses. Other dense copses of western chokecherry (*Prunus melanocarpa*), wild plum, and smooth sumac form miniature groves with virtually no ground cover below. Riverbank grapes climb over the shrubs making impenetrable thickets where skunks, mice, coyotes, and foxes find refuge and food and where prairie foraging birds build their nests.

In the river world of the open prairie woody vegetation finds a proper environment along with trees that grow around seeps, springs, and on stream terraces. The sloping banks of streams are favorable sites for many shrubs such as coralberry, elder (*Sambucus canadensis*), rough-leaf cornel, burning-bush (*Evonymus atropurpureus*), bristly greenbrier (*Smilax hispida*), poison ivy (*Rhus toxicodendron*), lance-leaved buckthorn (*Rhammus lanceolata*), and virgin's bower (*Clematis virginiana*). Many of these have showy, edible fruits carried by birds.

On sandy floodplains, along streams, and around lake shores at all elevations throughout the prairie one can find the sandbar willow (*Salix interior*). This shrub, with its clustered stems three to twelve feet high and long narrow leaves, is one of the easiest of all willows to identify. Its dense stands often are bordered by a belt of switchgrass and Canada wild rye.

The shrubs of the mixed prairie and the short-grass plains are a varied group. They are present because they are fitted to an environment which involves drought, shallow soils, drifting sand, and the depredations of gnawing and grazing animals. Many perish and many survive: among them the yuccas, saltbushes, winter fat, and various species of sagebrush.

Small soapweed (*Yucca glauca*) is a common plant on sandy soils of the plains from Montana to Texas. Its basal tufts of swordlike leaves grow from a very short semiwoody stem. At flowering time it puts forth an inflorescence from three to six feet in length. The flowers and the growing tip of the inflorescence are sweet and palatable and are especially attractive to cattle. It is a common experience while driving along roads on the western plains to see the showy flower clusters of small soapweeds along the roadside while not a single blossom remains inside the fence on grazed ranges. Yuccas undoubtedly served as emergency food for buffalo, antelope, and jackrabbits in time of drought. The Indians used the fleshy fruits for food and made soap from the roots.

Fourwing saltbush (*Atriplex canescens*) is eaten by deer, antelope, cattle, and buffalo. Its palatability and nutritive qualities are high, and it retains its leaves throughout a greater part of the year. Fourwing saltbush grows on moderately alkaline soils and is distributed from South Dakota to Mexico and west to Oregon. It is often erroneously called "shadscale" and even "sagebrush." It is a member of the goosefoot family and hence is closely related to Russian thistle, some of the pigweeds, and common winter fat, which also grows in the mixed prairie and in the western deserts.

The fine mealy covering on the leaves of fourwing saltbush gives it a grayish-white, scurfy appearance. The most conspicuous features are the fruits, which occur in dense clusters near the tips of the branches. These fruits each possess a pair of enlarged bracts consisting mainly of two broad wings which are more than one-half inch in diameter and

*Popularly reputed to repel fleas, fleabane blooms on the prairie in the summer and autumn.*

are net-veined. The flowers of fourwing saltbush are of two kinds, male and female, and they occur on separate plants; hence, not all the plants in a locality produce seeds.

Many species of sagebrush are found on the prairie. Fringed sagebrush (*Artemisia frigida*) is one of the most widely distributed of these. It grows from the arid deserts of Mexico through most of the western United States and Canada to the frozen regions of Alaska and Siberia. It also is found in Europe. Deer and elk use it for winter forage in many localities. Most authorities agree that its forage value is greatest in the

*Coneflowers are long-lived on the prairie. If not destroyed by continued overgrazing, a cluster of these plants with their showy yellow flower heads may persist for fifty years or more.*

southern part of its range, where cattle eat it readily, and least in the northern states and Canada.

Fringed sagebrush is a half shrub, a term used to describe perennial plants with woody bases from which annual stems arise to form small shrubs six to twenty inches high. The stems are densely gray, or silvery hairy as are the aromatic leaves. The leaves usually are less than one-half inch in length and are divided twice or three times into linear leaflets, a characteristic alluded to in the name "fringed." In late summer, flower heads consisting of many yellow flowers growing in spherical clusters develop along the upper portions of the annual stems.

Overgrazing and grassland depletion are indicated by fringed sagebrush when it occurs in abundance and the individual plants form mats instead of upright stems. J. Macoun, a botanical explorer, recognized this in 1875 in British Columbia. It has been recognized in a similar role by other investigators in Canada and the United States. Whether overgrazing by the buffalo contributed to its abundance on the original prairie we do not know.

Big sagebrush (*Artemisia tridentata*) is the one with which travelers become familiar as they journey through the West. Zane Grey made it famous in *Riders of the Purple Sage* in spite of the fact that it is silvery green instead of purple. Big sagebrush and other species of *Artemisia* border the prairie for hundreds of miles in Montana and Wyoming. The transition zone is many miles wide and is marked by gradual decrease in density of grasses in the understory as one goes westward until finally the shrubs form a pigmy forest in which grasses and forbs from the Far West are found.

Although the prairie is dominated by grasses, it is not completely treeless. West of the Missouri River in Nebraska and Kansas the dense forests no longer grow on the uplands but are confined to the river lands and lake shores. But one does not completely cross the prairie before he encounters the cottonwoods and willows along the streams that flow from the Rocky Mountains, or sees the outlying groves of pines along the ridges that extend eastward from the Black Hills. The transition to juniper can be seen far east along the Colorado-Oklahoma boundary. In Oklahoma and Texas one encounters the Cross Timbers, dominated by post oak and blackjack oak in the midst of the prairie sea.

One of the striking vegetational features of the plains region, recently emphasized by Philip V. Wells, is the widespread occurrence of woodlands along escarpments or breaks in topography, which protect the trees from fires. These wooded scarps are abrupt and are high above the long stringers of forests that grow along the prairie streams. The map prepared by Wells shows an astonishing number of scarps and areas of broken topography that support woodland in dozens of areas throughout the prairie province.

Quaking aspen and bur oak, for example, grow in mixture with big and little bluestem in the Turtle Hills, North Dakota. In Montana, eastern Wyoming, and the western Dakotas ponderosa pine and Rocky Mountain juniper are found with an understory of blue grama, western wheatgrass, and needle-and-thread. These same trees grow far eastward in the prairie that borders the Niobrara escarpment in northern Nebraska. The woodland of the Black Mesa–Mesa de Maya area of Oklahoma, New Mexico, and Colorado consists of pinyon (*Pinus edulis*), ponderosa pine, one-seed juniper (*Juniperus monosperma*), Rocky Mountain juniper (*J. scopulorum*), and wavyleaf oak (*Quercus undulata*), with an understory of blue grama and buffalo grass. This same combination of tree and grass species also is found on the Llano Estacado in New Mexico.

Plains cottonwood (*Populus sargentii*) is one of the most typical trees on the riverbanks in the central prairie. North of central Nebraska the cottonwood is the largest tree on the banks of the Missouri River. Farther south the cottonwoods intermingle with willows, elms, box elders, black walnut, and American basswood. These floodplain forests originally were best developed on the first bottom of the floodplain, where they were bordered above by sloughgrass or by big-bluestem prairie.

Westward along the rivers of the central prairie the deciduous woodlands were composed largely of floodplain species. Along the Niobrara River, for example, the floodplain supports stands of sandbar willow, peach-leaved willow, American elm, green ash, red ash, and hackberry. Bur oak and red cedar occur on some of the north-facing slopes east of Valentine, Nebraska. Red cedars also are found along the Smoky Hill River in the vicinity of Hays, Kansas, although the great drought which began in the spring of 1933 killed many of these trees.

Trees in the prairie were not mentioned extensively in the narratives of the explorers. Even in the early survey records much land was designated as prairie, although it supported trees up to two feet in diameter. Trees, to forest-minded men, meant commercial saw timber and for that reason the timbered prairie streams were mapped as being treeless. Hence we can only speculate on the real nature and distribution of trees in the prairie before white men saw them.

The tiny fungi and the bacteria of the prairie seldom come to our attention, yet the prairie and all its plants, birds, insects, and mammals could not exist without them. Without the help of decomposer microorganisms all nature soon would be clogged with the dead remains of plants and animals. The breakdown of dead matter by molds, bacteria, and protozoa in the soil and leaf litter involves a pattern of energy transfer quite different from that in a food chain in which a grass uses sun energy, a rabbit uses grass energy, a coyote uses rabbit energy, and a buzzard uses coyote energy.

Of all the lesser plants of the prairie, the fairy-ring fungi are among the most fascinating to me. I first saw fairy rings many years ago, without their fungi. The rings were conspicuous because of their dark green bands, one to two feet wide, in the yellowish green of the blue-grama sod in mid-August. By following the color bands I could walk

*Prickly-pear flowers are among the most delicate and beautifully tinted of all the prairie blossoms.*

around these circles, which were one hundred yards or more in diameter. I could follow one until it joined another circle or until the band was broken by changes in local topography. On close examination I found the remains of puffballs, which were mere fragments of the fungus bodies, with small amounts of brown spores still clinging to their bases.

When the puffballs are mature and white they can be seen for long distances; sometimes they are difficult to distinguish from white quartz stones. One can play a game with these fungi. When only two fruits, three to twenty feet apart, are visible, the problem is, Where is the circle? Here is a situation in which two are company, but a crowd would be desirable. When three fruiting bodies are present, and not in a straight line, you have an indication of which way the line bends and how large is the circle. By walking the edge of this imaginary circle you can find other fruiting bodies, sometimes dozens of yards ahead, even though they are hidden in tall wheatgrass in the swales.

Fairy rings are formed by many kinds of mushrooms and puffballs and are occasionally seen on golf fairways and lawns. These rings have been known for centuries and people once believed that fairies danced in the circles and caused the mushrooms to grow. In Holland they marked the place where "the devil churned butter." When Robin Hood's men saw Hob o' the Hill they thought he was an elf or troll whose friends made green rings that poisoned beasts that fed in the meadows. Thunder, lightning, whirlwinds, ants, haystacks, and the urine of animals also have been credited as the cause of these fungus rings.

There still is mystery in fairy rings, their kinds, their effects on vegetation, how long they grow, and their nutritional habits. But they are actually caused by the growth of fungi such as the common mushroom (*Agaricus campestris*), the puffball (*Lycoperdon wrightii*), and many others. The mycelium or moldlike threads of the fungus grows profusely underground, starting at a central point and spreading outward at the perimeter of the original patch.

Often the grass is stimulated as if fertilized, producing a ring of grass taller than that inside or outside the circle. Sometimes the soil becomes impervious to water in the mycelium zone and the grasses die, leaving a bare path through the sod. As the ring expands, grasses inside the circle invade the path, and their growth again becomes normal. Under favorable conditions—which may be years apart—the fungus produces the mushrooms or puffballs, which emerge from the soil in a ring.

The most extensive study of prairie fairy rings was made many years ago by H. L. Shantz and R. L. Piemeisel in eastern Colorado. A fungus which they called *Agaricus tabularis* made rings up to 230 feet in diameter. This fungus killed or badly damaged the grasses just inside the periphery of the circle where the fungus fruits were formed. Species of *Calvatia*, *Lycoperdon*, and *Marasmius* only stimulated the vegetation, and *Lepiota* made no noticeable effect.

Rings exceeding 600 feet in diameter were made by *Calvatia cyathi-formis*. Shantz estimated that a ring 200 feet in diameter could be 250 years old. On the basis of an advance of approximately one foot for each crop of fruiting bodies, some rings could be 600 years old.

As with all other plants and animals the fungi had their place in the scheme of things on the original prairie. The mycelium of the fungi, particularly the fairy-ring producers, caused chemical changes in the soil. They reduced the protein portions of dead organic matter in the soil to ammonia, or to other compounds which were changed by bacteria to nitrites. These in turn were changed by other bacteria to nitrates, which furnished nitrogenous material for the growth of green plants. When the old mycelium itself died it was decayed by bacteria and molds to more nitrogen, which was used by higher plants.

Where fairy rings temporarily caused the death of vegetation as the circles became larger, the bare areas were invaded by forbs that initiated plant successions. The first invaders included woolly Indian wheat, six-weeks fescue, false-pennyroyal (*Hedeoma hispida*), and pepper-grass (*Lepidium ramosissimum*). These were followed by various species of goosefoot (*Chenopodium*), stickseed (*Lappula*), and pig-weed (*Amaranthus*), which were replaced in a few seasons by short-lived grasses such as tumblegrass (*Schedonnardus paniculatus*) and squirreltail (*Sitanion hystrix*). Half shrubs such as snakeweed and fringed sagebrush then became established. Ultimately, blue grama and buffalo grass reappeared to make the prairie whole again. But the ever-expanding ring of fungus always made way for a supply of lesser forbs and grasses needed for repair of the vegetation when buffalo denudation, drought, or flooding scarred the grassy cover of the prairie.

Many other fungi grow in the prairie. I have seen giant puffballs (*Calvatia gigantea*) more than a foot in diameter in moist soil at the edge of the prairie near forest trees. One of these puffballs can produce seven trillion spores. Geasters or earth stars used to be numerous around our cattle corrals in the mixed prairie in northeastern Colorado. Mushrooms that grew on buffalo dung must have been numerous all through the prairie. The mealy ink cap (*Coprinus fimetarius*), which is attractive because of its pure white color when young, grows on freshly manured ground. Other fungi, such as the carved puffball (*Calvatia caelata*) and the bird's nest fungus with its tiny cluster of "eggs," grow among the prairie grasses.

One of the strange species of fungi found on dung is *Pilobolus*, which belongs to the group that includes the familiar bread mold. It dispenses

*Yucca seed pods split open in winter and the springlike stems snap back and forth and spread the seeds when brushed by large animals like bison.*

its spores explosively by building up pressure behind its sporangia or spore-bearing bodies. Because of this it has attracted the attention of biologists for three centuries. But it also is of interest because of the dramatic way in which it is adapted to its environment.

The threadlike mycelium grows in dung and after a few days produces sporangia on stalks that project above the surface of the dung. When sufficient pressure builds up the sporangium is propelled by a jet of cell sap with an estimated muzzle velocity of more than thirty feet per second. If the forcible shot strikes a grass blade at the end of its trajectory—which may be six or eight feet away—the sporangium adheres to it. If the grass blade is eaten by a grazing animal the sporangium with its thousands of spores passes through the digestive tract of the animal unharmed and is voided with the dung, ready to repeat the process of asexual reproduction.

Fantastic numbers of very small fungi and bacteria exist in the prairie. Counts have shown as many as 641,000 fungi and more than 20 million bacteria per gram of soil. Some of these fungi belong to genera many of us studied in school or have read about, particularly the genus *Penicillium*. But of greater interest is the finding of recent studies that the distribution of soil fungi parallels the distribution of the green plants we see aboveground.

Wet prairies have their characteristic groups of soil fungi, as do moist prairies and dry prairies. Some species occur mainly in one type of prairie and some are found in all prairies. But in general the associations of fungi follow a gradient with the change in moisture content from place to place. Thus when we explore the visible prairie we also walk over a hidden soil microflora that has its own distributional pattern.

There are fungi that grow parasitically on living plants and probably outnumber all the kinds of grasses and forbs on the prairie. Almost every plant has its own specific fungus parasite. Some plants are affected by many kinds of fungi. Buffalo grass, for example, is susceptible to several diseases. False smut (*Cercospora seminalis*) sometimes infects the fruiting structure of buffalo grass. Fortunately, this fungus does not infect all the seeds in a single bur. Leaf blotch is caused by a foliage disease which produces darkened patches on the leaves and causes them to curl. Leaf rust is a disease similar to leaf rust of wheat, which causes premature drying and thereby prevents food manufacture by the grass.

When we consider all the plants of the prairie, great or small, grasses or bacteria, we encounter the familiar situation of one population affecting the growth or death rate of another. When we include animals in the ecosystem we see that one creature or another is always eating or being eaten, competing or providing shelter, producing harmful wastes or playing the part of scavenger, acting or reacting with another. The complexity, the stability, and the beauty of the prairie derive from these adjustments, accomplished through the thousands of years that have enabled multitudes of grassland creatures to live together.

*The largest animals to roam the North American continent in recent times, bison are notable for their gregariousness. Huge herds of bison formerly grazed at the prairie margin and migrated between mountains and grassland.*

# 5

---

# Mammals of the Prairie

RECENTLY, I STOOD ON A HILLTOP in the sandhill prairie of western Nebraska, where the sky and the grass dominated the world. It was tranquil country with early fall in the air. The turkeyfoot was in bloom. So were the annual eriogonums, scattered like snow patches on the billowing hills lying golden-lighted in the early twilight.

This hilltop was a place to envision the prairie as it once was, as it might have been a thousand or five thousand years before. Standing there, I mentally pictured the antelope running swiftly, flashing their heliograph signals; the bear and elk roaming the draws and flat bottomlands; the bison moving across the land in herds ten miles square. I saw the lesser ones too—a coyote trotting to its den, the jackrabbits running tandem along their beaten paths, a ground squirrel sitting upright at its burrow. But mostly I saw the buffalo, or bison, the multitudinous ones.

Momentarily, I found it pleasing to mentally step further into antiquity, the better to review what is known of changes in the ever-restless prairie. Its boundaries, climate, plants, and animals have constantly changed through geologic time. With the retreat of the Cretaceous seas some sixty-three million years ago the emerging land was subject to invasion by seed plants, dominated especially in the north and east by forests of broad-leaved and evergreen trees. The rain shadow created by the rising Rocky Mountains resulted in increased aridity, favorable to grasses and drought-tolerant herbs, during late Oligocene and Miocene some twenty-five million years ago. Concurrently, many modern types of mammals, including large running animals, appeared.

Studies of the dentition and skeletal structure of fossil horses and other herbivores provide evidence that forests were in retreat from central North America more than forty million years ago and that modern types of grassland were developed about fifteen million years later during the Miocene and Pliocene epochs. Food thus became available for abundant grazing mammals, which in turn were eaten by the large carnivores so characteristic of the Pliocene.

The restlessness of the prairie flora and fauna continued when the earth's great cooling culminated in waves of northern glaciation during the million years of Pleistocene time, when early man, plants, and animals migrated to new territories and returned to old territories in the periods between the four major ice advances.

During the Ice Age, mighty mammals roamed the earth. The giant beaver, ground sloth, mastodon, and woolly mammoth lived in company with the sabertooth tiger and dire wolf. Even in the Far North there were lions, camels, and yaks, all of which disappeared in the Pleistocene. The horse and the woolly mammoth were present as well as caribou, moose, and bison.

Man must have witnessed, and possibly contributed to, the destruction of the large grazing mammals by fire drives and primitive hunting tools. At least, these are the methods described in the earliest historical records of the American Indians. The causes of the extinction of large mammals in late Pleistocene time, however, will not be well understood until paleoecologists have more case histories like the recent excavation of an imperial mammoth (*Mammuthus imperator*) in southwestern Oklahoma. Carbon-14 dating gives its age as 11,200 years. Found with the bones were projectile points from the weapons of early men.

Research into the past indicates that some of our recent mammals have been present a long time. Wood, bearing the unmistakable tooth marks of beaver, was dredged from peat in northern Wisconsin in 1965. Carbon-14 testing indicated that the cuttings were 2,834 years old. In the same region, bison bones recently have been dredged up and carbon-14 dated as being 6,960 years old. The last bison were killed in Wisconsin about 1832, but these mammals must have been in this locality at least 5,000 years before the Christian era.

The buffalo, or bison (*Bison bison*), were the big ones on the prairie —the largest mammals that have roamed the North American continent in recent times. The old bulls stood six feet high at the shoulder and weighed close to a ton. The cows were smaller and weighed half as much. In small groups, which were units of the great congregations, cows, calves, and young bulls grazed together while the patriarchs grazed or loitered at the edges of the herds.

The bison moved as the seasons prompted them and as the need for new grass urged them onward. Their shaggy coats were their shelter; their speed, strength, and numbers were their defense. Enemies they had—the Red Men who speared them with lances and arrows, the "buffalo wolves" that hamstrung the stragglers, and the giant grizzlies that came down from the western mountains when they were hungry for big meat. Intermingled with all were the pronghorns, which were the purest type of plains animals; elk which originally were prairie animals; and the deer, which were adapted to shrubby grasslands. The lesser mammals of the prairies and plains, both the significant and the insignificant, were there too—but the greatest of all were the bison.

The true home of the bison was on the plains and prairies. But in the beginning their range covered much of North America. Cortez and his men may have been the first to see a bison at Anahuac in 1521, in the menagerie of Montezuma. Later, Coronado saw them in Texas and Kansas, in 1542. Bison were seen near the Potomac River in 1612 and in the Great Lakes country in 1699. Father Dablon in 1670 first mentioned the Wisconsin prairies and their bison. He also noted that elk were frequently encountered in herds of four or five hundred in the area around the upper Fox River. Father Hennepin, the French missionary, also mentioned the herds of elk grazing on the plains and grassy

*The bison once used this pond in South Dakota as the cattle now use it. Water is essential to grazing animals.*

meadows at the site where Prairie du Chien now stands. Except for the explorers and the rudimentary beginnings of settlement by the Spaniards in the Southwest, the prairie still remained the unchallenged home of the buffalo until the great slaughter began in the middle of the nineteenth century.

Until they were brought to the brink of extinction, the bison were inseparably bound to the grasses of the prairie. Their forage requirements were similar to those of our modern cattle. An acre of tall grass, producing up to three thousand pounds of forage per year, could easily support a bison for two months or more. Several acres of the shorter grasses on the high plains were required for a month of grazing. In drought years on the Great Plains, seasonal grass production sometimes dropped to less than one hundred pounds of usable forage per acre, scarcely enough to feed a large bison for three days. But, on the average, we can readily accept an estimate of sixty million bison on the more than five hundred million acres of original grassland. On the other hand, there must have been gigantic fluctuations in their total numbers.

Blizzards sometimes decimated the herds in winter, and in prolonged drought through several consecutive summers, sometimes accompanied by prairie fires that ran for hundreds of miles, the bison must have died by the millions. In addition to these cataclysms, bison always were being killed by floods and lightning, by sinking in quicksand, by stampeding over cliffs, by accidents, by fighting, by Indian arrows and spears, and by large predators.

J. E. Haley, in his biography of Charles Goodnight, relates an incident of the starvation of bison by the thousands in the winter of 1876 near the Brazos River in Texas. Goodnight saw dead bison so thick "they resembled a pumpkin field." The lack of winter feed was so great that he estimated several million bison starved in an area 100 miles long and 25 miles wide.

Death is a normal part of the ecological pattern of life. Because of this, I used to visit regularly a spot on the mixed prairie near Pierce, Colorado. A cow had been killed by lightning and I found her body before the processes of dissolution had set in. Part of my motivation for these visits, I believe, was an undefined desire to see and to contemplate the processes by which bison bodies similarly had been returned to the earth through all the millennia on the prairie.

Among the early arrivals at the cow carcass were the blow flies. On the second day, magpies were present and there was evidence that

*Raccoons are common animals on the prairie. Their tracks may be seen in the mud near almost any prairie pond or stream.*

coyotes and skunks had feasted during the night. The job of removing the meat went on for many days and involved the efforts of birds, rodents, beetles, flies, and many other insects. The hide and the bones were most durable—they still were dried and intact during the following summer. The edible portions of the carcass, not carried away by birds and mammals, were taken into the earth during the first summer by burrowing animals and insects. Eventually the bones became scattered and at the end of seven years I could find only a small piece of jawbone and two teeth.

The place still was marked by growth of blue grama and western wheatgrass more luxuriant than that on the surrounding prairie when I visited the spot for the last time at the end of nine years of observation. I never made a sophisticated study of the insect scavengers on this carcass because I had neither the time nor the necessary entomological training. But my many pilgrimages told me a dramatic story of the dynamics of the prairie web of death and life.

The magnificent recuperative power of the bison herds, however, never failed the species in the periods following disaster. When the North American bison totaled sixty million head, approximately thirty million were females. Allowing for nonproducing female calves, young heifers, and old cows, only half of the females were required to produce fifteen million offspring each year. If, as some Indians believed, one-third of the calves were killed by wolves each year, ten million new animals still remained to replace those lost by natural death and the violent forces of nature.

The bison herds which were described by the early explorers as darkening the horizon and as incalculable multitudes were composed of many small groups of fifty to two hundred animals. Even though a herd might cover fifty square miles, and require several days to pass a given point, there were many miles of country not occupied by bison at any time. Thus they practiced a form of deferred and rotation grazing in which overgrazed areas might be untouched for several years. This allowed the vegetation to recover to its former productivity.

Ordinarily the herds moved at a slow, leisurely pace, each animal cropping the grass as it went along. If forage was abundant, the coarser tufts of grass were left untouched. These tufts provided protection for ground-nesting birds, mice, lizards, and other small animals. Burrowing mammals, of course, took refuge underground.

As the grass was exhausted in one place the bison moved on to fresh forage. The droppings or chips remained to fertilize the prairie. Their incorporation into the soil was hastened by a succession of insects. Some of these were flies that grew grubs in the chips. Later these larvae transformed into more flies, that pestered the bison. Tumblebugs or scarab beetles rolled the dung into balls, which they buried several inches deep. These provided food for the adults and for the young of the beetles and also enriched the soil.

When the bison came to water they came as a destroying horde to many wild things. I once saw a demonstration of what they undoubtedly did to thousands of ponds on the prairie. An errant herd of cattle, neglected by herdsmen, broke through the fence that protected a small pond we had reserved on our experimental range for scientific study by botany and zoology students from the local college. More than five hundred cows and calves were there for a week before we discovered them. In that time they destroyed a thousand Lilliputian plant and animal worlds.

They drank all the water in the pond. They trampled the cattails, arrowheads, sedges, and other emergent plants into the mud. They grazed and pressed into the soft earth the surrounding zone of grass and herbs for many rods beyond the shore of the pond.

We did not blame the cattle for the destruction—they were merely satisfying their needs for food and water. But gone were the duckweeds which had formed a green mosaic over the reflecting surface. With the duckweeds went the food supply for a pair of ruddy ducks that were nesting in the marginal sedge zone. Gone with the duckweeds were the water ferns (*Azolla*), the algae, the microscopic hydras, the tadpoles, the frogs, the garter snakes, the dragonflies, and the nesting redwing blackbirds. Gone with the cattails were the tiny cattail moths (*Lymnaecia phragmitella*) that lay their eggs only on the velvety pistillate flowers of the cattail clubs. Gone were the homes of the cattail-miner moths (*Arzama obliqua*) which live in the stems with never any contact with their moth neighbors in the flowers above. And when the pond floor dried, gone was the mud used by the cliff swallows to plaster their nests against the low cliff walls of a rocky outcrop on the hill above the pond.

From memory and notes the zoology students and I listed more than eleven hundred species of plants and animals that had been destroyed or ousted from their niches in this natural area of less than an acre. But no one despaired. We knew that the pond would fill with water in some future year and that the succession of little worlds would begin again, each interacting with others, and building upon one another, until the cycle of renewal had restored the little ecosystem to its former level. We knew that we had seen an example of how the cycle of bison visits to the prairie waters had been repeated a million times, or a thousand times a million times, in all the years of the prairie's existence.

In winter the bison cows and calves grazed together while the bulls tended to form protective circles around the groups that composed the herd. If snow was deep, the bison swept it away by swinging their large heads and long beards from side to side to expose the cured grasses. The pronghorns grazed on the uneaten spears of grass, but more frequently found their food supply of grass and shrubs on bare windswept hillsides and ridges.

The coming of spring was heralded by the booming of prairie chickens, the clamoring of migratory waterfowl, the congregation of sandhill cranes and legions of shorebirds around pond margins and in flooded bottomlands. By late March, wheatgrass spears were two or three inches high and the purple asterlike flowers of early-blooming townsendias were nestled among the blue grama and buffalo-grass leaves held over from the previous fall. Buffalo herd movements then were local since calving time was not far away.

*Extremely prolific, white-footed mice may be found everywhere on the prairie. They provide food for snakes, birds, and many mammals, but their great reproductive ability protects them from becoming extinct.*

The first calves were born in late April. The majority were born in May. Some were born in early June. At this time the bulls were more attentive to their guard duties, since the young calves were easy prey to wolves, marauding bears, and even coyotes.

Spring also was shedding time for the buffalo. As the hair came off in patches and streamers over a period of weeks, the great animals appeared to be tattered and torn. The hair, which had collected seeds of grasses, and multitudes of spiny burs, was dropped in ponds and wallows, scraped off on trees, or rubbed free by contact with other bison. Seeds thus were planted on ground that had been denuded by fire, overgrazing, or trampling hoofs. Birds and mice used the hair for nest construction.

Shedding of the heavy winter coats left the rear quarters of the bison nearly bare. They were pestered then by horse flies, deer flies, mosquitoes, and other insects. Magpies, blackbirds, and cowbirds perched on their backs to eat these insects. The best relief, however, was obtained by plastering themselves with mud from ponds, streams, and wallows. In summer, when ponds were dry, the bison wallowed in dust. Their activities created bare areas, which were planted with seeds that fell from their hoofs and from the wool on their humps and shaggy forelegs.

Much ground was disturbed and literally plowed by the bulls during the mating season in July and August. The bellowing of the excited bulls usually was followed by battles with rivals. Great lunges brought the animals together and the crash of heads frequently sent the bulls to their knees. With lolling tongues, bulging eyeballs, and straining muscles they sank their hoofs into the sod and pushed. Then they backed away, pawed the earth, raised dust with their horns, and fought again. Many battles raged at the same time. Many of the losers were gored, or left in weakened condition, so the watchful lobo wolves found it easy to finish the kill.

*Pronghorn antelope once were as numerous as bison on the western prairie. The white hairs on their rumps can be erected to flash danger signals that are visible to other antelope for several miles.*

The fierceness of the great gray wolves can only be understood in the light of their depredations on domestic sheep, cattle, and horses when their primary food supply, the bison, were killed off. In the 1870's a breed of men called "wolfers" or "Lobo hunters" attempted to exterminate the wolves for bounties ranging up to $150 for each wolf. Particular wolves became famous, such as the White Wolf of Cheyenne, the Pryor Wolf, and the Custer Wolf, which ranged the Black Hills of South Dakota for nearly ten years and killed thousands of dollars' worth of sheep and cattle. A government trapper finally caught the wolf after spending seven months on his trail.

If grizzlies, the only carnivores large enough to kill an adult bison, were present at a wolf kill, they fed on the carcasses. The coyotes generally ate some of the leavings, and eventually only the bones were left for gnawing by porcupines and mice, or for slow leaching, whereby their calcium phosphate was returned to the earth.

Second only to the bison, the pronghorn antelopes (*Antilocapra americana*) were the most numerous of the large grazing mammals on the prairie. What was important about the pronghorns was not what they were but what they did in the scheme of nature. They filled a niche somewhere between the limitless realm of the wandering bison and the localized habitat of the sedentary prairie dog. They did not seriously compete for forage with either of these associates since they mostly ate plants that competed with grass. Antelope also found prairie-dog towns congenial places in which to live because of the abundance of forbs that sprang up as the prairie dogs reduced the supply of competing grasses.

The pronghorns were distinctive creatures from the beginning. Apparently they originated from the extinct deerlike *Cosaryx* which lived in the Miocene age. They have some of the features of the true antelope of other continents, but are not antelopes. They have some of the features of a goat, including a variety of scent glands and a gall bladder. So when scientists classified them and gave them a scientific name, they placed them in a family of their own, *Antilocapridae*, meaning antelope-goat. They are native only to North America.

The pronghorns are distinctive in other ways. Both sexes may have horns, but the horns of the female never exceed the length of the ears. The horns are composed of fused hairs which cover a bony core. The horn sheath is shed annually. The rump patch, which resembles a huge powder puff when the hairs are erected, acts as an alarm device. When the white hairs are erected they reflect a large amount of light. Other pronghorns see this reflection and spread the hairs on their rump patches, thus passing the warning to still other pronghorns on the prairie. At close range you can see that mature animals have a mane along the dorso-median line of the neck. Bucks have a dark face which becomes jet-black in older animals.

Their eyesight, which has been compared with that of a man with eight-power binoculars, together with running ability, which for speed and endurance combined exceeds that of any North American mammal, admirably adapts the pronghorn for life on the endless terrain of the prairie. Even the fawns can run at a speed of twenty-five miles or more per hour when they are two weeks old.

Pronghorns have phenomenal running endurance in addition to speed. I once clocked a mature buck that ran just inside a fence that paralleled a road for seven miles south of Cheyenne, Wyoming. In that entire distance he never got under thirty-five miles per hour. Most of the time he ran at approximately forty miles per hour with occasional bursts of speed up to forty-five or forty-six miles per hour. Pilots have pursued antelope with planes for distances of fifteen miles, while engaged in live-trapping operations, without apparent injury to the animals.

Two anatomical characteristics contribute to the pronghorn's running ability. First, the large muscles of the legs are attached near the body so the long legs can be used with a minimum expenditure of energy. The body of the animal itself moves almost in a straight line, so that energy is not expended in lifting it up and down as is done by other galloping animals. Second, the pronghorn has a large-diameter trachea, which permits a large quantity of air to enter the lungs. Since the nostrils are not large enough to meet the capacity of the trachea, the animal runs with its mouth open and tongue hanging out to increase the supply of air to the lungs.

In large open spaces where pronghorns are unimpeded by fences or other obstructions they tend to run in a straight line for long distances when frightened or pursued by enemies. Undoubtedly this originally afforded much protection from wolves and coyotes, which like to run in relays in order to wear down their prey. The relay obviously did not succeed when an antelope decided to run clear out of the landscape. Mother antelope, however, were capable of protecting their fawns from attack by a single coyote or fox. If their strategy of offering themselves as prey failed to work, they turned and struck crippling blows with their sharp front hoofs.

The pronghorn formerly ranged at a variety of elevations and in various extremes of weather conditions. Temperatures far below zero and above 100 degrees F. in summer did not harm them. Pronghorns used water if it was available, but some herds lived and died without ever taking a drink, obtaining all the water they needed from the plants they ate. Prolonged summer droughts and severe winter storms made forage unavailable and undoubtedly inflicted heavy losses, as they did with the bison. In spite of these losses and the toll of fawns to predators such as golden eagles, coyotes, wolves, bobcats, and mountain lions, the pronghorns were able to maintain their numbers for thousands of years on the grasslands.

Overgrazing by bison tended to increase the supply of undesirable range plants such as locoweeds, snakeweed, fringed sagebrush, bindweed, yarrow, and larkspurs. The pronghorns ate all of these, including the poisonous ones, which the buffalo avoided.

Prickly-pear cacti were eaten, spines and all, apparently with no ill effects. Prickly pears increased greatly during drought periods. Their root systems, which grow horizontally for many yards in every direction from the cactus clump, and at a distance of only an inch or two beneath the soil surface, enable these plants to survive and increase even if only an occasional fraction of an inch of rain moistens the surface layer of soil.

The cactus branches or joints store moisture and at the end of a two- or three-year drought were practically the only green plants left on the landscape. At such times they furnished food and water for the pronghorns long after the buffalo had departed. Likewise, when prairie fires devastated the plains, usually only the spines of the cactus were singed. The fleshy plant parts remained for the antelope to eat.

The bison, pronghorns, jackrabbits, prairie dogs, pocket gophers, and other grazing mammals, of course, did interact with one another, and together they exerted a maximum effect on the growth of vegetation. There is reason to believe that control of the grasses by bison provided more forbs for pronghorns and better visibility for prairie dogs, thus aiding in their survival.

The blacktailed prairie dogs (*Cynomys ludovicianus*) next to the bison and pronghorns were the most important grazing mammals of the Great Plains portion of the prairie. Many authors have attempted to illustrate their astronomical numbers by citing the estimate of Vernon Bailey that an area of 25,000 square miles east of the Staked Plains in

Texas contained at least 400 million prairie dogs. But this Texas "town" was only one portion of the prairie-dog world. The "barking squirrel" or *"petit chien"* of Lewis and Clark lived in thousands of towns in the eastern parts of New Mexico, Colorado, Wyoming, and Montana, and in the western parts of Oklahoma, Nebraska, South Dakota, and in North Dakota west of the Missouri River. Now they exist only as remnants of their former numbers, owing to poisoning and destruction of their natural habitat.

Prairie dogs still are to be seen in western Oklahoma, western Nebraska, and in Dakota prairies and badlands. Several colonies are protected for the benefit of tourists in Wind Cave National Park in the Black Hills. John A. King's definitive study of one prairie-dog town in the park has revealed some of the fantastic social behavior and population dynamics of these paradoxical rodents, which still live in company with the pronghorns and the bison.

The prairie dog is a true ground squirrel, stout, short-tailed, short-legged, and remarkably adapted for digging. Adults are gray or grayish yellow on the back and paler below. Weight varies between one and two pounds, depending somewhat on the season of the year. When fat in early autumn, occasional animals may weigh three pounds. They are not strictly hibernating animals, although they may remain belowground for long periods of severe winter snow in the more northern regions.

Their eyesight is keen, and by means of a variety of chirps and "barks" they communicate many kinds of information to their neighbors. Because of this, I have always enjoyed a slow walk through a prairie-dog town. The prairie dogs one hundred yards or more ahead sit erect and chirp at a moderate rate. As you approach, the tempo of chirping increases, the dogs drop to their bellies on top of their crater mounds. At fifty to one hundred feet, just when they seem ready to explode with chirping, they dive below. The last thing you see is a flick of the black tail. I am inclined to believe this is a visual signal which pinpoints the location of an enemy for all the sitting dogs that form the periphery of your circle of disturbance.

The prairie dog digs a more elaborate burrow than any other rodent. The tunnel, which is six to eight inches in diameter at the opening, narrows to a vertical tube, which is dug to a depth of three to ten feet or more. A small "listening room" is dug about three feet below the entrance. At this guard room the tunnel generally turns horizontally and may branch, end in blind alleys, or rise to the surface many yards away. Side rooms sometimes are used as toilets, although the prairie dog is not too meticulous about this phase of housekeeping. The bedroom is a foot or more in diameter and is filled with dried grass or shredded plant stems.

Burrow entrances sometimes are only a few feet apart, but usually they are separated by distances of fifty feet or more. An acre may have fifty or more burrow entrances. Soil brought up from the burrow is carefully tamped by the animal's nose into a dome around the entrance. Back-door entrances to the tunnel system either may have no soil dome, or a crater of earth may be scraped from the surface soil outside the door. These domes or craters, which are kept in good repair, prevent flooding of the tunnel system during heavy rainstorms. The domes also serve as observation towers from which the prairie dogs detect enemies and communicate by voice with their neighbors.

Life in a prairie-dog town includes many activities. On clear summer days the inhabitants begin to appear soon after sunrise. They bask for a while. Then eating breakfast may require two or three hours, since there must be many pauses to watch for enemies, to greet near neighbors, to chase away intruders, and to explore the surrounding terrain. There is a rest period in midday. Then activities begin again in the afternoon and continue until sundown.

There are many enemies, including coyotes, badgers, foxes, bobcats, wolves, golden eagles, and hawks. Burrowing owls, weasels, snakes, and black-footed ferrets live in vacant burrows right in the town. In addition to these, fleas, ticks, and many insects live in the burrows. E. H. Taylor found large adult toads (*Bufo woodhousei*) in prairie-dog villages in Kansas at night. These toads hid in the holes during the day.

I have found many cottontail rabbits in abandoned burrows in eastern Colorado, and once I found a tiger salamander in a prairie-dog burrow. Ground squirrels, deer mice, and field mice also are found in prairie-dog towns but are mostly ignored by the rightful inhabitants. Snakes probably use the mice and smaller species of ground squirrels for their principal food, since prairie dogs, excepting their young, are too large to be swallowed.

On the original grasslands, the prairie dogs competed successfully with the bison, pronghorns, rabbits, ground squirrels, and mice for food. At least 98 percent of the prairie dog's food was vegetation. Occasionally cutworms, beetles, grasshoppers, and other insects were eaten. But the first choice was grass. When the grass cover was denuded, they ate forbs which replaced the grass. Scientists have wondered at their

*Once abundant on the prairie, mule deer were hunted almost to extinction. Now increasing in number, they prefer the brushy and timbered bottomlands along rivers and streams.*

ability to survive during drought when the ground is caked and nearly bare of green plants. But they are protected from starvation to a certain degree by the social organization which they have evolved.

Prairie-dog towns are distinct communities separated by natural barriers such as hills or ridges or rivers. The prairie dogs in different towns do not see one another and do not live in or cross the intervening area between towns.

Some towns have separate divisions, called wards, which are separated by moderately restrictive barriers such as differences in terrain or vegetation types. There is some exchange of animals between wards and the prairie dogs can vocalize between wards when enemies are present.

Within wards, closed social groups, called clans or coteries, consist of two to thirty or more prairie dogs. The animals of a clan have free movement within their territory, recognize one another, and cooperate in play, grooming, and other activities. The members use their individual burrows or sometimes share an elaborate common tunnel system.

The coterie is defended by its members against encroachment by members of other coteries. After the young are born and become capable of caring for themselves, the older prairie dogs move to the periphery of the town and thus expand its limits.

Many advantages of this social organization have been cited. The numerous burrows, which are available to any prairie dog in time of danger, provide a remarkable escape device. The defense of the coteries by their own members prevents overpopulation by invasion from surrounding areas. This results in an equitable distribution of animal numbers in the prairie-dog town and equitable demands on the food supply. The stable social organization within the coterie also provides a suitable environment for successful mating and rearing of young, since the local members are not antagonistic, and males and females are always present. Migration from coteries that otherwise would become crowded causes recombination of individuals into new coteries, thus insuring genetic variability from generation to generation.

A number of years ago, I watched the demise of a prairie-dog town on the plains northeast of Greeley, Colorado, without realizing at the time the importance of social structure and population abundance in rodent survival. This town was complete with prairie dogs, burrowing owls, rattlesnakes, and cottontails. The "poison experts" got in their licks and killed all but about a dozen prairie dogs.

Now, I realize that the coterie system had been destroyed, that the widely distributed remaining prairie dogs were probably unfamiliar with each other, and that they were uncooperative because of the long distances between them. Also, they were too few in numbers—the thousand eyes that formerly located enemies were reduced below the critical minimum for warning against enemies.

In the second summer after the poisoning, wheatgrasses, pigweeds, and other tall plants grew faster than the prairie dogs could clip them down for good visibility. At last, only one prairie dog remained. I saw it sitting lonesomely on its mound in the late summer of 1949. I suspect that a coyote or a golden eagle ended its existence.


On the prairie there always was an abundance of small mammals that ran aboveground, or burrowed in the soil, and used either plants or other animals for food. Some of these, such as the mice and voles, were more abundant locally than even the prairie dogs. But all locations in the prairie did not possess all of these creatures, since many were specialized for certain foods or were adapted only to certain environments in the grasslands.

One of the true specialists was the black-footed ferret (*Mustela nigripes*), which depended on the prairie dog as its principal food. Annihilation of the prairie dog in many areas did not cause the complete disappearance of the black-footed ferret, since it preys on other small mammals and birds. But it has been extirpated from most of its former range.

I treasure the memory of the first and only time I ever saw a black-footed ferret in the wild. It was near the border of Bates Hole in Wyoming. Dr. George Bird Grinnell had camped there in 1886. His account failed to mention coyotes, magpies, and other predators. But he saw sage grouse so numerous they reminded him of the legendary flights of the passenger pigeons. Sixty years later when I camped in this same locality, the sage grouse were scarce, but rodents were present, and golden eagles drifted down to perch on the rock pinnacles of a bluff behind our camp.

Suddenly in the sparse grass I saw a sinuous, loping, buff-colored thing that progressed in graceful leaps. Then it paused, sat upright, and stared with glittering eyes. The black band across its face, the black feet, and its size made it unmistakable. For a moment it remained immobile. Then like a serpent it vanished in the grass. I had seen one of the rarest mammals in North America.

Two "daytime" rodents, which formerly were extremely abundant in the western grasslands, are the thirteen-lined ground squirrel (*Spermophilus tridecemlineatus*) and the picket pin or Richardson's ground squirrel (*S. richardsonii*). On a recent trip through Nebraska, Wyoming, and Montana, my wife and I saw only one thirteen-lined ground squirrel and no picket pins. In 1929, when we camped in these states, the picket pins, sitting upright and resembling wooden stakes driven into the ground, were everywhere along roadsides, in grassy fields, and on the sagebrush-covered plains. I believe the extensive rodent-control programs of recent years have almost annihilated these interesting squirrels.

The secretive nocturnal rodents of the prairies, of course, are seldom seen by the casual traveler. Farmers and ranchers, at harvest time and haying time, probably see more rodents than most people. Depending on where one is, any of the following native rats and mice may scurry for cover when piles of new-mown hay are lifted with a pitchfork: plains harvest mouse (*Reithrodontomys montanus*), white-footed mouse (*Peromyscus leucopus*), deer mouse (*P. maniculatus*), northern grasshopper mouse (*Onchomys leucogaster*), bushy-tailed wood rat (*Neotoma cinerea*), and meadow vole (*Microtus pennsylvanicus*).

The meadow jumping mouse (*Zapus hudsonius*), which hibernates in winter, occurs both in lush upland prairies, and along the wooded borders of streams. The prairie jumping mouse (*Z. h. campestris*), which is a subspecies of *hudsonius*, is found in Manitoba, North and South Dakota, Montana, Wyoming, Colorado, and Missouri. Although this subspecies commonly lives in meadows and shows a preference for moist ground, I have found them in yucca patches on dry sandy soils.

Like Robert Burns, I have always had a tender sympathy for humble life, particularly the "wee, sleekit, cowrin, tim'rous beastie." The defenseless mouse, above all other mammals, provides magnificent opportunity for the study of populations, cycles of scarcity and abundance, and food chains in the natural world. The mouse is one of the smallest, but certainly not the least in importance, of the prairie mammals.

If mice could buy life insurance, the actuarial tables would require that they pay a high premium, for their enemies are legion. It has been well established that the majority of young meadow mice never reach maturity. They and their elders are chased into their burrows by weasels; snatched from their grass cover by hawks, owls, gulls, magpies and crows; ambushed in their runways by snakes; devoured by turtles and bullfrogs when they are swimming; and taken from their runways by badgers, foxes, coyotes, mink, skunks, and raccoons. In the face of all this persecution they have to find time to eat, sleep, build nests, dig tunnels, construct paths in the grass, store food, and rear their young.

A great many factors contribute to the survival rate of the meadow mouse. Food supply is one factor: food must furnish energy over and above that required for self-maintenance, if reproduction is to occur. Predation is another factor: if predators reduce the numbers of mice, the predators may turn to other sources of food, and thus allow the mouse population to increase. Reproductive ability is a third factor: the meadow mouse has it.

From five to nine meadow mice are born in a litter. The youngsters are weaned within two weeks. Three weeks later the young females are ready to mate. Three weeks after that their babies are born. In the meantime the original mother has produced another litter and is capable of repeating the process more than a dozen times within the year. This prodigality of reproduction can, when nature goes on a tangent, produce a population explosion that results in as many as eight thousand mice per acre. Usually before these eruptions get out of hand, unfavorable climatic conditions, diminution of the food supply, disease, and starvation reduce the population to normal numbers.

Ord's kangaroo rat (*Dipodomys ordii*) is one of the common species of the western prairies and plains. These clean, beautiful creatures occupy niches not duplicated by any other mammal. Sand for digging, seeds for eating, and roots of woody plants for protection from excavating animals are prime requirements in their lives. So they build their burrows beneath saltbushes, rose tangles, or yucca clumps, with numerous entrances for quick escape from within or without.

Kangaroo rats seldom travel far from home, but they must have access to seed supplies. Hence they dig their burrows where soil disturbance by fire, overgrazing by large herbivores, or drought has created conditions favorable for growth of their choice seed-producing plants. The soil in their tunnels must be pliable so the entrances can be closed during the day to preserve humidity and to impede the entrance of snakes and weasels.

*The "petit chien," or little dog of the prairie, was named by the members of the Lewis and Clark expedition. This vigilant prairie dog straddles its burrow, ready to dive to safety if an enemy approaches.*

Kangaroo rats seldom drink. Captive specimens have lived on rolled oats for three months without water. They are able to use metabolic water obtained from their diet of seeds, leaves, stems, and an occasional insect. In natural surroundings they may obtain some dew that forms on cool summer nights. Their kidneys are among the most efficient in nature—they excrete urine four times more concentrated than that of man. In addition, the renal papillae and the urinary bladder can resorb water for recirculation in the animal's body.

The kangaroo rat has no sweat pores to waste water. Moisture loss from breathing is reduced by the habit of working only at night when the humidity is highest. Moisture also is conserved in the daytime by closing the burrow entrance and remaining belowground, where the water vapor is much higher than in the outside air.

Seeds and other food materials are transported in cheek pouches which the kangaroo rat can empty instantly by shoving forward with the small forefeet. Kangaroo rats, like the harvester ants with which they associate, store seeds of different plants in different bins. And they are not above digging into the anthills and stealing the seeds the ants have so laboriously collected.

You should never believe that all the prairie-inhabiting mammals can be found in any one locality. Habitat conditions are different in each biotic province, in each vegetation type, and even in each plant successional stage within a local area. Likewise, every mammal has its own niche.

There is no simple way to find and study animals on the prairie. The best you can do, even if you live there, is to know certain places and return to them through all the seasons, year in and year out, piecing together fragmented observations into a continued story that gives understanding of the ecological pattern in nature.

The common ones, like the black-tailed and white-tailed jackrabbits, you may see by driving almost any prairie road at dusk. You may have to walk along the streams to see the eastern cottontail or among the tall upland grasses and in the yucca patches to see the desert cottontail. In late-summer evenings red bats, hoary bats, and the eastern pipistrelle, which is the smallest of the bats, may be seen flitting against the darkening sky just before the stars appear. If you are persistent, you may find their daytime roosting places in cottonwoods, willows, buildings, or in limestone quarries.

Count it your lucky day if you see a badger and can chase him, hissing and snarling, into his burrow. Badgers are becoming rare on the prairies. Dead skunks, both the large white-striped and the little spotted kinds, dead raccoons, and dead porcupines you can see on the highways almost anywhere in the western prairie country.

The minks, weasels, shrews, pocket gophers, moles, many of the mice, and the voles you will have to trap or understand the signs of their work if you want to be sure of their presence. Hunters who enjoy the chase with hounds can demonstrate that red and gray foxes are abundant in the prairie and along the forest edges. But you may not see the shy, mostly nocturnal little swift fox (*Vulpes velox*) once in your lifetime, since it is nearly extinct except in the southern part of its range, which formerly extended from Saskatchewan to northern Texas.

If you are just a tourist crossing the prairie you still can see bison at the wildlife refuge near Valentine, Nebraska, at refuges or on ranches in Texas, Oklahoma, and Montana, and Custer State Park. But, as Frank Thomson indicates in his *Last Buffalo of the Black Hills*, the park animals make trails like cattle, follow trucks loaded with hay, and stand peacefully for photos. (Don't get too far from your car when you photograph them.)

Visitors crossing the prairie, anywhere from Texas to Canada, can see some of the prairie mammals by leaving the four-lane highways and traveling the lesser roads. If, for example, you are going to Denver from the east, you can take the road from Sterling, Colorado, to Briggsdale and have good opportunities to see coyotes, antelope, jackrabbits, and even deer in late evening.

The road, which is paved but not excessively traveled, pitches down into saltbush-wheatgrass swales and winds over rolling grass-covered hills. For many miles the road parallels the Chalk Bluffs, which rise above the prairie level to the north near the Wyoming border. These bluffs are home for bobcats, golden eagles, and prairie falcons.

At sundown the silhouette of the Rocky Mountains beneath a flaming sky sets the scene for the crepuscular animals and the chain of food and survival. The rabbits leave their hiding places to feed. The last marsh hawks also are abroad, looking for a final unwary mouse or cottontail. And in the cottonwood trees along the stream courses, great horned owls come awake for their marauding. As the night comes on, the coyote chorus pinpoints the locations where the lobo wolves once howled. But in the dimness you will have to imagine that the dark forms of cattle slowly moving across the hillsides and flat uplands are wild buffalo.

Great blue herons nest in cottonwood trees and lay their eggs before the leaves appear. Composed mainly of sticks and twigs, heron nests are lined with grasses, rushes, and similar materials.

# 6

## Birds of the Prairie

THE DIVERSIFIED TERRAIN of the prairie makes for varied populations. The prairie waters—lakes, ponds, potholes, rivers, and streams—add to the variety of bird life because of the added habitat available for water-loving and migrating species. The mid-continental location of the central prairies also constitutes a transition zone where both eastern and western birds are found and where the southerly shift of northern species brings owls, longspurs, sparrows, and shorebirds along with migrating waterfowl from the Arctic tundra and boreal forests.

Many birds of the grasslands, especially the summer residents, are so common they can be seen daily on the prairie. Anywhere west of Illinois one can hear the melodious whistle of the meadowlark, the *jig jig . . . zig-zig-zig* of the dickcissel, the bubbling call of the male bobolink, and the buzzing sound of the savanna sparrow. The ringing note of the killdeer is a reminder that other shorebirds once traversed the prairies in countless millions during their annual migrations.

On the western plains small birds that have always belonged to the grasslands are still present: the horned lark, the chestnut-collared and McCown's longspur, Sprague's pipit, and the black-billed magpie. The birds of prey, hawks, eagles, and owls, are still there, but in diminished numbers. The birds of the prairie waters, herons, ducks, sandpipers, rails, coots, and grebes, can easily be seen. The two largest birds—the trumpeter swan and the whooping crane—that once made the prairie resound with their clamorous calls will not be seen by the casual traveler, even though they were saved from extinction by belated protection from the greedy hunters of the nineteenth century. But the geese, even though their numbers are reduced, still traverse the plains and prairies.

To me, geese have always been symbolic of the prairie, even though they were never really permanent residents. The memory of one great gander, after almost half a century, is still sharp and clear to me. I can still see the snow, sparkling under the November sun, the hoarfrost on the corn shocks; I can hear the sniffing of my two rabbit dogs nosing in the weed patches and see the solitary crow winging his way down to the timber that bordered Rock Creek on our Nebraska farm.

We were just a boy and his dogs, hunting rabbits with an ancient .22 single-shot rifle. We had crossed the old cemetery, never plowed and still filled with the plants of the native prairie, when I saw the great goose standing there on the hillside among the stubs of harvested corn. Ages went by as I tried to center him in my sights. An ague shook my hand and then the shot went wild as he launched his patriarchal bulk into the air, made a wide circle around the cornfield, gained altitude, and gradually diminished to a speck in the sky, going east over the hills to the Missouri River.

I think I cried a little when I told my father about the goose: big as our dooryard gander, a broad white patch on his cheek, light gray feathers all over the huge body. My father just smiled and said something about goose fever. Then he said I would never forget the experience. The thrill of the honkers would always be there when the geese came along. His words were prophetic.

This goose of my boyhood must have been one of that race of huge Canada geese that overshadowed all the lesser varieties. My grandfather, who was born in 1839, once told me how he killed seven of these giant birds by stalking them through the tall prairie grass. He was a strong man but he staggered under the burden when he carried them home. Later, my mother and her sisters and brothers had to herd the wild geese off the fields in autumn in order to keep them from eating all the green wheat plants. The flocks consisted of Canada geese of different sizes, including the exceptionally large ones.

According to a report published by Captain Thomas Blakiston in 1863, the Indians on the Saskatchewan River knew of these large geese. Since then scientific reports have noted the existence of exceptionally large geese in the plains region and the race apparently still exists.

Goose numbers and flyways have changed because of hunting, cultivation of the prairie, and draining of the ponds and lakes that once gave them sanctuary on their great migrations. The Army Engineers have channeled the Missouri River, so oxbow lakes are no longer formed by floods that formerly covered the bottom lands ten miles wide from bluff to bluff. Refuges have been developed by federal, state, and private agencies to the east on the Mississippi River. And former hunting grounds, once inaccessible except by horse and wagon, now are approached everywhere by automobile. And so the geese have learned to rest only in places of safety.

They make use of stubble fields where formerly they collected the grain of prairie grasses and nibbled the green shoots of autumn and early spring. Their migration is a pattern of resting—sometimes for several days—and moving on, then resting again. On the prairie they rested in the sloughs and in the Nebraska sandhills. The Niobrara, the Platte, the Republican, the Arkansas, the Canadian, and other rivers gave them intervals of sanctuary on the overland journey southward in the fall and northward in the spring. In between, when absence of storms allowed them leisurely travel, they rested on the prairie after posting sentinels so they could feed before nightfall.

From the time of the Ice Age, geese have lived essentially in a prairie world. During the Arctic summer they have always raised their goslings in a watery environment of grasses and sedges. During the southern winter for time without end they have sojourned in the swamps and meadows along the Gulf Coast. And in all the years when they were not alarmed by the intrusion of white men the innumerable skeins of geese cleaving the sky or cutting low over the oxbows of the rivers proclaimed the seasons with clamorous voices. Always when I see them in flight, following their ancestral traditions, gabbling, grunting, and honking, I associate them with the ever-restless prairie.

A great host of other waterfowl and shorebirds also migrated across the prairies. Some of the mallards, pintails, redheads, canvasbacks, gadwalls, and shovelers rested on the prairie ponds during late April and May, and in October when most of the migrations occurred. Varying numbers of herons, terns, long-billed curlews, and upland sandpipers nested in the sandhill meadows or on the western plains. The niches of these waterfowl and shorebirds extended far and wide and they bound together the food chains of such diverse habitats as upland prairies and lowland ponds and lakes.

I realized this many years ago while fishing for black crappies on Jumbo Reservoir, which nestles in the prairie-covered hills west of Sedgwick, Colorado. The crappies themselves were jumbos: the six-

and seven-year-old age classes averaged 13.2 and 14.5 inches long, respectively. Two-pound fish were not unusual, and their size and rate of growth were matched in early life only by those in Norris Reservoir, Tennessee.

It occurred to me that forty thousand ducks rafting on Jumbo Reservoir might have some connection with the size of crappies, perch, and other fish that grew there. I reasoned that thousands of ducks, over a period of several months each year, produce a lot of fertilizer; and fertilizer in a lake grows lots of *Daphnia, Cyclops,* algae, pond weeds, and other things that feed little fish which feed larger fish. Then, with further research, I learned that Reelfoot Lake in Tennessee, and other well-known crappie lakes in Ohio, Iowa, and other states, rafted thousands of ducks each winter. Lakes which were polluted, or contained too many carp, or had no spawning beds, or suffered excessive irrigation draw-down each year, had few or no crappies. But the inference was clear: waterbirds and fish do have their connections, as do most other creatures in nature, if we have only the wit to see them.


The year-long resident birds of the prairie, of course, have to adapt themselves to life in their individual localities through all the seasons. The prairie chickens above all were the unique ones. These children of the sod lived in the vast prairie wedge that spread from its eastern point in Illinois to its southern edge in Texas and its northern boundary in Canada. Historical accounts tell us that prairie-chicken numbers once ran into the millions in this vast territory of rolling prairie and never-ending plains. My grandfather told me that he used to fire once across his corncrib in the 1870's to kill enough prairie chickens to furnish a meal for his family of eight.

The greater prairie chicken (*Tympanuchus cupido pinnatus*) originally lived in a variety of grassland types extending from Alberta and Saskatchewan south to Texas and eastward to the grassy openings in Ohio. The lesser prairie chicken (*T. pallidicinctus*) occurred chiefly in the western parts of Kansas, Oklahoma, and Texas. Atwater's prairie chicken (*T. cupido attwateri*) inhabited the open coastal prairies in southern Texas and southwestern Louisiana.

The courtship drama of the prairie chickens and their mode of living intrigued even the earliest travelers. Throughout the fall and early winter the bird flocks moved as units between their feeding and roosting grounds. They used grassy shelter but were capable of roosting in trees in company with their cousins the sharptail grouse. During blizzards they burrowed into the snow.

In January or February—later in the far north—the flocks separated by sexes as the males began their displays on the booming grounds. The resonant calls that accompanied the dance could be heard for a mile during the morning and evening meetings. The booming displays increased in frequency until they were performed daily throughout the spring. Only the males occupied the strutting stages, which were many rods in diameter and large enough for even a hundred birds to display at one time. Some authorities believe that these booming grounds were used for centuries and were not abandoned even after the buffalo trampled them to dust.

The booming notes of the prairie chicken have been likened by Charles W. Schwartz to "that of the lower notes of an ocarina or the sound made by blowing across the open neck of a bottle." When the cock has selected his spot on the booming ground he runs forward, stops, pats the ground with his feet, inflates his orange air sacs, lifts his orange eyebrows, erects the pinnae on his neck, spreads his tail with a flick, and begins to boom. His display sometimes provokes fights. Opponents approach each other, necks outstretched, wings drooped, and air sacs deflated. Then they hop into the air, clash with wings beating, and then repeat the performance like domestic roosters fighting. Usually, little harm is done and the males then resume their booming.

Some ornithologists believe that the elaborate display of the males serves to intimidate the less virile males from mating. The performance also is involved with courtship since the cocks boom more frequently when the females are in their presence. Mating is polygamous and is done both on and off the booming ground when the females signify their acceptance of the males of their choice. Nest sites are chosen in meadows, lightly grazed grasslands, or under shrubs. As many as fifteen eggs are laid and the chicks hatch in May in the central prairies.

Juvenile prairie chickens eat more insects than adults. On the original prairie, seeds of grasses, flower heads, legume leaves, weed seeds, leaves of grasses and forbs, and rose hips made up their principal diet. Prairie chickens in the forested borders ate hazelnuts and acorns. According to the early writings of Audubon, prairie chickens in Missouri and Kentucky ate tree buds, wild grapes, mistletoe, and hazel catkins.

Prairie chickens come together in late summer in flocks which fly from roosting sites to feeding grounds. Most people do not think of them as high fliers. But I have seen them flying hundreds of yards high in the Nebraska sandhills in late October. They can be mistaken for high-flying ducks unless one watches closely and sees their wings alternately twinkling in the morning or evening sunlight and then setting in momentary glides.

Numerous enemies plagued the prairie chickens in their ancestral homes. Spring floods always were a menace, especially on river bottoms, where silt was spread over their nests and eggs. Many chicks were drowned when cloudbursts turned the level prairie into a miniature ocean. Hail from sudden storms also destroyed many birds where protective cover was absent. Drought was the greatest enemy of all. When droughts occurred for years on end, both the present and future food supply was destroyed. The birds were exposed to the elements because of lack of vegetation shelter, were weakened by excessive heat, and became subject to disease and predators.

Wolves, coyotes, and foxes caught some of the adult birds. Skunks and smaller predators ate the eggs, destroyed the nests, and preyed on the chicks. Marsh hawks annoyed the cocks on their booming grounds or flushed them from hiding places in the grass. When flushed the prairie chickens became more vulnerable to duck hawks, goshawks, the ferruginous hawk, and bald eagles. Badgers and ground squirrels were major sources of nest destruction.

In spite of these enemies the prairie chickens prospered and were in balance with their environment. The hawks that caught an occasional bird also acted as natural checks on destructive rodents. Badgers checked the increase of ground squirrels, which preyed heavily upon bird nests. The hawks, eagles, and owls also preyed heavily on rabbits and mice that tended to destroy shrubs which furnished food and shelter for the prairie chickens.

Other summer birds on the prairie are numerous. Birds such as the horned lark, lark bunting, bobolink, Smith's longspur, chestnut-collared longspur, Sprague's pipit, and lark sparrow can be seen and heard singing on the wing. They sing and fly to notify other birds of their kind that "This is my territory." In contrast, forest birds rarely sing on the wing, since their presence would not be noted visually because of the dense vegetation. More than half of the prairie birds build their nests on the ground; about a third of all species use weeds or low shrubs for their nests; the burrowing owls use prairie-dog tunnels; and the swallows, eagles, and hawks use rock ledges, cliffs, or tall trees. The magpies use tall shrubs and trees with thorns.

*The magpie, one of the most resourceful birds of the western prairie, subsists on bird eggs, young birds, mice, and dead animals. Resembling a robin's nest, the nest of the magpie is protected by an intricately woven mass of sticks and thorny twigs.*

The black-billed magpie (*Pica pica*) was a resident bird of the western prairies noted by the early explorers. These jay-sized black-and-white birds with the unmanageable tails were accused by Zebulon Pike of pecking holes in his mules. Since then they have been guilty of many other depredations, including nest robbing, pecking into the kidneys of live sheep, stealing young chickens, and building their monstrous nests in farm buildings and among telephone wires.

Magpie nests usually are constructed in shrubs or small trees. The inner cup, which is comparable to a robin's nest, is made of mud, plant fibers, and small twigs. If mud is unavailable the magpie substitutes cow manure. Undoubtedly they formerly used bison dung. Below, above, and around the inner nest the magpie builds a veritable trash pile of interwoven sticks two to six feet long and one or two feet in diameter. Only with difficulty can one tear this tangle from the shrub or tree in which it has been built.

Magpies on our experimental range north of Greeley, Colorado, used to build stick nests on our windmill platforms. Then when the wind shifted, the fan would swing around, lodge in the nest, stop the pump, and leave our cattle without water. One summer I destroyed three of these nests in as many weeks. Then I decided to leave the mud cup of the fourth nest on the windmill platform. Soon it contained seven eggs. The eggs hatched and the youngsters eventually prospered. But their exposure to the hot sun raised blisters that remained on their bare backs and sides until the feathers grew in.

We never bothered the magpies if they did not interfere with our windmills or fill the sliding-door track on our machine shed with trash. They are great scavengers, especially on dead rabbits and similar carrion, and are excellent grasshopper catchers. On the prairie the nests of the meadowlarks, sparrows, horned larks, and other grassland dwellers are so well hidden they suffer little from magpie depredations.

If the gods were to choose a bird typical of the summer prairies they probably would designate the meadowlark. No one can watch this bird stalking through the grass without recognizing it as a dominant factor in the control of insects and weeds that can become too numerous at times. Practically all school children recognize the complex, melodious whistle of the meadowlark, especially the western form (*Sturnella neglecta*), which has a more complex cadence than the eastern one (*S. magna*). The nests with their white eggs speckled with lilac or brown are quite completely hidden from view in tufts of prairie grass. All through the summer one can hear the cheery whistle of these birds, even when driving fast on the highways.

We always considered it a good omen when the cliff swallows (*Petrochelidon pyrrhonota*) returned to our ranch on the plains in eastern Colorado. Our birds did not follow the legend of the cliff swallows' return to San Juan Capistrano Mission in California on the same day of March in each year. Instead, they arrived about the tenth of May, just when we were driving the cattle out to summer pasture. Before our buildings were constructed the swallows nested in the Chalk Bluffs a few miles north of our place near the Wyoming border. They adopted us soon after we arrived in 1937, since the overflow from our new windmill always provided a supply of mud for making their globose or retort-shaped nests beneath the eaves of our cookhouse. Their original homes were along the walls of canyons in the escarpments of the prairie and on the vertical sides of rocky river bluffs. They were seen along the Missouri by members of exploring expeditions and their nests were observed on the bluffs of the Niobrara River in Nebraska. Their nests also were seen by Edwin James on July 9, 1820, when Major Long's exploring party went up Clear Creek in Colorado.

Although the cliff swallows may not be the most typical birds of the prairie, their animation and enthusiasm in both nest building and insect catching always infect one with pleasure and admiration. The nearest mud puddle, pond, or buffalo wallow is surrounded by a twittering circle of dark blue sprites with reddish brown throats and whitish foreheads. They duck their heads to pick up mud, which they roll into little round pellets and transport forthwith to the wall or rock cliff to be laid, brick on brick, until the domed nest is complete. When the young can fly they stand in the circle with ecstatic quivering of wings, watching their parents roll more pellets to repair the nests that shelter the colony until the flock leaves on the southern journey in September.

One of the most familiar birds in the summer evening skies is the common nighthawk (*Chordeiles minor*). It arrives on the prairies in late May or early June, long after the other migrant species have appeared. It departs in early September to a winter home in South America. The nazal *peent*, uttered by the bird as it courses through the air, is a characteristic evening sound. The brief vibrant boom of the male is caused by air rushing through the wing primaries as the bird power-dives. This booming display is pronounced during the courtship period and may be a form of aggressive behavior. I have heard it many times, however, in early September when the breeding season was long past, and believe it is caused when the bird power-dives for flying insects.

The nighthawk makes no nest but lays two oblong eggs on the bare ground among the grass tufts. The eggs and young are remarkably adapted to the extremes of temperature on the hot earth. One report tells of eggs being laid on a roof where the temperature reached 130 degrees F. and the eggs became embedded in tar. But they hatched and the young developed normally.

Nighthawks have a predilection for sitting on fence posts and fence rails. They nearly always face into the wind and appear to sleep with their eyes half closed. Their diet is almost exclusively flying insects, which are caught in the wide-gaping mouth surrounded by bristles that trap moths, beetles, flies, and mosquitoes. On the western plains flying harvester ants are especially abundant in mid-August and are eagerly sought by the nighthawks.

Among the most exciting of the prairie migrants are the sandhill cranes. These giant long-necked, long-legged wading birds are quite at home in meadows, on open grasslands, and even in cultivated fields where grain, tender herbage, insects, spiders, toads, mice, lizards, and small snakes are available for food. They are seen frequently in the Platte River Valley in western Nebraska in late March and early April. J. V. K. Wagar once told me of a flock that got lost in the fog behind the Rampart Range a few miles north of Colorado Springs. He heard their sonorous trumpeting during the night while they rested in an open meadow near the ponderosa pines. When he saw them in the morning there appeared to be a solid acre of cranes huddled together. When the fog lifted they circled upward until they were mere flecks in the sky. Then they flew southward past Pikes Peak.

According to Lawrence H. Walkinshaw, cranes have inhabited the continent for as long as the prairies have been here. Fossil remains have been found from the Eocene period; remains of *Grus canadensis* are also known from the Pliocene of Nebraska and from the Pleistocene of California, Florida, Wyoming, and Nebraska. The greater sandhill cranes formerly were abundant in most of the prairie states. Their rapid disappearance began about 1870 and continued as human populations increased, the grasslands were plowed, and ponds were drained.

In the Pine Ridge country of western Nebraska, where scarplands, badlands, buttes, valleys, and canyons provide conditions for junipers, pines, and prairie to mingle, a mixture of eastern and western birds occurs. The pines and shrublands provide habitat for pinyon jays, rock wrens, loggerhead shrikes, western tanagers, and violet-green swallows. Upland sandpipers and long-billed curlews frequent the grassy places, and in early fall mourning doves congregate in flocks of fifty to three hundred or more. On windy days one can flush them from weedy patches and unplowed fields. They generally vanish with the first hard frost of autumn.

The limitless expanse of sky is the domain of the hawks, eagles, and falcons, and they remain in view for hours on end. The turkey vulture circling above broad valleys, the golden eagle silhouetted against a fleecy cloud, the peregrine falcon stooping for an unwary duck, the kestrel twinkling in one spot, all give clues to the weather, wind conditions, and what is stirring below.

The birds of prey and the scavengers, in addition to stirring the imagination because of their mastery of the air and the chase, have an ecological significance that generally goes unappreciated. They are primarily flesh eaters, although some forms include insects, reptiles, and even fish in their diets. But of greater import is the fact that they live near the top of the pyramid of life.

The small plant-eating animals have their predators, which in turn are preyed on by larger predators in nature's pattern of energy exchange. Roadrunners, magpies, jays, crows, shrikes, grackles, and many other birds in addition to the raptors prey on other birds and small animals. But the hawks, eagles, and falcons stand more or less at the top of the food chain. Since each predator may eat one or many birds or smaller animals each day or week, the animals in the lower links of the food chain must necessarily be more numerous than their predators in order to maintain their populations.

When I see the black form of a turkey vulture drop from the sky, and then another and another, none of which was visible before, I know that an animal has died and an ecological niche is momentarily vacant. But another of its kind will come to replace the dead. The replacement may involve another food chain, beginning either with grass or with a series of small and numerous animals being preyed upon by larger and less numerous creatures, until the niche is filled and the interacting creatures of the prairie are again in dynamic equilibrium. The vulture, even though it does not kill its prey, jiggles the balance of nature by depriving meat-eating insects and mammals of some of their food. But when it dies it pays its debt to the coyotes, beetles, and worms.

The eagles, hawks, and falcons likewise make an impact on animal populations since their prey includes shorebirds, waterfowl, rabbits, rodents, and other animals that compensate for their losses by rapid reproduction. If the diseased and overabundant prey of the raptors were not kept in check by predation and the natural elements, many of the lesser inhabitants of the prairie would become injurious to their own environment and their own kind.

More than a dozen and a half species of hawks, eagles, and falcons are common in the prairie region. The large rodent-eating species include the golden eagle, bald eagle, ferruginous hawk, Swainson's hawk, red-tailed hawk, and rough-legged hawk. One of the most common is the marsh hawk, the harrier of the prairies, distinguished by its white rump and upward position of the wings in flight. It is a familiar sight on the prairie in late evening as it skims low over the marshes and grasslands, quartering back and forth, occasionally hovering, and then dropping swiftly on its prey. Common items in its diet are rodents, snakes, lizards, grasshoppers, and small immature birds. It does not pursue its quarry on the wing, and unless food must be transported to the nest, it devours its prey where it is caught.

When one thinks of eagles on the western prairie he must think primarily of the golden eagle (*Aquila chrysaetos canadensis*). Before white men came to the grasslands, the golden eagle bred all across the continent. Had it limited its food to rabbits, gophers, ground squirrels, snakes, and carrion it might have persisted in greater numbers. But with the coming of "civilization" it broadened its diet to include the young of domestic stock, game animals, ducks, and other forms considered valuable to man. Now it is uncommon except along the western borders of the prairie.

Golden eagles are the largest birds of prey found over many large areas. Adults weigh from eight to twelve pounds and have a wing spread of seven feet or more. Their size alone distinguishes them from the hawks. Their feet, which are feathered to the toes, distinguish them from the bald eagle, which has bare toes. Whenever this great bird is sighted it adds a touch of romanticism to the landscape. But it is not the invincible model of prowess and lordly courage given to it in romantic fiction. The golden eagle will resort to carrion eating when living game is scarce, and it will desert its eggs or young when human intruders climb to its eyrie.

At close quarters, however, when the eagle is wounded or cornered it stands foursquare and stares with relentless gaze that makes man or beast beware of its steel fists. The talons that break the backbones of rabbits, or even fawns of antelope or deer, can pierce a man's leg to the bone, and their grip is unrelenting. The eagle's size becomes apparent when it is at hand or in a trap from which it must be removed. And when it is freed to unfurl its mighty wings it then truly becomes magnificent.

For nearly ten years I knew one golden eagle on our experimental range in northeastern Colorado. He was distinguishable from all others by the pure white primaries in his right wing—probably the replacements of feathers lost by accident or from a gunshot wound. Daily the great bird made the seven-mile trip from the eyrie in the Chalk Bluffs to the telephone poles near our headquarters. His mate, a much larger bird, seemed to have a different hunting territory, but occasionally they appeared together, cruising the sky over our pastures. The pair remained faithful to one another and to their eyrie for six years. Then she disappeared, probably the casualty of a stockman who had seen them eating the carcass of a young lamb, many of which were killed by rattlesnakes in that territory.

*Male prairie chickens inflate bright orange air sacs on the sides of their necks during courtship displays. In the early-morning and late-evening hours these birds gather on their "booming grounds" on the grass-covered hills to perform elaborate dances. (Nebraska Game Commission)*

Once we had the old man eagle in our hands. He had dropped through the opening in the top of one of our panels, made of two-by-fours and chicken wire, used to keep cattle from grazing our observation plots. He had killed and eaten a jackrabbit that somehow had entered the cage through a hole beneath the wooden frame. Then he had been unable to fly through the narrow opening. We judged that he had been there for more than a week. When we released him he could hardly fly to the nearest fence post, where he sat for several hours. In the evening he was gone. But a week later he was perched on his favorite telephone pole south of our headquarters. He maintained his regular routine for several more years and then in the tenth year he appeared no more.

The maximum age of the golden eagle in the wild state is unknown. James Dixon studied one that lived for thirty years under natural conditions. The wariness of eagles when one approaches their nests undoubtedly is a factor in their survival. Lee W. Arnold has speculated that wariness in golden eagles may have developed as a result of the use of tail feathers for headdresses by generations of North American Indians. The two central tail feathers from immature birds were used because of the white bases of the feathers.

The golden eagle eats a great many kinds of food. On the original prairie the birds taken by eagles undoubtedly included the prairie chicken, sharptail grouse, geese, ducks, quail, plovers, curlews, crows, hawks, and owls. Prairie mammals listed as food of the eagle include skunks, ground squirrels, prairie dogs, raccoons, jackrabbits, cottontails, foxes, coyotes, native rats, mice, and the young of deer and antelope.

If the eagle is the daytime symbol of power among birds, the great horned owl should be ranked first among the nocturnal birds for efficiency in marauding over the prairies. The eastern race (*Bubo virginianus virginianus*) is common along the wooded prairie streams west of the Mississippi River and probably overlaps the range of the western subspecies (*B. v. occidentalis*), which occurs along the cottonwood-bordered creeks and rivers east of the Rocky Mountains. Nesting of these large birds begins on the prairies in mid-February or early March, even when snow and blizzards are possible for several weeks after egg laying.

Great horned owls occasionally use crow, magpie, and heron nests. In 1948 a pair of these owls raised a brood of three in the entrance to a hole in a clay bank on Owl Creek near Rockport, Colorado. The hole had been dug by coyotes, which were poisoned by a member of the Fish and Wildlife Service. After the young had left the nest the adults regularly sat in a cottonwood tree on the edge of Owl Creek. The pellets cast by these owls indicated that their principal food was cottontails. I collected 147 rabbit skulls beneath this tree in 1950.

Of all the owls that frequent the prairie the most amusing are the burrowing owls (*Speotyto cunicularia hypugaea*), which seem to spend much of their time staring at visitors in their domain, whether the visitors are coyotes or people. If the owls are found in company with Richardson's ground squirrels, which also sit bolt upright and stare, the meeting of animals, birds, and humans becomes even more amusing.

A prairie-dog town, complete with dogs and burrowing owls south of Pierce, Colorado, used to attract travelers on the highway between Denver and Cheyenne as bears attract tourists in Yellowstone National Park. Cars would stop and sometimes a dozen people would watch the antics of the birds for an hour or more. The long legs of the adults and the variations in sizes of the young, which were constantly preening themselves or flapping their wings, made the family seem ludicrous in comparison with other owls. Occasionally the adults would pursue grasshoppers among the prairie dogs, which paid little heed to the birds.

This colony of owls lived among the prairie dogs but not in the same holes. They used abandoned tunnels made by the prairie dogs. These owls are not known to dig their own tunnels but are capable of enlarging and cleaning out old burrows. They kick the loosened dirt backward in a shower that includes soil, animal manure, and debris from prey they have captured.

Burrows occupied by the owls can be distinguished from those of prairie dogs by the pack-rat-like accumulation of hair, pieces of bone, insect scraps, parts of dead animals, and owl pellets around the entrance. The nest occupies a chamber up to eighteen inches in diameter and several feet underground from the entrance. It is almost invariably lined or floored with an inch or two of dried horse or cow manure. As Bailey and Niedrach point out in *Birds of Colorado*, the owls no doubt used bison dung in former years.

A lot of hogwash has been written by various authors and perpetrated by story-tel'ing cowboys of the West about the cooperative society of burrowing owls, prairie dogs, and rattlesnakes. According to some of the stories, the owls mount sentry duty and watch for enemies; the prairie dogs dig the holes; and the rattlesnakes, which use the holes for shelter, die fighting in defense of the prairie dog's young. This nonsense was debunked as early as 1874 by Dr. Elliott Coues, who explained that the owls and prairie dogs used the same holes only in time of imminent danger when the nearest shelter was the only choice. The owls sometimes make a meal of young prairie dogs as they do of mice, lizards, small birds, and insects. But the owls and their eggs are eaten by snakes. Snakes also eat the prairie-dog young. Mainly, the association between these three very different animals is one of convenience: the burrows made by the prairie dogs are the binding attraction for all.

One summer I watched the development of two young barn owls (*Tyto alba pratincola*) in a nest in our haymow. I first saw them in their natal down, which was replaced within two weeks by the whitish woolly covering that remained for almost two months. When I last saw them they had the full mottled plumage, speckled with gray and black. Two more different creatures in the same nest I have never seen. The larger one was long of face, irascible to the point of viciousness, and hissed constantly when handled. The smaller one was gentle, round of face, and sat contentedly on my gloved hand each time I visited the nest.

The pellet collection around the haymow nest indicated that kangaroo rats, meadow voles, white-footed mice, and jumping mice were the principal food items brought in by the parents. I never found evidence that birds were captured by this pair, although blackbirds, horned larks, lark buntings, doves, and many other species were present in the vicinity.

The usual presence of many rodents on the prairie would make it a natural habitat for barn owls, except for the scarcity of desirable nesting sites. These owls, which are found throughout much of the temperate zone, make their nests in hollow trees, holes in clay banks, and crevices of rocks and cliffs in the prairie escarpments.

Many of the prairie waters are fringed with shrubs and trees which are productive of fruits and insects not typical of the prairie itself. In these borders catbirds, thrashers, quail, hawks, herons, cormorants, kingfishers, and owls find nesting sites or resting places from which they move out into either the environment of the prairie or the world of the prairie waters. The herons particularly range far from their homes in search of food.

One summer I spent many hours in a tree blind on an island in Terry

*The first baby out of the egg in this redwing-blackbird nest already appears to be hungry for insects from the grasslands.*

Lake, east of the Rockies, observing and photographing great blue herons, double-crested cormorants, snowy egrets, and black-crowned night herons, all of which fish in prairie waters. Most of the herons and cormorants did their fishing in lakes that lay from one to five miles distant from their nests. Possibly the fishing was better away from their home lake, but the habit of leaving their nests unguarded allowed many raids on their eggs and young by crows and magpies.

Many years ago Herbert Schwan and I were assigned the task of selecting a natural area for biological study in the Nebraska National Forest in the sandhill country. We drew the boundary around Signal Hill, where a heronry was located. These great blue herons had to fly from six to ten miles one way in order to do their fishing on the Dismal River.

Birds in the prairie marshes, on the other hand, stay close to home. Early in March the peepers fill the air with their resounding chorus. Soon after, the melodious *gurgle-lee* of the redwinged black bird is heard and then we know that the secretive ones, the American bittern, Virginia rail, gallinule or "water chicken," and common snipe, will be there among the cattails and sedges. The long-billed marsh wren will build several nests of brown sedge leaves among the reeds before his impish wife arrives. And somewhere in the tangle at the edge of open water the pied-billed grebe will build a floating nest that is nothing more than a platform of trash collected from the marsh.

Originally, the shorebirds visited the prairie in immense flocks. Many used the marshes with their shallow water and endless beds of reeds, bullrushes, and sedges as feeding and resting places during the annual migrations. The American golden plover, a charming bird, was one of the abundant species. In their winter home on the Argentine pampas, W. H. Hudson saw them in such multitudes that they resembled a deep brown floor around the pools of water on the plains. He likened the sound of their voices to that of the wind vibrating thousands of tight-drawn wires.

The golden plovers on their northward migration seemed at one time like a vast river of birds flowing from an inexhaustible source. Audubon on March 16, 1821, watched the shooting near New Orleans and estimated that forty-eight thousand golden plovers fell that day. Their numbers were likened by other observers to those of the passenger pigeons.

The great shooting by the sea was the decisive factor that nearly eliminated the sandpipers, curlews, godwits, avocets, and other shore-birds that spent part of their lives on the virgin prairies. Much of this shooting was done on the Eastern Seaboard. In the estuaries around Chesapeake Bay, on the South Carolina coast, and near the Georgia line countless numbers of wild ducks came to garner wild rice. Reed birds were everywhere, along with the curlews, willets, sanderlings, ruddy turnstones, and sandpipers along the tidal creeks and on the sandflats left by the receding tides.

The early-day hunters were not nature lovers: they sought only to kill, mostly for the market. But they were not the whole cause of the demise of the shorebirds. Hydropolitical projects began to divert river waters of the coast so that salt water ruined the deltas. Estuaries were filled, swamps drained, and cities built where the migrating birds once fed. On the prairies the land was plowed, ponds and marshes were drained, and the rivers were channeled for navigation or for flood control. Almost too late have we realized the bounty of nature we lost by drastically changing the land.

We still have one common and widely distributed shorebird remaining in North America, the killdeer (*Charadrius vociferus*). Its summer range extends from coast to coast and from the Canadian Arctic to central Mexico. It is found almost everywhere on the prairie, and not always beside the nearest water. This trim, medium-sized, vociferous plover is distinguished by its two prominent bands across the white breast and its orange-tan rump. The alarm call *killdee* or *dee-ee kill-dee kil-dee* resounds from the mud flats, lake borders, and grasslands from the Yukon to Chile and Peru. At breeding time the call attenuates into a trill as the birds display with spreading tails and drooping wings.

The nest is not camouflaged. It consists merely of a depression in the soil of a field or the sand gravel of a lake shore. The usual four eggs, with brown and black splotches on a gray background, are difficult to see among the pebbles. The precocial chicks, immediately after they are hatched, follow their parents to the nearest shoreline. The food of chicks and adults is mainly insects and small invertebrate animals.

The killdeer is not especially alarmed by man and adapts readily to his fields, pastures, and even the grassy strips near airports. Grazing animals are scolded vigorously when they approach the killdeer's nest. The broken-wing act, however, is used when coyotes, foxes, cats, and other predators prowl in the vicinity of the nest or young.

In the wildlife refuges in the central prairie the piping plover

(*Charadrius melodus*) is seen occasionally, while the semipalmated plover (*C. semipalmatus*) and the black-bellied plover (*Squatarola squatarola*) are seen only rarely. These three are transient visitors in the Dakota and Nebraska prairies. In these same areas the upland sandpiper (*Bartramia longicauda*), American avocet (*Recurvirostra americana*), and Wilson's phalarope (*Steganopus tricolor*) are summer residents, as are the black terns (*Chlidonias niger*), which sometimes are abundant.

The greater yellowlegs (*Totanys melanoleucus*) and lesser yellowlegs (*T. flavipes*) are relatively rare transient visitors in the prairies that stretch from Oklahoma to the Dakotas. These large long-legged shorebirds, that call noisy alarms, frequent the mud flats, river bars, and shallow pools in marshes while hunting for insects, snails, and even small fish. These birds breed from Alaska eastward and in the northern parts of the Canadian prairie provinces.

If any shorebird typified the untamed spirit of the virgin prairie it was the long-billed curlew (*Numenius americanus*). In their former abundance they must have presented a notable sight as the large loosely assembled V-shaped flocks wheeled over the grassy plains, whistling while on the wing or when feeding on the boundless prairie.

I have seen a few of these magnificent birds and the sight of them always brings long thoughts of myriad winged creatures and mighty bison roaming the prairies. In 1941 a pair of long-billed curlews nested on the Central Plains Experimental Range north of Greeley, Colorado. Four greenish-olive eggs were laid in their nest hidden in a swale dominated by desert saltgrass. The nearest water was in a pond half a mile away. When we could take time from our work we watched the male flying overhead as we came within two hundred yards of the nest. He showed so much distress at our near approach that we never examined the nest during the brooding time. Then a flood washed out our fences and when the repairs were done the curlews had vanished. We never knew if an eagle, coyote, or other predator destroyed the brood, or if the flood caused the parents to leave the locality.

Since then I have seen the long-billed curlews in Texas, Montana, and Oregon. The flocks always have been small, never more than ten to twenty flying in their V-shaped squadrons on the late-summer southward migrations. In order to imagine their former abundance I have to wait for the multitudinous ducks that come out of the northland in autumn to settle on ponds and rivers for a while and then rise with a sound like attenuated thunder before they separate into swift-moving skeins against the October sky. But the musical notes of migrating myriads of curlews I am unable to imagine.

*Tiger beetles run over sandy areas in the prairie in search of insect prey. Their larvae are also fierce predators of insects; they live in burrows and snatch any unwary insect that wanders too near the burrow opening.*

# 7

## Insects of the Prairie

WITHOUT INSECTS, the prairie—its plants, mammals, birds, reptiles, and amphibians—would never have existed. The relationship between such birds as the meadowlark or the nighthawk and insects is readily apparent. The link between ants and toads is a little more obscure since most of us do not watch toads, on the prairie or elsewhere. Some of us who are botanically inclined are conscious of the coaction that involves mutual benefits between insects and plants in the process of pollination. Seed production by innumerable forbs and by plants with highly specialized flowers, such as the yucca, would be impossible without insect aid.

If one looks closely at the prairie many of its principles and processes can be traced back to the activities of insects. A male bird, for example, establishes his territory at the beginning of the breeding season and defends it against all other males. His proclamation of ownership is instinctively determined by the probable food supply, shelter, nesting material, and resting places afforded by the vegetation of his chosen territory. His food supply and that of his family, whether it be seeds, insects, or meat of animals, depends ultimately on the plants in his niche. And the presence of these plants depends not only on how well they are pollinated by wind or insects, but on how extensively their flowers, leaves, stems, and roots are eaten by insects. Those greatest of plant eaters among the insects on the prairie, the grasshoppers, can spell success or failure to a multitude of birds and other living things.

Even the mighty buffalo, pestered as they were with flies and other insects, both external and internal, owed their existence directly and indirectly to insects. The wind-pollinated grasses were not the only food of the buffalo. These mighty beasts needed the variety of high protein and other essential food elements found only in forbs and shrubs in the grassland. Many of these plants existed on the prairie because they were pollinated by insects.

Insects also buried the dung of the buffalo and thus fertilized the soil, which made it productive for succeeding generations of buffalo. And when the trampling feet of the vast herds destroyed the plant cover and compacted the soil so water could not readily enter, hosts of burrowing beetles, bees, wasps, and ants helped loosen the earth so it could absorb moisture and once more bless the landscape with endless leagues of asters, mints, goldenrods, shrubs, and grasses.

The insects of the prairie are beautiful, useful, destructive, deadly, and endlessly strange and interesting. The extraordinary behavior of some is almost beyond belief. Many are highly evolved, especially the social groups such as the ants and some of the bees and wasps. Most are delicately attuned to special and restricted ways, including those that bury animals and act as scavengers for both plant and animal debris. Above all, they are a vast, varied, and pervasive group, the most numerous of all animals on land.

A who's who of the insects of the prairie would include nearly all the orders of the class *Insecta*. How many species live in the innumerable habitats and niches of the prairie no one knows. For the entire world the number of described species has been estimated at more than 685,000. In North America north of Mexico more than 84,000 have been estimated. The book *Common Insects of Kansas* contains the estimate that somewhere between 15,000 and 18,000 species exist within the borders of that state. In the whole prairie the orders of insects certainly are represented by species that range from the primitive forms such as the springtails, mayflies, and dragonflies to the advanced social groups of wasps, ants, and bees. In between are the dozens and hundreds of species of grasshoppers, termites, sucking lice, bugs, aphids, lacewings, beetles, butterflies, moths, flies, and fleas.

In many bluestem prairies, grasshoppers (*Orthoptera*), flies (*Diptera*), and bugs (*Hemiptera*) are the dominant orders of insects. Beetles (*Coleoptera*) are numerous throughout the prairie as are moths (*Lepidoptera*) and parasitic wasps (*Hymenoptera*). But, of all insects, grasshoppers are generally conceded to be the most important from the standpoint of their potential destructiveness.

Like most boys who have spent time in the outdoors, I enjoyed the antics of grasshoppers on the prairie. They ate the corks out of our water jugs at haying time. They chewed the binder twine and snapped open our bundles of wheat until the manufacturers learned to impregnate the twine with substances distasteful to grasshoppers. I used to catch them—and still do—to make them spit "tobacco" juice. I would wipe their mouths with my finger to see how many drops they could produce before they ran out of spit. I also knew which plants they preferred and hence where to find them when I needed them for fish bait. I learned that early morning, when dew is still on the grass, is the best time to collect them, since they are not early risers.

Not until I studied zoology, however, did I become aware of some of the details of their life histories. The eggs are laid in late summer and fall. The female thrusts her abdomen into the soil to a depth of an inch or two and starts laying eggs at the bottom of the tunnel thus formed. A glutinous substance excreted by the female as the eggs are laid hardens into a sac or "pod" which contains from fifteen to seventy-five eggs, depending on the species of grasshopper. A single female lays from eight to twenty pods. The eggs remain in the ground during winter and hatch during the following spring.

The young resemble miniature adults and can hop almost immediately after they hatch. They require from one to two months to mature, during which time they molt or shed their skins five or six times. The growth periods between molts are called instars. In the final growth period fully developed wings appear, except in wingless species, and the grasshopper is then ready to mate and reproduce.

In later years, I became more seriously involved with grasshoppers. In my range research on the grasslands of Wyoming I studied the effects of poisoned bait spread by airplane to kill grasshoppers on the short-grass prairie. The infestation was so serious that the grasshoppers had eaten the grasses into the ground and then transferred their attention to the leaves and bark of sagebrush. In the previous year I had stood on top of the Big Horn Mountains with an entomologist who showed me eggs of migratory grasshoppers he said would hatch and produce grasshoppers that would move to the plains in the following year.

During the drought of 1939, I counted 112 grasshoppers per square yard on the prairie in northwestern Oklahoma. They were eating every green thing on the landscape, including prickly-pear cactus. The sound of their moving as they jumped ahead of my footsteps resembled the crackling of small flames in a grass fire. When flights of grasshoppers

*When flying in the vicinity of their native pond, dragonflies usually have a favorite twig where they alight.*

passed overhead during the heat of the day the rattling tumult of the first swarms changed to a sibilant rumble as additional hordes joined the legions already in flight. Thus I was able to envisage the awful reality of the former plagues of grasshoppers that once devastated hundreds of square miles of prairie. Although there is no proof in history, I could imagine that the thousands of dead buffalo described by explorers as resembling gigantic pumpkin patches on the endless plains could have been there because unbelievable multitudes of grasshoppers had left no living plants for them to eat.

Throughout recorded human history migratory grasshoppers, commonly known as locusts, have swarmed across deserts and grasslands, destroying all green vegetation and leaving starvation for man and animals in their paths. Ancient civilizations in Asia and Africa were threatened by plagues of locusts. At present, swarming locusts still are found in India, China, Australia, Africa, and on both continents in the western hemisphere.

Grasshopper injury to crops in New England was noted as early as 1797. In 1818 vast hordes destroyed the crops of early settlers who plowed the prairie in the Red River Valley in Minnesota. During the period 1874 to 1877, the Rocky Mountain grasshopper, or locust, did so much damage that its depredations were considered a national calamity. Congress, on March 3, 1877, created the United States Entomological Commission and authorized it to investigate the grasshopper problem.

Much has been learned about the seasonal development and habits of grasshoppers since the formation of this commission. But it was not known until 1921, when Boris Uvarov published his discovery, that migratory grasshoppers live as solitary animals, like ordinary grasshoppers, until they become crowded. Crowding may not occur for many generations, but when high temperatures in the fall provide conditions for long periods of egg laying, and cool weather in the following spring delays hatching until adequate food is available, then a complete hatch of eggs may occur. If no wet periods long enough to stimulate grasshopper diseases occur, and if natural enemies fail to destroy their usual quota, enormous increases in grasshopper numbers are likely to occur. If several favorable years follow in succession, their numbers pyramid and they aggregate into swarms that contain millions or even billions of grasshoppers.

The dramatic swarms of grasshoppers that impressed the public in 1874 were made up of the Rocky Mountain locust (*Melanoplus spretus*), a species which now appears to be extinct, since no specimens have been taken for more than fifty years. But entomologists have warned that the migratory phase of this species might reappear in a series of years favorable to swarming.

Each state in the prairie region contains at least a hundred species of grasshoppers. Nearly two hundred have been listed for Kansas. Many of these, of course, are rare; some are common; and a few are so abundant as to cause noticeable damage to vegetation. The migratory grasshopper (*Melanoplus mexicanus*) is most abundant on the western prairies. It is reddish brown with a black patch on the neck or collar. It is a strong flier and is similar to the supposedly extinct Rocky Mountain locust. The differential grasshopper (*M. differentialis*), which is occasionally destructive on grasslands, is yellow with contrasting black markings. The thighs of the hind legs are marked by black bars arranged like chevrons. This grasshopper is about one and one-half inches long.

Other grasshoppers common on the prairies are the two-striped grasshopper (*M. bivittatus*), the red-legged grasshopper (*M. femur-rubrum*), and the clear-winged grasshopper (*Camnula pellucida*), which is primarily a grass feeder. The big-headed grasshopper (*Aulo-cara elliotti*), a gray-brown insect with blue hind tibia, is destructive on short-grass prairies. The lubber grasshopper (*Brachystola magna*) is interesting because of its size—up to three inches in length—and its mixture of greenish, brown, bluish, and black colors. Its front wings are pink with small black spots. This hippopotamus of grasshoppers feeds not only on grasses but on the dead bodies of its own kind.

The feeding habits of grasshoppers on the prairie are not as well known as one might expect. Many studies of grasshoppers have been made in cages in the laboratory but these insects do not have the ecological behavior of grasshoppers in nature. In an investigation of grasshoppers on Montana rangelands, Norman L. Anderson and John C. Wright found that an observer in the field often had to wait as long as thirty minutes, prone or sitting, before grasshopper activity in the immediate vicinity returned to what could be considered normal. They found that the mere presence of grasshoppers upon certain kinds of plants did not mean that the insects were eating those plants. Most rangeland grasshoppers are not omnivorous but are selective and have food-plant preferences. Many species differ widely in their feeding and roosting habits. The spotted bird grasshoppers (*Schistocerca lineata*), for example, like shaded ravines and gullies in which shrubs are growing. They are most commonly found perched on wild rose bushes. They eat stiff goldenrod (*Solidago rigida*) and coralberry (*Symphori-carpos orbiculatus*) but do not usually feed on grasses. They are seldom seen on the ground.

In contrast, the migratory grasshoppers are commonly found on the ground. The first two instars eat mainly dry materials consisting of plant debris and cow manure. As they pass through succeeding molts and instars they add more and more green grass to their diet. As they approach the adult stage they change from grass to a large variety of forbs and shrubs. If rain comes in August and induces a new growth of grass, many of these grasshoppers return to flats where green forage is abundant.

*A fly is laying its egg on the manure ball which these scarab beetles are starting to bury. Scarab beetles or tumblebugs can digest enough manure in one day to equal their own weight.*

One must not imagine that the whole world of grass-eating insects on the prairie consists of grasshoppers. Their near relatives, the katydids and crickets, are there in multitudes and present a richly diverse and interesting group of familiar insects for study and contemplation of prairie niches. Katydids are large, usually green, grasshopperlike insects, which are mostly nocturnal in their activities. Like their relatives the crickets, they are accomplished insect musicians. The familiar sound of their stridulation is produced by rubbing together roughened areas on their front wings. Katydid "songs" sometimes are astonishingly loud and function as courtship calls. The rasping notes are so distinctive that experienced observers can name the species without seeing the insect. Unlike grasshoppers or locusts, which have ears on the sides of their abdomens, katydids and crickets have ears below the "knees" on their front legs.

Most of the katydids are grass eaters but a few capture grasshoppers and other insects, or eat dead insects, including their own kind. The common meadow katydid (*Orchelium vulgare*) ranges from Canada to Georgia and west to Wyoming and Texas. The round-winged katydid (*Amblycorypha rotundifolia parvipennis*), found in Oklahoma, Arkansas, and Texas, is distinctive because of its oval wings, which are rounded at the tips. It is usually green but may be pink. Its song, *tsip-i tsip-i tsip*, is distinctive. Another common species is the broad-winged katydid (*Microcentrum rhombifolium*), distributed from New York to Indiana to Colorado and Kansas. It occurs across the southern United States from coast to coast.

On the prairies, and almost everywhere else, the familiar crickets are known for their chirping and for their love of food whether it be leather gloves, starched clothes, plant tissues, or dead insects. The true crickets (*Gryllidae*) and their relatives the tree crickets (*Oecanthinae*) are songsters of the night. Their stridulation is accomplished by rubbing together a double file and scraper on their front wings. The tree crickets synchronize their chirps in a given area so they all call in unison. The sound is so penetrating I have been able to locate chirping crickets more than 150 yards away on still nights.

Various formulae have been suggested for determining temperature by the rate of tree-cricket chirping. A common method is to count the chirps per minute, divide by four, and add 40. When the temperature is above 50 degrees F. the calculation is surprisingly accurate. I have found that tree crickets, even in the same shrub or tree, sometimes chirp at different rates. When I placed my thermometer at the exact locations of the crickets, I learned that their microhabitat temperatures also were different.

The common field cricket (*Acheta assimilis*), found in almost every vegetation type in the United States, reaches its climax in numbers on the prairie in autumn. These crickets hide beneath stones and among grass stems. Their black or brown bodies usually are from one-half to an inch long. The antennae are sometimes one and one-half inches long. Both male and female crickets have a pair of cerci, or appendages, that project to the rear like twin tails. These appendages possess hairs that are especially sensitive to vibrations from the earth or from the air. Female crickets have an egg placer, or ovipositor, which projects behind like a stiff tail. This ovipositor is thrust into the soil to lay some three hundred tiny oval eggs, which must be alternately frozen and thawed during the winter to make them hatch in May or June.

The young crickets spend a good part of the summer growing up. Then when September comes, they are adults and are everywhere searching for food. They are omnivorous, and dine ravenously on green vegetation or on the meat of dead insects, particularly grasshoppers. Since adult crickets can eat the equivalent of three-fourths of their own weight each day, and since there may be ten thousand of them on an acre, their impact on the prairie sometimes equals that of the rabbits, mice, and other small mammals that search for vegetable and animal food among the grass stems.

No insects have more fascinating ways of life, or more useful places among the prairie inhabitants, than the dung beetles. The pre-eminent ones are the "tumblebugs" or ball rollers. Many of us have known them from our childhood days. But few of us have had the patience or training to ask, "Where do they come from? Where are they going?" I doubt that the ancient Egyptians were aware of the life history details of the sacred scarab or dung beetles, which to them were emblems of eternity. They believed that the ball represented the earth and that the movements of the beetle were influenced by the heavenly bodies. The male beetle typified the god Kheperi, the rising sun. In ancient embalmings, beetles were placed on the eyes in the belief that this would enable them to see again. If substituted for the heart, the heart would beat again. The beetle also denoted reincarnation. In one sense the dung beetles do participate in a form of reincarnation by returning the manure, left by grazing animals, into the ground. Much of this fertilizer becomes available for growth of new grass. Thus the beetles help perpetuate the web of life on the prairie.

The dung beetle's life history is as fascinating as are the theories of their place in creation held by the Egyptians. In order to see their life cycles you have to follow the insects until they have buried their manure balls in the soil, mark the locations with stakes, and dig one up every few days. The beetles are not hard to find on the prairie. The species *Canthon laevis* is common almost everywhere as is the large *Pinotus carolinus*. One has only to find a cow path worn several inches deep by the passing of many animal feet. The beetles will be there, since many of them accidentally roll their balls over the edge and are unable to push them back up the steep sides of the path.

In order to shape the balls the beetles tear off pieces of fresh manure and roll them by pushing upward with their hind legs. Whether the balls accumulate a coating of dust or not seems to matter little to the insects. Sometimes two beetles join in the task. When a suitable spot is reached the beetles bulldoze with their heads around and under the ball of manure. Gradually it sinks and follows the beetle into the earth. Sometimes one beetle does all the work and the other rides the ball down out of sight. The soil heaves for a while and then is still.

In the underground chamber, which is excavated several inches below the surface, the beetle dines until the food is gone. The feast may last for a day or a week. A coiled food tube, ten times the length of the beetle's body, produces the juices that enable it to digest in one day manure equal to its own weight. When the ball is eaten the beetle comes to the surface and searches for more manure.

In spring and summer the females of some species bury a ball of manure, add soil, and mold it into a pear-shaped body within the spherical cavity at the bottom of the burrow. One of the largest eggs—nearly one-fifth of an inch in diameter—in the insect kingdom then is laid in a saucerlike depression at the small end of the "pear." The mother then digs her way to the surface. When the larva hatches from the egg it feeds on the dung and plasters the walls of its home with fecal cement

*Lubber grasshoppers grow to lengths of nearly three inches. Thousands of these grasshoppers with big appetites can denude large areas of prairie in the few weeks they require to grow to adult size.*

that protects it until the pupal stage is complete and the new tumblebug digs through the soil to start a life of its own. Since the scarab beetles live for several years it is possible for the mother to see her children and their children's children. But they show no sign of family recognition when they meet.

Many variations exist in the habits of tumblebugs. Some do not make their own balls of manure but use deer pellets. Some females remain in the underground chamber guarding the egg and the pupa; then the mother and her adult child emerge together. Others, like the European *Copris hispanus*, shape several smooth ovoid bodies of manure in the underground chamber. The female lays an egg on each ball and then smooths and polishes them while the eggs hatch and the larvae develop. Other species of dung beetles are unsophisticated in their habits. One kind, for example, does not roll a ball through the grass; instead, it forms its ball in a burrow at the edge of the pile of manure. Another merely fills its burrow with manure. The laziest one of all simply lays its eggs in the manure and the larvae develop there.

Many of the dung beetles are beautiful and are prized by collectors. Some are large, black, shining, and marked by shallow striae on the wing covers as, for example, *Pinotus carolinus*. The somewhat smaller *Phanaeus vindex* is decorated with a bronze head, a copper thorax, and metallic bluish-green wing covers. A small species, *Psammodius interuptus*, less than one-fourth inch in length, has a black thorax and a brown head and brown wing covers.

When we contemplate all the rolling, burying, digging, and sanitation carried on by the dung beetles, who can say that they do not perform an important ecological function on the prairie? What better and more constant means of tilling, aerating, and fertilizing the soil can we find in nature? The manure carried underground by these insects is quickly acted on by bacteria and transformed into substances useful to plants. And its removal from the ground surface minimizes the habitat of flies that pester modern livestock, as they once pestered the buffalo.

Some of the most important insects on the prairie are the scavengers or meat eaters found on carcasses of mammals, birds, and reptiles. Without these insect morticians the world soon would be an unpleasant, if not impossible, place in which to live. When an animal dies, most of us are aware that blow flies and carrion beetles soon visit the carcass, as do scavenger mammals and birds. Bacteria and fungi also speed the processes of decomposition. But few of us realize that the major role played by many insects is the disposal of carrion and the conversion of its energy into forms useful to living things.

In a revealing experiment, Jerry A. Payne recently demonstrated in South Carolina how efficiently insects can reduce dead bodies to the dust from which they came. He placed stillborn baby pigs in screened cages in a hardwood-pine community. The screened cages protected the carcasses from mammal and bird scavengers. Some of the cages permitted the entrance of insects and some excluded insects. Then the stages of decay were watched for several weeks.

In the cages open to insects, flesh flies arrived on the pigs within five minutes. Blow flies began feeding within ten minutes. These insects also began to deposit eggs. Soon after, yellowjackets were feeding on the liquids produced by the pig bodies. The yellowjackets also captured adult blow flies that had come to the carrion to lay their eggs. Ants also began feeding on the first day.

By the second day scarab beetles had buried themselves in the soil beneath the carcasses. They remained in their tunnels during the day and fed on the pigs during the night. In succeeding days the procession of insects included fruit flies, coreid bugs, soldier flies, hister beetles, carrion beetles, and skin beetles. Meanwhile, many fly larvae developed and migrated from the carcasses. By the eighth day only dry skin, cartilage, and bones remained. Still the succession of insects and other small animals continued. As many of the beetles and flies abandoned the remains, centipedes, millipedes, snails, and roaches appeared beneath the carrion. Payne found a total of 522 species that were attracted by the pigs.

Pigs which were protected from insects went through several stages of decomposition and disintegration, including bloating, dehydration, and mummification. The drying stage proceeded slowly and the mummified appearance lasted as long as two months. Body form was still clearly apparent after three months. Thus the experiment demonstrated the effectiveness of insects in the decomposition of carrion. It also demonstrated a microsuccession among the small fauna that came to bury the dead. What a job insects must have done when thousands of buffalo died of starvation or natural disaster on the prairies!

A multitude of insect species perform the important work of pollination on the prairie. It matters little if these insects are seeking pollen, sucking nectar, or are predators hunting other insects on the innumerable flowers of the grassland. If the pollen is carried from the anthers to the stigmas of the flowers, the plants can reproduce. The miracle is that both the plants and the insects benefit.

Insect pollinators include such diverse forms as beetles, butterflies and moths, bugs, flies, leafhoppers, and walking sticks. Many of these insects spend dual lives in foraging for food. The bright-colored soldier beetles (*Chauliognathus marginatus*), which resemble fireflies, commonly feed on goldenrod flowers and aid in their pollination; but their larvae live in the soil and are carnivorous. Moths and butterflies pollinate many of the conspicuous flowers and are repaid by the plant which furnishes leaves as food for their caterpillars. The flower flies of the family *Syrphidae* are a numerous clan and many are beneficial to plants. These bright-colored insects, some of which resemble bees or wasps, are confirmed flower visitors. The larvae of many syrphids are predators on aphids, which because of their reproductive capacity are serious plant pests.

Among the most specialized of the pollinators are the moths and butterflies. Although many of these produce larvae with strong jaws and voracious appetites for leaves and other plant organs, the adults are responsible for cross-pollination of innumerable prairie plants. Thus, they are essential for the production of seeds, fruits, and plants upon which other animals depend, either directly or indirectly.

Probably the best known of the moths are the sphinx or hawk moths, some of which are so large they resemble hummingbirds. The bodies of these moths are relatively stout and torpedo-shaped. The larvae are brown or green caterpillars with either a horn or a colored spot near the tail end. The adults hover in front of flowers while they uncoil and thrust their long tongues deep into the nectaries of flowers with long tubular corollas.

The butterflies of the prairie are numerous and show great variety in size, color, and habits. Many are flower visitors and some of their larvae feed only on certain species of plants. The best-known and most-widely-distributed butterflies are the monarchs, which feed mainly on milkweeds. The monarchs migrate southward across the prairie, just as they do along the Atlantic and Pacific coasts. At night the swarms of monarchs roost in trees along stream courses as they go southward in easy stages toward the Gulf of Mexico.

Among the other butterflies common to the prairie and its borders are the red admiral (*Vanessa atalanta*), which flies from March to September, and the painted lady (*V. cardui*), which is fond of thistle flowers. The goatweed butterfly (*Anaea andria*) is of interest since its larvae feed on croton leaves. The great spangled fritillary (*Speyeria cybele*) has larvae that feed on violet leaves. The giant swallowtail (*Papilio cresphontes*), which is one of the first butterflies captured by young collectors, is predominantly black with a yellow V pointing toward the tail end of the body. The cloudless sulphur (*Phoebis sennae*) is one of the puddle butterflies that congregate around ponds and moist places.

Skippers, the dull-colored butterflies with recurved hooks beyond the club of the antennae, are common throughout the prairie. Some of their caterpillars feed on grass; some make webs on tree leaves; and some, like the checkered skipper (*Pyrgus communis*), feed on plants of the mallow family. The larvae of the giant skippers such as *Megathymus yuccae* bore into the stems and roots of yucca, which depends on pollination by the pronuba moth. Adult giant skippers have a wingspread of one and one-half inches or more and their larvae are large. In Mexico the two-and-one-half-inch-long larvae of the skipper that feeds on the leaves of the century plant are sold for human consumption and can be bought in cans labeled "Gusanos de Maguey."

Of all the pollinating insects on the prairie the bees are probably the most important. Many of the rose-family plants, many forbs with conspicuous and strongly scented flowers, and most of the legumes are pollinated by bees, flies, and wasps. Bees, along with beetles, pollinate goldenrods and other forbs that bloom in late summer and autumn.

On the original prairie there were no honeybees. These were introduced from the Old World after the discovery of America. But the native bees were exceedingly numerous—possibly a thousand species could be listed as inhabitants of the central prairie. Unlike the honeybees, most of the native bees do not store honey. And, with the exception of the bumblebees, the great majority of wild bees are not social insects; instead, they live solitary lives and make individual nests.

The bees of the prairie are similar to their relatives the wasps in that most species nest in underground burrows. Most of the wild bees carry pellets of pollen to their nests, either by collecting it in so-called pollen baskets as do the honeybees and bumblebees or by packing dry pollen among the hairs on their bodies. Some of the bees have become parasitic and lay their eggs in the nests of other bees that collect pollen for their larvae. All the native bees can sting, and unlike the honeybee, which cannot withdraw the ovipositor, they do not die when they sting.

Scientists differ in their opinions as to the proper classification of bees.

For our purpose it is sufficient to recognize some of the groups by what the bees do in their life activities. The bumblebees, like honeybees, are social insects that live together in nests, cooperate with the queen, and practice division of labor. Most of the other bees are solitary in that each female prepares her own nest, where her eggs are laid on small particles or pellets of pollen. The nests, however, may be placed close together and thus produce colonies of solitary bees. In addition to the bumblebees, some of the groups found on the prairie include leaf-cutting bees, mining bees, short-tongued bees or sand bees, deceptive bees, silk bees, and wasp bees.

Bumblebees are recognized by most people because of their large size and stinging ability when disturbed. I learned this early with my boyhood friends when we played an exciting game with the bees near our swimming hole. We made paddles out of shingles, and when we were completely undressed someone would stir up a bumblebee nest with a stick. The object was to bat the bumblebee with the shingle before the bee could sting one of us. Being naked, we believed we were giving the bees a sporting chance. The bees flew like bullets and hitting them required excellent eyesight and coordination. There were many casualties on both sides, and when one of us was stung the cure was to lie with the injured part of the body in warm mud at the edge of our swimming hole.

Several dozen kinds of bumblebees live on the prairie. One kind has a red band across the abdomen and a black band across the thorax (*Bombus ternarius*). Others are characterized by various markings of brown, black, and yellow on the head, thorax, and abdomen. The queens of all bumblebees mate with the males in summer or autumn and then hibernate during the winter. In spring the queens build their nests in old mouse nests, in burrows made by rodents, or in cavities under stones. The eggs are laid in waxen cells and when the larvae hatch they mature in about three weeks. The queen feeds them with nectar and pollen. The first workers are small but as succeeding broods are produced their workers become nearly as large as the queen.

The leaf-cutter bees are interesting because the females cut oblong and circular pieces from leaves to line their nests and to make partitions between the cells. The nests are made in hollow stems and in holes in the ground. The leaf-cutter bees in my garden are especially fond of lilac leaves, which they use to line their nests in the hollow bamboo sticks we use for wind chimes on our front porch. The clicking together of the bamboo pieces and their musical notes do not deter the bees or the hatching and growth of their larvae. On the prairie, numerous leaf-cutter bees of the genus *Megachile* visit and pollinate a large number of flowers. The nesting habits of the various species of leaf cutter and other bees of the grasslands have not been studied in detail.

Short-tongued bees of the genus *Andrena*, which range from quite small to larger than a honeybee, are noted for their seasonal habits. The different species follow closely the appearance of certain flowers and many of them seem to be limited to a single kind of plant. In spring the different species of these so-called sand bees visit the flowers of willows, wild plums, wolfberry, and meadow parsnip. In early summer a new set of bee species visit the flowers of violets, sweet clover, western wallflower, wild spirea, and smooth sumac. The late-summer species have available a great variety of asters, goldenrods, gumweed, and other plants and do not seem to be closely restricted to particular kinds of flowers.

*Kneeling near a harvester-ant mound, the author is examining seeds collected by the ants.*

A great many other bees of the prairie are so deceptive in appearance they could pass for ants, flies, or other insects. Some of these have black, unbanded, shining bodies that are devoid of hairs. Some are partial to yellow flowers of gumweed and sunflowers, and may be rare or absent when these flowers are not present. One species (*Panurginus malvastri*), which was first described from Nebraska in 1907, visits the brick-red flowers of scarlet globe mallow.

Certain kinds of solitary bees, known as alkali bees, are efficient pollinators of alfalfa. Farmers sometimes provide them with artificial nests made of thousands of soda straws with the open ends facing in one direction. Each bee knows its own straw and does not interfere with neighboring bees using other straws. Artificial nests also can be made by boring holes in blocks of wood which are placed aboveground and sheltered from the sun and rain with a roof. The bees thus are not molested by skunks and ground-dwelling birds.

The mining bees of the subfamily *Halictidae*, most of which nest in ground burrows, build communal nests with a common opening through which the bees pass to their individual cells. A guard is posted at the entrance to keep out wasps and other parasites. Sharing in communal labor by these bees, such as preparation of cells in the nest and pollen gathering while fertilized females are laying eggs, make these groups true temporary societies. The social structure, however, is not as advanced as that of the bumblebees or the highly organized societies of ants.

The direct and indirect effects of ants on the prairie have been inadequately studied. Ants have been on earth for nearly one hundred million years and undoubtedly they have been on the prairie since its beginning. Their highly efficient social organization has contributed to an adaptability and behavior that has enabled them to persist in the midst of all natural enemies and all climatic adversities.

The most conspicuous signs of ants on the prairie, of course, are the large mounds of the harvester ants (*Pogonomyrmex occidentalis*). The hills made by these ants are Gargantuan in comparison with the Lilliputian hills of the garden ants most of us see at home. The mound usually is a round-topped cone, six to twelve inches high, and three to five feet in diameter at the base. This cone generally is situated at the center of a bare circle which varies in diameter from a few feet to ten yards or more. These circles are kept clear of vegetation by the ants, and when the colony prospers the mound and cleared area may grow for twenty years or more. Some of the mounds I marked with iron stakes in Colorado in 1939 were still present when I visited them in 1968.

The seed-collecting habits of harvester ants were mentioned by the writers of antiquity, but the Old World ants of which they wrote belong to the genus *Messor*. Undoubtedly the harvester ants of the genus *Pogonomyrmex* were seen by Coronado when he led the conquistadores up from Mexico. The Reverend Henry C. McCook, however, was one of the first to study them in detail. His books about the harvester ants of Texas and those of the Great Plains were published in 1879 and 1882. More recently, many studies have been made of the taxonomy, colony life, and ecology of the harvester ants.

The ant mound is made of gravel and other particles of solid material, most of which are collected from the ground surface in the vicinity of the nest. I have found nests covered with lava particles in Idaho, with green jade in Wyoming, with fossil shark teeth in western Colorado, and with colored fragments of broken bottles in Oklahoma. The mound usually consists of gravel and earth cemented together near the surface to make a rind that is more or less waterproof.

The opening into the mound is usually on the southeast in spring and on the southwest in autumn. This position may be related to the incidence of the sunlight and its greatest warmth during these seasons. The large permanent mound probably has utility in relation to the need for early spring and late autumn warmth, since a dome in these seasons receives nearly twice as much solar energy as the surrounding level ground surface. I can only speculate that the harvester ant (*Pogonomyrmex barbatus*) of the southwestern prairies frequently makes only a cleared circle, without a mound, because the added temperature in a cone or hemispherical dome is not needed.

The doorway of the harvester-ant mound opens into a lobby or foyer from which tunnels lead to a labyrinth of dome-shaped chambers and connecting galleries which are excavated by the ants to depths of nine to twelve feet. In the upper galleries and chambers the queen, eggs, larvae, pupae, immature workers, and adult workers live during the summer. In winter the queen and adult workers hibernate, without eating food, mostly below the frost line. With them live a motley array of insect guests, intruders, and parasites, including beetles, smaller ants, crickets, termites, bugs, and worms.

At harvest time thousands of ants search the prairie for the seeds they store in chambers that serve as granaries. The ants explore for seeds on the ground and also climb plant stems to obtain ripened seeds of many grasses and forbs. Since the ants may number 500,000 per acre in certain prairie types and since they can run at the rate of ten feet or more per minute when the temperature is high it is evident that every square foot of soil surface may be covered daily in their explorations for seeds. The ants in a single large colony can easily collect a pint of seeds in a single day. In a growing season they exert an important influence on the seed supply of forbs and grasses.

Harvester ants have a cosmopolitan appetite for seeds. On the prairie they fill their granaries with seeds of pigweeds, goosefoot, squirreltail, prickly poppy, needle-and-thread, hairy goldaster, and rubber rabbit-brush. Like good farmers, they store the seeds in different bins. As a supplement to the starch and fat in seeds, they collect dead insects and bird dung, which provide protein in their diet. In this respect they are small but abundant scavengers on the prairie.

The utility of the circle of bare soil around harvester ant mounds has been the subject of speculation by many observers. One theory is that the ants chew down the vegetation to afford protection from enemies. But since they must run across many feet of bare space to reach the surrounding grassland it appears to me that they are exposed rather than protected from enemies. The absence of plants near the mound, however, does allow the sun to dry the cleared circle after rainstorms and thus tends to alleviate the danger of mold's destroying the seeds in the granaries below.

The constant clipping of vegetation by the ants also prevents the formation of roots which might decay and leave channels in the soil through which rainwater could enter the nest. And when fires burn over the prairie, as they have for centuries, the soil around the mounds is not heated to an intolerable degree. Thus the ants are spared and with their stored seeds they are able to live until the prairie becomes productive again.

*Poised to strike, the prairie rattlesnake detects odors with its tongue. The heat pits in front of the eyes also enable the snake to locate its prey.*

# 8

---

# *Reptiles and Amphibians*
# *of the Prairie*

WHEN THE FRIGID NIGHTS OF WINTER give way to longer
days and the turbulent winds of March subside, the warming sun brings
a new season to the prairie. The bleak foreverness of the landscape,
given a few weeks of life-renewing heat, suddenly teems with growing
things and becomes a living world. And, as the chill of winter releases
its cruel grip, the cold-blooded inhabitants in the earth begin their adjustment to the meliorating environment.

The prairie rattlesnake (*Crotalus viridis viridis*), a dweller of the
flat western grasslands, ventures forth from his prairie-dog burrow to
bask in the midday sun. Or he coils on a south-facing ledge of a plains
escarpment outside the den where he has spent the winter with others
of his kind, deep in the crevices of fractured rocks. He does little exploring and the unwary deer mouse that passes his rock elicits no attack.
At night he returns to his rocky chamber. Not for several weeks will
he actively explore the surrounding territory, relentlessly searching for
mice, horned lizards, and newly born rabbits before he migrates possibly a mile or more to better summer hunting grounds.

In another den that once was home for a badger family a six-foot-
long bullsnake (*Pituophis melanoleucus sayi*) stirs sluggishly but does
not emerge to hunt. Higher soil temperature ultimately will quicken
his movements and impel him to venture forth and establish his domain

among the kangaroo-rat burrows or in the bordering vegetation near a sandy creek bed where he can be near the water and the numerous rodents and cottontails that live there in abundance.

Beneath a stone on a southern prairie hillside, a plains blind snake (*Leptotyphlops dulcis dulcis*), less than eight inches long and thin as a darning needle, burrows upward in search of worms and small insects. This reddish brown degenerate serpent, with vestigial eyes imbedded beneath translucent scales, lives a subterranean life and is seldom seen. But the warm rains of spring moisten the soil and it comes out of its earthen burrow at dusk to explore and then to return to its hiding place in the soil. Its tail is as round as its head and it has teeth only in its lower jaw.

On a warm night in early April, when gentle rains have moistened the hard-packed ground, the soil surface heaves in ten thousand places and the snouts and eyes of a multitude of plains spadefoot toads (*Scaphiopus bombifrons*) emerge. If the weather remains favorable they leave their burrows and go abroad in search of food. Before morning they retreat underground and may not emerge again for many nights. But ultimately a torrential rain floods the lowlands and fills the buffalo wallows and shallow depressions. Then the bleating of the toad congress shatters the stillness of night and announces that mating time has arrived.

Throughout the prairie other subterranean cold-blooded creatures begin to stir in their earthen chambers. The eastern collared lizard (*Crotaphytus collaris collaris*) moves slowly from his rock crevice to bask atop a heat-absorbing basalt boulder. Soon he is warm enough to catch insects or even lizards smaller than himself. And he is quick to take cover if a fox or other enemy appears on the scene.

Throughout the prairie, as spring advances, many other reptiles and amphibians resume the active phases of their existence. On the Kansas grasslands ornate box turtles dig their way up through the soil and emerge from hibernation. From the mud of ponds, streams, and rivers, painted turtles, mud turtles, snapping turtles, and others of their kind emerge to take up their tasks of feeding, breeding, and avoiding enemies in their individual ways. With them come the frogs and salamanders. Once more, wet and dry habitats are populated with cold-blooded creatures that have ended their half year of suspended animation. Now they occupy their niches, along with the birds, mammals, and insects in the living world of the prairie.

The most spectacular, but not the most numerous, of all the cold-blooded creatures of the prairie are the rattlesnakes. I have encountered many of them while wandering over the prairies of North America. These meetings have never caused me undue alarm, but I have nearly always treated these snakes with respect, especially the large western diamondback rattlesnakes (*Crotalus atrox*) of Texas.

The smaller prairie rattlesnakes are less fearsome than most people suppose. In general, I have found them less aggressive than some of the harmless garter snakes, or the water snakes of the genus *Natrix* which inhabit prairie streams and ponds. Only once have I been struck by a rattlesnake and that was on the ankle of my leather boot while walking through tall grass in the state of Washington. I made the mistake of following directly behind a companion in an area where rocky outcrops provided abundant dens for rattlesnakes. Probably the passing of my friend disturbed the snake and it was ready to strike when I followed in his footsteps.

On the Central Plains Experimental Range in northeastern Colorado we kept a record of all rattlesnakes encountered over a period of fifteen years. The largest prairie rattlesnake, out of 318 examined, was 46 inches long. It had 9 rattles. The shortest snake we measured was 11 inches long. It had one rattle and a button. The average length was 27.1 inches and the average number of rattles was 5.6. Our earliest sighting of a rattlesnake was May 1 and the latest was November 10. We saw the greatest numbers of snakes in July and August, mostly in blue grama and saltbush vegetation where mice, kangaroo rats, and cottontail rabbits were abundant. Only once in fifteen years did we see a rattlesnake at night although we constantly traveled in darkness the fifty-two miles of dirt road on our experimental pastures.

Most of the rattlesnakes we encountered on the prairie did not rattle upon discovery. Usually they remained coiled and motionless and many tried to escape without rattling even when prodded with a stick. A few showed fight, especially on hot summer days. On one occasion a large rattlesnake became aggressive when I teased it with a shovel. It repeatedly advanced toward me, forming a loop, striking at least one-third of its length, and rattling continuously.

Only once have I smelled the anal scent which angry or frightened rattlesnakes can spray a distance of several feet in the form of fine droplets. One spring, a number of us decided to kill rattlesnakes that hibernated in a rock den near Grover, Colorado. In their migration from this den they became a menace to schoolchildren and also killed newborn lambs that examined them out of curiosity. We killed sixty-three rattlesnakes that day and the chemical alarm of their scent, which resembles the odor of green apples, caused snakes to rattle all around us. We finally abandoned the task because of the danger of other snakes hidden in the cover of dried weeds and grass.

On the original grassland, prairie-dog towns were favorite habitations for rattlesnakes. The dog burrows provided shelter from the heat on hot summer days and places of hibernation in winter. Food was usually abundant, since mice, rabbits, lizards, toads, salamanders, and other creatures were usually present. The young of prairie dogs and of burrowing owls undoubtedly also served as food for the rattlesnakes. In other places in the prairie, gophers, ground squirrels, and mice provided food for the snakes.

The rattlesnakes themselves had enemies on the prairie. The sharp hoofs of stampeding buffalo probably killed many snakes on the surface of the ground. Deer have been known deliberately to jump on snakes to kill them. And coyotes, foxes, hawks, eagles, and owls have always been predators of snakes, especially young ones. The red-tailed hawk is one of the most important destroyers of rattlesnakes. The roadrunner on southwestern prairies is believed to take more young rattlesnakes than all the other predators combined. Extended exposure to sunshine also can kill rattlesnakes; such accidents, however, are not common.

Many other snakes are found in prairie environments, although relatively few are seen by the casual observer. Raymond L. Ditmars has pointed out that numbers of snake species increase greatly as one goes southward. There are no snakes in the Arctic tundra. Only a few, including the prairie rattlesnake, are found in southern Canada. In the Mississippi Valley and westward, bullsnakes, garter snakes, water snakes, and hognose snakes become more abundant. Copperheads, prairie rat snakes, and king snakes are encountered in increasing numbers from Kansas and Missouri southward. Among the largest of the prairie snakes are the Texas diamondback rattlesnakes, which may measure six feet or more in length. The prairie bullsnake occasionally reaches a length of nearly eight feet. It is capable of destroying a whole clutch of young rabbits at one meal.

The intriguing eastern hognose snake (*Heterodon platyrhinos*) and its relative the plains hognose snake (*H. nasicus nasicus*), both of which are widely distributed, live largely on toads. Occasionally they eat frogs,

*Harmless to humans, the hognose snake feeds principally on toads. These nonvenomous snakes are characterized by flattened heads and prominent snouts.*

and they will accept dead birds and mice. The hognose snake is called the "spreading viper" by some people because of the snake's habit of flattening its head and body and hissing loudly in the presence of a presumed enemy. Sometimes the snake writhes as though it were in the throes of death and then turns belly-up. If turned right side up, it instantly goes belly-up again. I have seen them repeat this performance half a dozen times in succession. They are perfectly harmless even though they can be teased into striking repeatedly, with mouth closed.

On the prairie, as elsewhere, many more snakes exist in varied niches than are ever seen. A four-foot bullsnake used to live under a concrete platform on our prairie ranch. Occasionally it made the one-hundred-yard round trip from its burrow to the water tank near our windmill. Sometimes it climbed into the tank and swam in the cool water; then it returned home, leaving a clearly defined trail in the dust. Many similar snake trails were made at night in our dooryard but the snake under the platform was the only one we ever saw regularly over a period of several years.

I am inclined to believe that the secretiveness of snakes explains in part our lack of knowledge of their impact on animal populations through predation. To my knowledge, no one has made a careful estimate of the biomass of snakes and reptiles on the prairie, or elsewhere. Biomass, the total weight of animals on an acre or a square mile, provides a useful measure of the productive capacity of the environment. It also indicates which level in the food chain is occupied by a given animal. We know, for example, that a square mile of productive prairie can support twenty thousand pounds of cows grazing there for a year. We know that a productive lake may produce seventy-five pounds of fish per acre per year. Perhaps, if we knew how many pounds of box turtles, lizards, and snakes live on a square mile of upland prairie we would agree that these animals have an important place in the prairie food chain.

We do know that predation is a necessary and natural process in a balanced wildlife community and that all animals living in a given environment must ultimately die in one way or another. In this process, whereby animals live and die, the first step is the conversion of green plants into animal substances. These substances are then passed on to other animals until the ultimate consumer—man, a bear, or an eagle— is reached. This ultimate consumer finally is felled by parasites, disease, starvation, accidents, or old age.

In the prairie food chain, turtles, lizards, toads, frogs, and snakes are only a few of the animals involved in the series of consumers. They are aided, or inhibited, by other consumers such as meadowlarks, weasels, badgers, and a host of other animals all engaged in maintaining populations more or less in balance with what the environment offers them in the way of food and shelter. Their combined efforts are necessary to the maintenance of populations that do not permanently exceed the biological capabilities of the land.

Thus, when a snake falls victim to a red-tailed hawk, some of the burrowing owls in a prairie-dog town may be spared. In turn, more mice may be eaten because the owl still lives. But with fewer mice, many insects and spiders will survive, and because of the decrease in mouse population, hawks, foxes, skunks, coyotes, and other predators will shift their diets to include grasshoppers, rabbits, or bird eggs. Ultimately the food chain will adjust until its links fall back into their normal sequence again. The point of this discussion that we should remember, however, is that we do not know how vigorously reptiles jiggle this prairie food chain.

There are at least a dozen kinds of turtles to be seen in prairie habitats. Some turtles live in muddy ponds; others prefer clear streams; and a few inhabit dry uplands where water, other than that from rainstorms, may not be encountered for years on end. Most of us think of turtles as "mud turtles" or snapping turtles with vicious dispositions when brought out on dry land from their watery homes.

As a boy I realized how numerous turtles were on our prairie farm. I always felt sad when the cork bobber on my still-fishing outfit slowly descended into the depths of our prairie creek instead of jiggling up and down with the nibbling of a sunfish or catfish on my worm bait. The slow descent of the bobber, with hardly a ripple on the water surface, meant that I had a turtle on the hook and that the line would have to be cut, even if I succeeded in pulling the ungainly creature to dry land.

The common snapping turtle (*Chelydra serpentina serpentina*) is found in prairie waters. It prefers mud-bottomed ponds and streams and seldom leaves the water except at egg-laying time. From twenty to forty spherical eggs about the size of golf balls are laid in June. They hatch in August and September. The hatchlings tend to migrate toward open horizon and not necessarily toward water. Many of the young become prey to raccoons, skunks, snakes, bullfrogs, herons, and other large birds. In the water they are eaten by large fish. The adult turtles eat plants, fish, swimming birds and animals, carrion, and various invertebrates. In the original prairie environment they undoubtedly served as useful scavengers that helped keep their ponds free of decaying animal matter. In winter they hibernate in mud on pond and stream bottoms and in muskrat burrows.

The western painted turtle (*Chrysemys picta belli*) is widely distributed throughout the central prairies. It prefers shallow water in swamps and muddy ponds. This turtle, with its olive-green carapace, or upper shell, marked with a pattern of yellow lines and marginal red or yellow borders, loves to bask on sunny banks of ponds and on partially submerged logs. They quickly drop into the water when danger threatens.

The map turtle (*Graptemys geographica*) inhabits the larger streams and rivers in the Mississippi Valley and is found eastward to New York

*Ornate box turtles have been named for their ability to close their shell, thus protecting withdrawn limbs, head, and tail in a sort of box.*

and West Virginia. Map turtles do not always hibernate in winter and they may be seen moving about under ice. A longitudinal yellow spot behind the eye aids in their identification. Their food consists largely of snails, clams, and crayfish. Insects are eaten to some extent.

The typical "land turtle" of the prairie, of course, is the gentle little ornate box turtle (*Terrapene ornata ornata*). Its favorite habitat is dry open grassland on sandy soils, but its wide range covers the central states between the Mississippi and Missouri rivers to the Rocky Mountains and southwest into northern Mexico. Almost every tourist in the West sees these turtles since many are killed on highways where traffic is heavy.

Box turtles are characterized by two movable lobes hinged to the shell so the turtle can pull in its head and feet, close up its armor, and become impervious to the prying claws and teeth of enemies. The forefeet have five claws and the hind feet, which are stumplike and adapted for walking on land, usually have four claws. The dark brown or black carapace consists of plates marked by radiating yellow lines.

Hibernation by box turtles is accomplished by digging into sand or leaf mold. On the western plains they frequently enter prairie-dog burrows and also hibernate in these ready-made tunnels. They emerge in April and for a time are relatively inactive. Mating generally occurs in May and June. The eggs are laid from June to July and require somewhat over two months to hatch. The young box turtles are seldom seen since they are usually covered with mud or cow manure. This serves as a protective device. Undoubtedly the young turtles on the original prairie associated themselves with buffalo dung, which attracted insects that served as turtle food. Grasshoppers form a conspicuous part of the food of the adult turtles, although their omnivorous diet also includes a considerable amount of succulent plant material, including poisonous mushrooms. The turtles are immune to the poison but people who eat their flesh do so with risk since the potency still remains for man.

Box turtles make excellent pets and require only a place for digging, an occasional supply of water, fresh meat, vegetables, insects, or table scraps for food. There are numerous reports of captive box turtles living for twenty or thirty years. If one makes persistent inquiry it is generally possible to find someone who has a pet ornate box turtle in almost any town or city on the prairie. But few people, even those who own pet box turtles, ever think of them as more than gentle, lackadaisical creatures that are durable and easy to handle.

Box turtles, however, are worthy of contemplation. When they eat grasshoppers, they compete with magpies, skunks, snakes, and mice. When grazing animals, including insects and coyotes, eat succulent vegetation, they compete with the turtles. When skunks, ground squirrels, badgers, foxes, and ants eat turtle eggs, their predation adversely

*Toads of many kinds are found on the prairie. Born in the water, they spend most of their life on land, searching for worms and insects.*

affects the turtle population. But somehow a balance in turtle numbers is struck, probably because adult turtles are so long-lived and have so few natural enemies.

Among the seldom-observed creatures of the prairie are the salamanders. The salamander hunter's paradise, of course, is in unglaciated Appalachia, where isolated mountain masses have provided the proper conditions over millions of years for the development of numerous species and races. But a roll call of salamanders on the western prairie and in its waters yields its quota of these strange creatures.

Only an amphibian watcher can appreciate and understand the fascinating life cycles of amphibians, whether they be frogs, toads, or salamanders. The nuptial dances of salamanders, for example, and their double lives as larvae and adults present enthralling possibilities for contemplation of the evolution of aquatic and terrestrial animals through geologic time. Most people, however, are not familiar with their life cycles, and in many instances do not recognize salamanders when they see them.

Mudpuppies are salamanders, known to many fishermen. The species *Necturus maculosus* inhabits lakes, ponds, streams, and rivers where the water is usually three feet or more in depth. The gills of these salamanders, which reach a length of a foot or more, wave like dark red feathers in moving water. Their food includes crayfish, plants, insects, small fish, snails, and other organisms. These salamanders are found from the eastern Dakotas and Kansas to southern New York and northern Alabama.

Among the giant salamanders found in eastern prairie waters is the hellbender (*Cryptobranchus alleganiensis*). A few specimens have been recorded from the southeastern corner of Kansas but they are more common east of the Missouri River through Iowa, Illinois, and into the Appalachians. These grotesque creatures, which attain lengths up to two feet or more, are unique among salamanders in that they practice external fertilization somewhat in the manner of frogs and toads. The eggs are laid in rosarylike strings and the male emits a cloudy seminal fluid over them. The females of other salamanders pick up the spermatophores, or jellylike masses containing sperm, and are fertilized internally.

The one species which comes near to being a prairie-going amphibian is the tiger salamander (*Ambystoma tigrinum*). There are several subspecies, which differ in their markings, geographical distribution, and larval development. These salamanders, with the yellowish or white blotches on brownish or gray backs and sides are inhabitants of ponds, temporary pools, and moist places throughout the prairie. For many years we had tiger salamanders in the dirt-floored basement of our cookhouse in northern Weld County, Colorado. I also have seen them emerging from prairie-dog holes and have found them beneath stock-watering tanks where the overflow from windmill pumps kept the ground water-soaked throughout the summer.

The original prairie habitat undoubtedly provided favorable conditions for tiger salamanders, since ponds and buffalo wallows were frequently filled with water during the breeding season in late February and March. The eggs hatch in two or three weeks and the larval sala-

[155]

manders eat tiny crustaceans and insect larvae. Later, they eat worms, tadpoles, and each other. When they transform into adults they eat almost any moving object and in turn are eaten by raccoons, skunks, snakes, and other predators. The tiger salamanders hibernate and spend much of their lives underground in burrows and tunnels.

Most people are unaware of the countless numbers of frogs and toads on the prairie and in its waters. The deep bass voice of the bullfrog (*Rana catesbeiana*), of course, is a sound familiar to those who live almost anywhere east of the Rocky Mountains. The bullfrog now is more abundant than it was originally since thousands have been planted by game commissions to provide "frog fishing" for sportsmen and lovers of crisp fried frog legs. In some instances these plantings are to be regretted since the bullfrog's omnivorous diet includes insects, crayfish, mice, small snakes, small birds, and other frogs. Some of our native and most interesting frogs are in danger of being exterminated by bullfrogs.

Frogs and toads are prime examples of creatures that live double lives and hence occupy different niches during their existence on the prairie. In many respects they are intermediate between the fishes and reptiles. Their eggs are laid in water and in their larval, or tadpole, stage they have gills and swim like fish. In ponds or streams they affect the growth and development of other animal populations by eating or being eaten and thus are a part of the web of life in aquatic environments. When they transform to adults they lose their gills, breathe by lungs, and emerge into a drier environment where another web of life requires different adjustments to food, shelter, and enemies. A frog or toad on the prairie is not only a link between two environments but it is a link between past and present, repeating in its own lifetime that ages-long metamorphosis that enabled it to climb out of the slime and live on land at last.

Adult frogs, more than toads, still depend on two environments: land for their food-gathering territory, water for protection from land-based enemies, and pond or stream bottom mud for winter hibernation. Usually it is only a quick jump from one of these environments to the other. The leopard frog (*Rana pipiens*) nicely illustrates this adaptation.

Wherever water is found, leopard frogs usually are present. The adults live almost exclusively on nonaquatic insects and other arthropods that exist in a very narrow zone between grassland and water. In this zone they eat and also are eaten by innumerable enemies that

*Bullfrog tadpoles have gills and swim like fish. Like all amphibians, frogs and toads link two environments—land and water.*

pursue them from land, water, or air. Among these legions of preda-tors are fish, large salamanders, snakes, raccoons, mink, skunks, bull-frogs, herons, and hawks. The toads, on the other hand, by abandoning water for the greater part of their lifetimes, have escaped many of these enemies. But they have acquired new enemies and have had to adapt themselves to new kinds of existence in places where water is only an occasional factor in their environment.

The spadefoot toads, for example, are essentially dry-land creatures and are among the most abundant of the prairie amphibians. These se-cretive animals are confirmed burrowers and spend much of their lives underground. Only during the breeding season, which is triggered by rain in abundant quantity, is the deafening chorus of a toad "congress" heard after the males emerge from the ground and enter newly formed pools. Their loud calls are an invitation to females to come and enter the pool since the time for mating is right.

The spadefoots are unique among toads in that they possess a tubercle or "spade" in the ankle region of each hind leg. This prominence with its sharp cutting edge enables the animal to dig and sink backward into the soil. The burrows, which vary in depth from a few inches to three feet or more, are used for daytime protection and for winter hibernation. The toads emerge at twilight, or in darkness in midsummer, to feed; they return to the earth before morning. The same burrow is used by an individual for days and weeks at a time, although some toads have several burrows. Many toads remain in their burrows for days or even weeks without feeding.

There are both eastern and western spadefoot toads and they are widely distributed. The plains spadefoot (*Scaphiopus bombifrons*) is found in the western prairies from Texas and Oklahoma to the Dakotas, Montana, and southern Canada. Hammond's spadefoot (*S. hammondi hammondi*) is at home on the short-grass plains and prefers "hard" soils, although they are also found in sandy soil.

Arthur N. Bragg, in his book *Gnomes of the Night*, points out that spadefoots do not have a breeding season synchronized with the calendar as do other toads and frogs. On the prairie the presence of water in breeding pools is too uncertain to coincide with a definite time of the year. Instead, the spadefoots are adapted to breed when water comes in quantities sufficient to keep pools and ponds supplied until the tadpoles have metamorphosed into young toads.

Rainfall of two inches or more within a short time is conducive to spadefoot mating. The males stream into ponds, flooded pools, and ancient buffalo wallows, from all directions on the prairie. The loud call, which is a *wah* for the plains spadefoot and a gutteral *ye-ow* for Couch's spadefoot (*Scaphiopus couchi*), stimulates other males to come and call to attract females. Hammond's spadefoot males call as they swim about, while Couch's spadefoot males call from the shore.

When a female touches a male spadefoot he immediately clasps her with his forelegs in front of her hind legs. As they swim from place to place egg masses containing up to one hundred or more eggs are laid by the female and fertilized by the male. Clasping continues until several hundred eggs have been deposited and the female's body has been reduced in size.

In the semiarid prairie environment, development of the young toads must be accomplished before the pool dries. The eggs usually hatch within two days. In another day the mouth parts develop and the tadpole is able to feed on very small organisms in the water and on organic material in the mud of the pool. As the tadpoles grow they feed on larger organisms, including dead tadpoles. Metamorphosis to tiny toads is complete in four to six weeks. When the tadpole tail has been absorbed the new generation on dry land begins the process of finding cover, burrowing into the soil, and emerging periodically to find food that they might ultimately grow into mature toads.

The toads of the prairie, of course, have their tribulations and their enemies. Evaporation of pools kills many by drying them out. The tadpoles are eaten in semipermanent ponds by dragonfly nymphs, diving beetles, birds, and snakes. On land, skunks, badgers, raccoons, and other mammals take their toll as do hognose snakes, which seem to specialize on toads. On the other hand, the toads themselves eat insects and worms, and thus are links in the food chain that begins as always with plants and ends with the higher orders of predators.

The toads and other amphibians of the prairie challenge the curiosity of layman and scientist alike. Much remains to be learned of their life histories, adaptations, and niches. The metamorphosis from tadpole to toad is just as startling as the change from a caterpillar to a moth or butterfly. But it differs from insect metamorphosis since the amphibian change from young to adult involves continuous food gathering in a precarious environment. We must admit, however, that the amphibians have been successful. They have been around, in various habitats, more than three hundred million years. During the eons of their existence, the dinosaurs dominated the earth and vanished. On the prairie the ancient camels, horses, and mammoths also disappeared. And, under the dominance of man, the bison nearly reached extinction. But we still have with us the salamanders, the frogs, and the toads.

*A prairie river is formed when many tributary streams add their flow to the main stream. This is a fork of the Republican River in western Kansas.*

# 9

---

# *The Prairie Waters*

WHEN WE EXAMINE THE WATERS of the prairie—rivers, lakes, ponds, flooded buffalo wallows—we find a tremendous variety of plants and animals linked together in aquatic food chains that are interwoven with dry-land food chains. This dependency of a multitude of creatures on a combination of wet and dry habitats binds plant and animal communities into a web with strands that extend far from the water into the prairie itself. The buffalo, for example, fed largely on grasses, but they made regular trips to water. While at water they trampled many small animal food chains out of existence. When they shed their thick winter coats and became exposed to biting flies and other insects they covered themselves with mud from ponds or wallowed in the dust and created shallow circular depressions in the soil. When these wallows filled with rainwater they became breeding places for toads, salamanders, and aquatic insects.

The rivers, streams, and ponds of the prairie never were entities in themselves. Their physical dynamics and the nature of the life they contained depended on the sources of their water and influences from the surrounding land. Nutrients came from the land with the water which flowed into the streams and ponds. Food energy moved from water to land when the kingfisher plunged from his tree and snatched a minnow, or the raccoon extracted crayfish, clams, and other aquatic animals for food. Aquatic insects in millions emerged from their larval stages to complete their adult lives on the prairie, while prairie insects were blown by the wind or fell from shoreline vegetation to be used as food by fishes. And always the large grazing mammals came from the hinterlands to drink. In so doing they left trails across the face of the prairie. These trails eroded, became valley grooves, and changed the appearance of the broad landscape itself.

The prairie waters are vastly different from one locality to another. Rivers vary from their headwaters to their places of final discharge into the sea, and differences in size of stream, temperature of water, rate and volume of flow, and surrounding vegetation, create many environments. The waters of prairie ponds and lakes are more static but less permanent than those of streams and rivers. In time the ponds and lakes are invaded by vegetation and filled with silt and organic matter until they die and finally change from swamps to prairie.

All prairie waters have similar characteristics in that they support food chains which start with plant producers and end with animal consumers. A chain may lead from aquatic plants to muskrats to mink; from insect to sunfish to snapping turtle; or from fish to bird to mammal, with final prey and predator on land. In general, the types of plants and animals that link water with land are similar, wherever fresh water is found.

The role of water, however, does not end with the production of plant and animal food chains. The very existence of the prairie as a whole is the result of water that comes from the far ends of the earth, moves through its cycles on the prairie, and resumes its travel around the world. We can best understand its impact by considering its travels in space and time. It heaves and rolls on the restless face of the ocean; it rises as vapor in the atmosphere; it travels with the winds and descends as mist, rain, or snow. On and under the soil it seeps or runs into ponds, lakes, streams, and rivers. It rises through the roots and stems of plants to become part of their body substance or to be evaporated once more into the freedom of the roaming winds. Some of its molecules are detained for a time as part of the substance in animal bodies. Some are held in the ice of glaciers for centuries. And some are locked for eons in the rocks of the upper crust of the earth. But most water eventually flows through the great river systems back to the sea, carrying with it the soil and the organic substances of continents.

The North American prairie exemplifies on an enormous scale this ceaseless functioning of the hydrologic cycle with its varied effects on all living things. If one looks at a map of the Mississippi–Missouri River watershed he will see that it roughly coincides with the location of the original prairie. Many of the far-flung tributaries of this river system have their beginnings in eastern forested country at the edge of the

*Beginning in the Rocky Mountains, the Platte River crosses the prairie and flows into the Missouri River. The Platte River is so shallow that it is not navigable.*

Appalachians; others originate in the Rocky Mountains of the West. And, finally, almost innumerable tributaries originate on the prairie itself.

In order to understand a prairie stream, one should begin at its headwaters and work downstream, noting its changing environments as it grows larger, accumulates water from its tributaries, becomes a river, and then flows into still larger rivers that finally go to the sea. The beginning of a prairie river is not always easy to see. I remember how I once wandered over the short-grass sward east of Amarillo, Texas, searching for tumblebugs rolling their manure balls. They were there, as were the familiar blue-grama plants and prickly-pear cacti. The endless plain seemed so flat that I wondered how water could run. Then I saw little erosion channels among the grasses and realized I was standing at the headwaters of one of the tributaries of the Red River of the South, that collects water from the rolling plains in northern Texas and southern Oklahoma and carries it across the prairie to the Mississippi. Since then I have stood at the headwaters of many other streams of prairie origin and have seen how they begin.

*Prairie ponds illustrate the dynamics of nature by providing food, shelter, and water for an immense variety of living creatures. Spring and summer flooding fills all the prairie ponds.*

A prairie stream usually begins where water from rain and melting snow flows to slightly lower ground and then seeps into the soil. This beginning of a stream may be marked only by more luxuriant growth of prairie grasses and forbs. No trees or water-loving shrubs are present since deep soil moisture is only intermittently present.

Farther downhill, sometimes miles from the beginning, floodwaters from heavy thunderstorms may cut a channel in the prairie sod. This channel, which carries water only occasionally, exposes bare soil where seeds of willows and hardy shrubs may germinate and produce the first woody vegetation. On the Saline River in west central Kansas, for example, such woody shrubs as coralberry and wild currant are present. The prairie grasses still border the stream even though they are periodically subjected to flooding.

As other channels join the main stream, some of which may be spring-fed, the creek bed becomes wider and deeper. Water runs here throughout the year. Ash, hackberry, box elder, and cottonwood trees appear along the banks and their shade modifies the habitat and permits the growth of sumacs, elders, wild gooseberries, and other shrubs and vines. Sometimes the stream flows through a meadowland where water-loving species prosper, especially the bullrushes, reeds, and cattails.

Still farther down, the stream builds a small floodplain to which the fertile soil of the prairie is added during times of flood. Thus an environment is created favorable to larger trees and greater abundance of shrubs, vines, and shade-enduring forbs. Now, in addition to box elder, green ash, cottonwood, and hackberry, the forest may include honey locust, cherry, and walnut trees. Near the riverbank may be elms and willows. Beyond the edge of the floodplain, where the narrow band of forest meets the prairie, may be bur oaks and numerous shrubs, of which the most common are sumac, rough dogwood, and coralberry. These form the real contact with the prairie. Thus we see the beginning of segregation of the woodland species along a prairie stream into tree associations which will become distinctive woodlands in their own right as the stream flows onward and becomes a large river.

The ultimate development of a prairie river is exemplified by the Missouri River itself. Its forested bluffs along the Iowa and Nebraska sides, for example, with their varied slopes and numerous ravines endlessly repeat the sequence of transition from prairie on the highlands through oaks, hickories, walnuts, lindens, and elms to cottonwoods and willows on the vast level floodplain.

Prairie rivers that arise in the mountains may have calm or turbulent beginnings. The Yellowstone River, for example, which starts near Yount's Peak east of the Continental Divide in northwestern Wyoming, winds through marshy meadows and between forested hills, behind which are the rugged peaks of lofty volcanic mountains. Tributaries from the mountains augment the slow-moving current as it flows into Yellowstone Lake. Beyond the lake the river flows quietly until it plunges over two high vertical falls into a deep canyon. The current then is swift and many tributary creeks contribute white alkali from hot springs, crystal-pure water from deep ravines, and seepage water from swamps filled with dense growth of vegetation which blossoms in midsummer. This is fishing country since the river is cold and contains the minerals and plants to support the web of life that leads to trout production.

Northward to Livingston, Montana, and eastward toward Billings the river flows through mountainous country. Picking up tributary waters as it goes, it winds through miles of sagebrush country and grassy plains, and it becomes a prairie river before it empties into the Missouri west of Williston, North Dakota.

The Powder River, on the other hand, which begins in the dry sagebrush plains of central Wyoming, and flows northward to the Yellowstone near Terry, Montana, is the stream of cowboy legend: "A mile wide, and an inch deep." This is a river of sand, and water warmed by the prairie sun, but a river where the buffalo once came to drink, and the otters went down their icy slides when winter was on the land.

All the rivers of the prairie do not follow the sequences of development described above, nor do they have similar vegetation along their courses. The Platte River, for example, is shallow through most of the year and flows for hundreds of miles over a sandy bottom so unstable that few perennial plants ever gain a foothold in its channel. Thousands of sandbar willows, however, line the banks of the Platte and cottonwoods are numerous on its floodplain all the way from the Rocky Mountains to the Missouri River. On nearly level, wet, sandy soil, big bluestem mingles with switchgrass. Many swales near the river's edge support pure stands of cordgrass. The transition from cordgrass to big-bluestem prairie through belts of switchgrass and Canada wild rye is characteristic not only of the Platte but of many other prairie rivers.

The animal life of prairie rivers has never been as extensively studied as has that of eastern rivers. Under comparable aquatic habitats, however, most rivers have essentially similar organisms. The bottom of the stream, whether composed of rocks, sand, or silt, largely governs not only the nature of the vegetation which grows there, but also the kinds and abundance of animals, including fish. The streamside vegetation likewise tends to control the kinds of mammals, birds, reptiles, amphibians, and insects that live beside the stream and commute between grassland and water.

Few of us have the training or the inclination to observe in detail the fascinating adaptations and life cycles of creatures that live in rivers. The swarming millions of mayflies dancing over a placid stream with its surface dimpled by trout snatching the molting nymphs is a sight to delight the heart of any fisherman. But how many of us, including fishermen, pause to contemplate the chain of creatures, starting with bacteria, paramecia, hydras, copepods, water fleas such as *Daphnia* and *Bosmina*, and insects that make trout life possible? And how many of us think of the enemies, including water bugs, tadpoles, frogs, snakes, turtles, herons, mink, otters, and floods the trout have to avoid between egg and rod-bending fish?

In the prairie waters, as in most rivers, the numbers of kinds of fish are small near their sources as compared with the variety to be found in the lower courses. In the cold waters of mountain streams, trout are almost universally present. Farther down are dace, darters, suckers, and minnows of various kinds. In the deeper rivers that flow into the Missouri and the Mississippi are buffalo fish, catfishes, sunfishes, crappies, basses, sturgeon, and gar pikes. Improbable as it may seem, pike and sturgeon once were common in the larger streams and rivers of Wyoming. There, at the far western edge of the prairie-sagebrush transition, in such seemingly unsuitable streams as Bittercreek near Rock Springs, and Teapot Creek near Midwest, native suckers and minnows are found.

If there is a typical prairie-water fish, the western white sucker (*Catostomus commersonni suckleyi*) might be it. This fish is found in most of the streams of the Missouri River drainage and occurs from Montana to New Mexico. It is an insectivorous fish but large adults also feed on bottom slime, algae, molluscs, and plant material. The western white sucker also lives in lakes. Specimens weighing up to three pounds are sometimes caught at depths varying from sixty to ninety feet.

One species or another of the catfishes is found in most waters of the prairie. The southern channel catfish (*Ictalurus punctatus*) is not abundant in the northern prairie streams but it ranges through the lakes and large streams of the Mississippi system south to Mexico. Of equally wide range is the black bullhead (*Ictalurus melas*) which small boys, and big boys, catch from New York to Colorado and from North Dakota to Tennessee. This is a fish of muddy bottoms, where it lays its eggs in depressions that are guarded by the adults even after the young have hatched.

A fish I always greet as an old friend is the plains killifish or zebra topminnow (*Fundulus kansae*). It has no value as a game fish but it is an attractive creature with its dark olive-green back, orange-yellow sides, and dusky vertical bars that cross the sides from head to tail. It makes a good aquarium fish. But I always view it as one of the true and original natives of western prairie waters.

There are so many other kinds of fish in the prairie streams and lakes that only an ichthyologist or fish expert could identify them properly. At least 135 kinds have been listed for Iowa. More than 90 species are found in South Dakota, which is one of the semiarid prairie states. Colorado has more than 50 native species. Some of these, of course, are found in high mountain streams and lakes. But the fact remains that wherever water exists permanently it is likely to have an abundance of fish and other aquatic organisms.

Among the interesting aspects of prairie lakes and ponds are the great numbers of habitats they produce. On the northern prairie there once were an almost astronomical number of lakes, ponds, potholes, and moist depressions. These occurred in many stages of senescence, varying from bodies of deep water without perennial aquatic vegetation to shallow depressions which had been filled by vegetation and silt until they were merely marshes where water remained aboveground for only a part of each year. Many of these prairie waters have been drained for agriculture and now grow corn instead of fish, ducks, geese, and other wildlife.

In the prairie pothole region of Minnesota and the Dakotas, agricultural drainage mopped up more than 156,000 acres a year in the 1959–64 period. The same thing is going on in the country as a whole. During the calendar years 1940–64, more than 45 million acres of United States wetlands were drained. Drought has also contributed its periodic effects to the wetlands of the prairie. This is happening in Canada, too. In mid-1955 there were some five million small ponds in the southern portions of the Canadian Prairie Provinces. By 1962, drought had

*The water in this prairie stream flows the year around. The moist banks of the stream support shrubs, willows, and cottonwoods.*

reduced these to only half a'million. When these ponds dried the duck and shorebird populations dropped and a multitude of mammals, insects, and other wildlife species vanished.

On the original undisturbed prairie, ponds and lakes served as a waterbank and tended to keep the water table high enough that droughts did not always devastate the landscape. Now we are learning that drainage contributes to flooding and rapid drying of the land. Rather than holding water where it falls, drainage bleeds the flow into creeks and rivers, often exceeding their channel capacity and flooding agricultural lands, towns, and cities.

Many lakes and potholes in the prairie are intermittent; they contain water in the spring and become dry in late summer. Others hold water long enough for waterfowl to nest on the adjoining prairie and then find refuge in the water for their broods until the young are large enough to fly and care for themselves. Permanent and deeper lakes, of course, are found in the moraine systems in the Dakotas, Wisconsin, Minnesota, and in northern Illinois, Indiana, and Ohio. These lakes occur in the depressions between the sandhills of the terminal moraines left by the continental ice sheet.

Lakes of different origin occur in the sandhill region of Nebraska. They occur in the depressions in thousands of acres of wind-drifted sand, where their bottoms are below the water table. They are not connected with any river system and they do not drain. There are hundreds, if not thousands, of these lakes. Most of the larger ones have been named. Some of these lakes are surrounded by large meadows and prairie-covered hills. Game fish now found in the largest lakes include northern pike, walleye, largemouth bass, rock bass, bullhead, yellow perch, bluegill, crappie, and green sunfish. The principal waterfowl nesting in the sandhills are blue-winged teal, mallards, pintails, redheads, gadwalls, and shovelers. Peak populations of several million ducks have been reached in October. Long-billed curlews and upland plovers nest in the marshlands. Mammals that frequent the lake borders and surrounding prairie include pronghorns, whitetail and mule deer, coyotes, muskrats, beavers, badgers, mink, raccoons, skunks, weasels, and porcupines. In the lakes themselves are found the usual multitudes of plants, microorganisms, and orders of lower animals.

As long ago as 1887, Stephen A. Forbes wrote that a lake is a microcosm—a little world in itself. Today, we call it an ecosystem, an area where living organisms and nonliving substances interact with an exchange of materials and energy. A lake or a pond, however, is never a completely self-sufficient unit, especially in the prairie. There always is an interaction between land and water whereby some nutrients make successive trips from land to water and back again. They are washed downhill and trapped in the aqueous environment. Then plants and animals synthesize them into food chains, from which some of the constituent plants and animals emerge on land and through death and dissolution are released again into the soil and air. If they are washed into rivers they may be lost to the sea; if they return to lakes and ponds they may be recycled again and again.

Many of these uphill movements from water to land occur on the prairie. The nymphal insects leave their aquatic environment and live as adults on land, where they become food for birds, reptiles, and mammalian predators. An exodus of living substance from a temporary pond occurs when spadefoot toad tadpoles metamorphose into thousands of adults and begin their burrowing activities on the grassland. Ducks and waterbirds that feed in lakes and ponds scatter their fertility over the prairie during their aerial journeys. And what a mass of debris, organic matter, and living organisms must have moved out of water holes and ponds when the bison rolled in the mud to escape the summer clouds of insects and then hastened to their grazing grounds on the slopes and hills.

Intermittent ponds on the prairie frequently support unique communities of animals and then go through a rapid plant succession during several years of drying during which they literally return to grass. I studied and mapped one of these for fifteen years on the mixed prairie in northeastern Colorado. Torrential rains in July 1941 filled this pond to a depth of nearly five feet. The buffalo grass on its bottom died immediately. Avocets and killdeer waded the shallow margins as the water evaporated throughout the summer. In autumn, hundreds of mallards and pintail ducks rested there for several weeks before they continued their southward migration.

In March of the following spring, tiger salamanders were present. Later, innumerable cyclops, fairy shrimp, and copepods appeared. Whirligig beetles, diving beetles, and water striders were abundant in late spring. And suddenly countless tadpole shrimps (*Triops*) were swimming there like so many tiny horseshoe crabs of the seashore. How did the fairy shrimps and other crustaceans arrive in this pond which had been dry for many years? I know that some of these organisms can survive in the egg stage in dry soil for many months. But could they survive for nearly ten years? I do not know.

*Floods on the prairie are produced when summer storms pour down as much as ten inches of water in a few hours.*

In midsummer of the third year the pond was dry once more. The deepest part was densely covered with vervain (*Verbena bracteata*). Bordering this mat were concentric zones of squirreltail, western wheat-grass, buffalo grass, and finally a mixture of buffalo grass and blue grama which had never been covered with water. In succeeding years, these zones gradually moved inward and obliterated each current vegetation stage in the center of the pond. By 1953, the predominant vegetation once more was buffalo grass interspersed with numerous forbs. Grasshoppers and pronghorn antelope were the principal native grazing animals.

Plant life in prairie lakes and ponds, in general, consists of rooted plants and of floating or buried plants such as algae and the bacteria in the mud and on organic debris. Plants are essential in the water life, since they provide food, shelter, and oxygen for the animal inhabitants. Dead plant bodies provide organic substance for insects, crustaceans, fish, and other animals in the food chain; they also fill the lake, and along with silt and other matter, eventually promote its succession through swamp or marshland to prairie.

This succession begins with submerged plants which are well adapted to withstand wave movement because of their long, narrow, or finely divided leaves. Among these are the many species of pondweeds (*Potamogeton*) and other common hydrophytes, such as milfoil (*Myriophyllum spicatum*), water weed (*Elodea canadensis*), and water crowfoot (*Ranunculus delphinifolius*). Duckweeds are usually present in floating masses in areas of quiet water.

Where wave movement is not severe, and in protected lagoons, yellow cow lily (*Nuphar advenum*) commonly occurs in small colonies. The floating and submerged leaves which arise from thick rhizomes or underwater stems provide excellent protection for fish. Wild rice also grows in protected waters not over two or three feet in depth. This grass passes through a submerged and a floating stage and develops as a land plant when the water recedes into the soil in later summer. Its seeds provide food for innumerable prairie waterfowl in autumn.

Emergent plants, which grow at the margins of lakes and ponds, are able to endure seasonal fluctuations in the water table. Many of these form a zone between the water and the adjoining moist prairie. This zone frequently is defined by arrowheads, cattails, and reeds. Beyond the reed zone the wet meadow frequently is dominated by bluejoint, various sedges, and forbs such as milkweeds and sunflowers. In the upper and drier zone of the wet meadow big bluestem, Indian grass, and switchgrass are frequently dominant. Above this zone are the usual grasses, forbs, and shrubs of the prairie.

*Mallards, the commonest wild ducks, rest on the ice of a prairie pond.*
*When the ice melts, the ducks will begin their love dances.*

# 10

## The Great Wanderers

EACH SPRING, during my years on the prairie, I welcomed the return of the cliff swallows, the mountain plovers, the long-billed curlews, the ducks, and the geese. It was a special occasion when I saw the first bittern, the first snowy egret, or the first Virginia rail in the marshes. I used to ask these migrants, "How are things in Bongo?" I would ask as a farmer might ask his neighbor who had been away on a visit, "How are the crops at Julesburg, or at Shenandoah, or at Joplin?" But when I mentioned Bongo, I was really asking my feathered friends, "How are things in Texas, Louisiana, or Patagonia?"

I invented Bongo, not because it was a fanciful place like Shangri-la, to be attained only by a fearful journey over almost impassable mountains, but because it was any place, or every place from which visitors came to my place on the prairie, to pause momentarily or to stay throughout the summer or the winter. Tied down by routine and the continuity of my job, I had to remain essentially in one spot on the prairie. Even though I drove twenty thousand miles each year in my car, it was mostly in circles or in zig-zag patterns which caused me to cross my own tracks repeatedly, seeing the same landscapes dozens of times. I used to think that if I could string out my twenty thousand miles to Labrador, across the Atlantic, across the jungles, the Pampas, the Andes, and back again, I'd be in Bongo every month of the year. Some of the birds did it, but they never could tell me about the bug crop in Argentina, the storms across the Gulf of Mexico, or the cotton crop in Texas.

The long-billed curlews sometimes whistled as they ran before me, possibly telling me they had spent the winter on the southwestern prairie near Brownsville, Texas. Then I would ask them to give my greetings to their bird neighbors on the Canadian meadows and prairies. To the marsh wren among the cattails I would say, "It was cold here while you were away. We had thirty-seven degrees below zero on February 1, but it warmed up in March. Still, the snow was three feet deep where you built your nest in the sedge swamp last spring."

Then I would turn to another great wanderer of the western prairie: the tumbleweed. There are many kinds of tumbleweeds, but the greatest traveler of them all is the Russian thistle (*Salsola kali tenuifolia*). It was not an original inhabitant of the prairie; instead, it came from Russia and was first noticed in Bon Homme County, South Dakota, about 1873. In twenty years it established itself in every state in the Great Plains region. Now it is an integral part of the plant succession that perennially tends to return plowed fields and bare areas to permanent prairie.

In order to appreciate this wanderer, you have to live with it and understand that, like old Proteus of the sea, it has many forms. The tumbleweed or globelike form enables it to run over the prairie with all the winds that blow. Its prodigious seed supply is dribbled out over a period of several months, since some of its twenty thousand seeds are loosely attached while others are virtually buried in its stems and branches. Seedlings can even grow from the seeds in these branches when they are covered with drifting soil. With the whims of the winds every bare area is sure to receive its supply of seeds and in spring to produce from one to several thousand seedlings per square yard. The resulting black-green carpet frequently dies because the seedlings compete with one another and wilt if life-giving rain is long delayed. But scattered plants on barren land produce three- to five-foot globes of wirelike branches with spiny bractlike leaves and greenish flowers that turn pink at maturity. Until they mature and dry, the plants make sedentary prickly shelters for rabbits, mice, and birds. Then when the roaring winds of autumn pluck them from their moorings, they become swift-moving balls that race across the landscape, jostle through fences, and pile up among streamside shrubs. When the wind shifts, they become free again to move in another direction and sow their seeds in every niche.

The wanderings of most of the plants of the prairie are not as conspicuous or seemingly exuberant as those of the tumbleweeds. Many have been on the prairie for thousands of years, spreading their clans a

*Family groups of geese create much activity by dabbling for food in prairie ponds.*

few yards with each yearly seed crop. Others traveled faster by moving with the windblown sand or by hitching rides with their spines or burs in the coats of mammals. The fast travelers have taken their gigantic strides across the prairie on the muddy feet of birds. By these modes of migration the prairie has always been supplied with propagules, both plant and animal, to fill its empty niches caused by fire, erosion, trampling, and the major cataclysms of drought and climatic change. Even the prairie itself has wandered over the mid-continent.

The prairie has always been dynamic, not only in its continual turnover of plant and animal constituents in each and every part of its expanse, but in the great boundary movements of the grassland itself. The north and south geographic drift of the whole grassland formation was caused by the irresistible advance and retreat of the Pleistocene glaciers.

Some scientists believe that the first grassland began under forest trees and that it evolved through survival of plant forms that increased in abundance and dominance as the forests retreated from the center of the continent. They believe that the great central grassland did not migrate from elsewhere, but developed in place while the forests migrated westward, northward, and eastward. The prairie then followed behind the moving forest boundaries. Indirect evidence of this grassland development and subsequent migration comes from indications that horses and other herbivores, which originally were forest animals, developed teeth specialized for grinding grasslike vegetation. They also developed skeletal structures which adapted them for speed and escape in open country and in areas of high visibility. This evolution of plant and animal forms occurred before the appearance of the Pleistocene glaciers.

The forests of seed-bearing trees which occupied much of the northern part of the continent in late Cretaceous time contained maples, beeches, spruces, and other genera like those of today. In western North America, fig trees and other semitropical elements were present until the rain shadow of the uplifting Rocky Mountains produced a drier climate on the plains and in the interior lowlands and forced an outward retreat of the forests, leaving a great grassland in the central third of the continent. A cooling trend, begun in the Oligocene, was followed by the glaciation of the Pleistocene.

The four major ice advances, the Nebraskan, Kansan, Illinoisan, and Wisconsin, caused major displacements of both forest and grassland in the northern part of the continent. During the advances and retreats of the glaciers, and in the warmer interglacial periods, many plant and animal species disappeared. Others migrated to new territory or returned to old territory and mingled with species from different localities to form new associations which ultimately gave rise to the distributional patterns of the modern prairie.

Paradoxical as it may seem, apparently there was no great distance between the ice of Pleistocene time and the vegetation south of the glacial front. Studies of fossil pollen in bogs of central and northern Illinois, for example, give evidence that forests were within fifty miles of the ice sheet that laid down the terminal moraines in which the bogs were formed. Studies made in Manitoba have led to the conclusion that the ice practically touched the grassland. As the ice melted, the resulting waste area was vegetated first by marsh grassland, then by western upland grasses, and finally by the boreal forests that form the northern borders of the modern prairie.

There has been much speculation about the migration of prairies following the retreat of the Wisconsin ice, and the movement of many of its characteristic species from their distant retreats in the southeast and southwest back to the mid-continent. A warm, dry period followed the recession of the Wisconsin glacier and allowed the eastward extension of the prairie into Ohio. Then an increase in rainfall permitted a western migration of deciduous forests from the Ohio Valley and from the Allegheny Mountains until the forests bordered the eastern prairie in much the same proportions as were found by the first white men in America.

When we contemplate the botanical composition of the whole prairie it is well to recognize that many plants have undergone little change since the Cenozoic. The theory of their migration through contraction and expansion of their original areas of distribution with the changing climates of the Ice Age and the interglacial periods presents a more realistic picture than the romantic concept of whole floras marching equatorward and then poleward. As a specific example, we can visualize easily how desert species, that developed originally in the far Southwest and in Mexico, have gradually moved eastward and northward into the prairie. Some of these species, having affinities with the southwest deserts, have invaded or migrated as far as North Dakota. Among them are the yuccas and the prickly-pear cacti.

The geographical affinities of many other species have been studied by plant geographers. Their research has given us an understanding of why we find many familiar plants of deserts in not necessarily uncongenial places on the prairie. On alkaline soils in the western prairie, fourwing saltbush is a common shrub on stream terraces. Frequently it grows in company with such saline-soil-enduring shrubs as winter fat and greasewood. It seems strange to see these shrubs, so common on western deserts, growing in the blue-grama and buffalo-grass sward until we remember that they are great wanderers and that they still may be marching away from their ancestral homes.

In my own wandering over the prairie I often find myself asking some living creature, even a fish, "How did you happen to get here?" This is a legitimate question, especially in the North, since it is obvious that when the last Pleistocene glacier blocked off the outlets to Hudson Bay, covered the land far south in the lake states, and fed torrents of water from its melting edge into the Missouri River in the Dakotas, it forced the fish to move. Later, they returned, not only to the river and tributary drainages in the northern prairie but to the lakes in innumerable moraines left by the melting ice.

The upper Missouri River provided refuge for fish from its northern tributaries when the last glacial advance came down from the Keewatin center, west of Hudson Bay, moved southward over the eastern

*Since the killdeer makes no nest, its eggs are often difficult to find
among the prairie grasses or on gravelly shores. Soon after hatching,
the young killdeer instinctively follows its parents, searching for
crawling insects, which are its principal food.*

Dakotas and deflected the Missouri River, which continued to flow
southward along the western margin of the ice sheet. At the same time,
as the ice moved southward, it dammed north-flowing river systems
and formed Lake Agassiz, where the present Red, Saskatchewan, and
upper Nelson rivers now flow. At one time, Lake Agassiz occupied an
area greater than that now covered by the Great Lakes and was 650
feet higher than the present Lake Winnipeg, which is its remnant and
successor. Drainage was southward through glacial river Warren to the
Mississippi. When the ice retreated, drainage from Lake Agassiz returned to Hudson Bay.

The fish of the Red River drainage apparently used the Warren River, following the recession of the glacier, in their northward movement from the upper Mississippi drainage. Some fish probably were laterally dispersed, east and west, by migration routes through glacial lakes in the northern reaches of the Mississippi-Missouri drainage basin. Others merely moved down the rivers as the ice advanced and returned upstream as the ice retreated.

Glaciation left some of the northern fish stranded as relicts in habitats far south of their normal distribution. Cold-hardy fish, such as the pearl dace (*Semotilus margarita*), now native in far northern Canada, were able to tolerate Pleistocene conditions in the northern plains. With the recession of the glacier they returned to their normal habitat. But relicts, or remnant populations, are still found in cool, permanent spring waters of the Nebraska sandhills and in southern South Dakota. Reeve M. Bailey and Marvin O. Allum state that, "Of the 94 species and subspecies of fishes . . . listed from South Dakota, at least six are believed to have persisted during the last glaciation in the western part of the state or in adjacent areas in the upper Missouri basin."

Of all the modern wandering fish, the eels are among the greatest travelers and have the most fabulous of life histories. Many years ago, my grandfather used to catch eels, along with enormous catfish, that came up from the Missouri River into the Nemaha River in southeastern Nebraska. At the end of high-water time he would set his trammel net, made with different layers and different-sized meshes, to catch buffalo fish and catfish as they returned with the receding waters to the Missouri. The fine-mesh net occasionally would capture eels, which he considered a great table delicacy and which pleased him more than some of the six-foot "blue cats" (*Ictalurus furcatus*) that formerly were common in those waters. He was unaware, however, of the fantastic life cycles of eels, since he believed they passed their entire life cycles in the local rivers near his home.

The American eel (*Anguilla rostrata*) ascends the Mississippi and Missouri rivers and many of their tributaries in the prairie region. Eels have been caught at Yankton, South Dakota. They are caught occasionally in Colorado in the Arkansas River. In Iowa they have been reported from most of the major streams and a few lakes. They are common throughout the lower Mississippi Valley.

Eels are found in many parts of the world and are in great demand where they are abundant since their flesh is rich and delicious. Housewives sometimes are reluctant to cook them since they are long, serpent-like fishes with paired pectoral fins and minute scales so imbedded that the fish is slippery and appears to be scaleless. Eels are most common in the larger rivers since they prefer habitats with deep bottom mud. They live on other fishes, frogs, crayfish, and even dead animals. They can move overland in damp or marshy places, an ability which explains their presence in lakes and ponds not connected with running streams.

The American eel reproduces only in the Atlantic Ocean, in the Sargasso Sea northeast of the West Indies. After a period of seven to fifteen years in the rivers of the prairie the females drift southward in autumn on one of the great migrations known in nature. In the Gulf of Mexico they meet the males that have lived in bays and estuaries through all the years the females have been wandering in inland waters. Together they pass eastward beyond Florida and into the Atlantic Ocean. After laying several million eggs each, the females die in the waters of their births, just as salmon do in the rivers where they were hatched.

When the young eels hatch they are ribbonlike, transparent, and only a quarter of an inch long. Along with their European cousins they gradually arise from great depths and drift northeast with the Gulf Stream to the latitude of Bermuda, where they separate—the European eels going eastward and the American eels going westward. When they appear at the mouths of American rivers, after a period of nearly three years, they transform from ribbonlike larvae to miniature eels. But only the females leave the salt water and work their way up the major rivers and finally into the inland waters.

The systematic migrations of eels, shorebirds, and waterfowl are entirely different from the former erratic wandering of the buffalo. Even without historical authentication of buffalo roaming, we can rationalize that the mighty herds had to move in order to persist in front of the advancing Pleistocene glaciers. But from early postglacial time to the time of their near extinction in the nineteenth century they had to wander over the prairie in search of food and water as droughts scorched the earth in one place and then another.

Droughts can be destructive of both plant and animal life, as some of us have seen in our own lifetimes. The great drought of the 1930's left the land barren over thousands of square miles in the southern plains. The loss of vegetation cover allowed the wind to carry the prairie soil in a yellow haze over Chicago, Washington, D.C., and eastward over the Atlantic Ocean. The black dust storms that brought midnight at high noon to southern Colorado, northern Oklahoma, and Texas were caused in part by poor cultural practices and plowing of more than eight million acres of native grassland in the Great Plains.

I was there and I saw the blue-grama leaves shrivel to powdery dust while the grasshoppers ate the stunted forbs and shrubs into the earth. No ponds remained. The streams ceased to flow. No cow could exist. Had the buffalo been there they would have died, or would have moved to more productive prairies, as they apparently did in historic times.

The buffalo originally wandered as far east as New York and Washington, D.C. Early maps of Kentucky included the location of salt licks used by the buffalo. Their trails were followed by the early explorers and later became the overland routes that paralleled the Erie Canal, or came through Cumberland Gap, or followed the watershed of the Monongahela to the Ohio River.

In the West, buffalo bones have been found with those of mountain sheep on mountain summits where horses could not go and which a man could reach only by climbing. The buffalo regularly moved up the river bottoms from the plains, through the Front Range of the Rocky Mountains, and into South Park, where the grasses were kept luxuriant by the cooler climate at altitudes of seven thousand to ten thousand feet.

Before the mighty winter of 1851–52, which decimated the buffalo herds, they left trails in and around the Black Hills of South Dakota. These trails still can be seen between Spearfish and Whitewood. Thousands of buffalo once grazed in the Black Hills around Signal Knob and then made trails by going to water on Castle Creek. Animals in the vast herds on the western plains, of course, were too numerous for all of them to live on the highlands beyond the western prairie border. And so they made treks of several hundred miles in search of food and water and to escape the summer heat on the southern plains. They did not, however, make the great north-south migrations once ascribed to them.

The roving of the great herds was matched by that of the gray or buffalo wolves. These tireless beasts of prey trotted in packs at the edges of the herds but were ignored by the buffalo as long as no individual was singled out for prey. In good seasons the wolves killed buffalo calves or aged animals that became isolated from the herd. In times of dire necessity they attacked even the large bulls, when deep snow impeded their movements or when enduring blizzards weakened their ability to remain in the herd, where all the animals crowded together to present a solid front of bony heads, lowered horns, and crushing hoofs. When the wolves isolated an animal from the herd they attempted to "hamstring" it by severing the tendons of its hind legs. Once the animal was down at the rear the wolves tore at its flanks and virtually ate it alive as loss of blood weakened the mighty beast and caused it to crash to earth.

By the end of the nineteenth century, wolves were nearly extinct on the prairie. The packs were disseminated and the remaining animals lived in isolated pairs or families. J. Knox Jones believes that the wolf in Nebraska was extirpated between 1915 and 1920 in the northern and western parts of the state, and much earlier in the southeast. In the days of the buffalo, however, it was one of the greatest of all wanderers, ranging from southern Mexico to northern Alaska and over all of the continent excepting the Pacific Coast and part of the states that bordered the Gulf of Mexico.

Twice each year, for how many centuries no one knows, the geese, the ducks, and countless lesser birds have made incredible journeys up and down the prairie in response to stimuli we have yet to understand completely. After their sojourn in southern lands, the lengthening days trigger the urge to migrate and the great flocks rise from the marshes along the Gulf Coast and begin cleaving the air in V-formations with clamorous conversation that proclaims the northward-marching spring. Those of us who have lived on the prairie and have heard the honking of March geese have always known that their arrival heralded the end of winter and offered the promise of spring to come. Most of us, aside from enjoying the sight and sound of geese on migration, have given little thought to the complexity of the phenomenon and its relation to history, climate, geography, and food.

From the geographic standpoint, the prairies in America provided the great bird wanderers an open route of travel between temperate and tropical regions with no barriers such as birds encountered in crossing the Sahara Desert or the great ramparts of the Alps and the Pyrenees in the Old World. In America, the Appalachians and the forests on the east and the Rocky Mountains on the west bordered the prairie and tended to guide the migrants up and down the mid-continent.

It was Frederick C. Lincoln who described the flyways, as a result of studies of migratory waterfowl. He gave us the concept that flyways are geographic regions of breeding and wintering areas connected with each other by migration routes. Two great flyways crossed the prairie from north to south. Birds from all across central Canada funneled down the Mississippi flyway and spread east and west along the Gulf Coast. Birds of the central flyway came down a broad travel band that originated in Alaska and the Mackenzie River delta, covered much of the Great Plains and ended along the Gulf Coast of Texas. There were, of course, many digressions from these main routes of travel and much

*Russian thistles, commonly called tumbleweeds, form large globes which break away and tumble, each one sowing thousands of seeds.*

overlap between flyways by birds of the same species and of different species.

Whatever their migrational origins may have been, I know that the primal urge to migrate still lies deep in the breasts of tame geese. When the wild geese passed over our farm in autumn our tame gander always heard or saw them long before our own poor senses detected the clarion notes of the flocks coursing southward to their winter homes. His flock would set up a great clamor in our barnyard and the migrating flocks would honk in return, inviting their earthbound friends to join the high-flying throng. The old gander would marshal his group like a drill sergeant assembling his squad. Then, in answer to his strident honk, and with great tumult of voices and beating of pinions, our geese would use the whole runway of the barnyard to become airborne. But alas! Their weight, brought on by soft living, would bring them fluttering to the ground in our garden, or in the field beyond. Their enthusiastic clamor then would subside into small talk and they would nibble at things without eating, or stand with heads turned sideways, looking up into the sky.

Ducks, as well as geese, are one of the most visible manifestations of bird migration up and down the prairie. In autumn especially, they arrive in such numbers that even the most casual observer is aware of their presence. They do not come with the punctuality of swallows arriving at San Juan Capistrano. Perhaps, if the Franciscan Junípero Serra had named a mission after a patron saint of ducks, the ducks would arrive at their stopping places on the prairie waters on precisely the same day each year. I suspect, however, that the unpredictable prairie weather would throw them off schedule in most seasons. Fall ducks, especially, are regulated to a large extent by the whims of the storms. One day there will be no ducks on the lakes and rivers. Then an October northwester will blow out of the night, bringing gray skies and a horizontal blizzard. The next day the ducks will be there in hordes, dabbling, quacking, or lifting off the water with the attenuated thunder of thousands of wings, flying out to the fields for corn and wheat where once the prairie covered the land.

The different ducks do not all come at the same time. The blue-winged teal are among the first, often arriving in warm September sunshine. Nor do they tarry for long periods. With them go many other birds, including the avocets, nighthawks, eastern kingbirds, upland plovers, and some of the killdeer. With the coolness of fall come the gadwalls, baldpates, and buffleheads. The local mallards and the Wilson's snipes may have left the central prairie waters in late October, but they are replaced by other mallards from farther north. Some of these stay through the winter since they are only partially migratory, as are the green-winged teal, Barrow's golden-eye, the marsh hawk, and the ferruginous rough-leg.

I wish we knew more of how ducks and other waterbirds act as carriers of seeds, spores, and minute animals of pond and river life. I am inclined to believe that the circumboreal distribution of many of our aquatic plants is due to ducks. And how do intermittent prairie ponds that have been dry for years become suddenly populated with all manner of plants and animals soon after water has filled the depression again? Muddy duck feet must surely be part of the answer. Recent research has shown that viable freshwater algae, protozoans, nematodes, and rotifers are found on the external surfaces of birds. Other studies have demonstrated that small crustaceans can be carried internally in the digestive tracts of waterbirds.

In a recent study, Charles R. Malone found that two species of freshwater snails were found capable of attaching themselves to the feet of killdeer and remaining viable long enough to effect passive overland dispersal. Since killdeer are among the most widely occurring shorebirds in North America, their habit of walking and standing in water containing an abundant growth of aquatic plants, which provide a favorable habitat for small animals, probably makes them significant dispersal agents for small organisms that live in prairie waters.

Still more recently, Vernon W. Proctor, Charles R. Malone, and Victor L. DeVlaming have reported that vegetative cells and spores of algae, various crustacean eggs, and living adult seed shrimp can be retained within the digestive tracts of killdeer, and to a lesser extent, mallard ducks. These viable organisms are retained longer by killdeer than by ducks, and hence can be carried across greater distances. When we consider how widely killdeer, sandpipers, and other waterbirds travel, it is obvious that with the help of birds many aquatic organisms are among the great wanderers over the prairie.

A great many other wanderers travel under their own power across the prairie. Among the smallest of these are insect migrants, especially the dragonflies, butterflies, and locusts. We ordinarily think of dragonflies as inhabitants of stream sides and lake sides. But dragonflies are great travelers even around the localities where their nymphs have spent their more or less sedentary aquatic lives.

On June 14, 1967, while camped near Crater Lake in the Wichita Mountains Wildlife Refuge in western Oklahoma, I saw many large dragonflies cruising through the upper branches of oak trees and out across the prairie, where tame buffalo were grazing more than half a mile from water. Later that day, on the way to Lawton, Oklahoma, and still later on the way to Amarillo, Texas, I encountered dragonflies moving northward across the prairie. I am not certain that they were migrating, but they were many miles from water.

Butterfly migrations are well known and those of the monarchs (*Danaus plexippus*) certainly are not unusual on the prairie. Monarchs are common all across the United States and their winter clusters have

*Seeds planted by the tumbling weeds in the fall and winter produce countless millions of new plants the following year. These compete for moisture and sometimes die without producing seeds, clearing the way for the longer-lived forbs.*

been noted along the Gulf Coast and of course in Pacific Grove, California, where they are protected by city ordinance and are a noted winter tourist attraction. Monarchs migrate southward over the plains and prairies in a great band that spreads from the Rocky Mountains to the lake states. In September, I have seen them resting overnight on oak trees in Milwaukee, Wisconsin, in western Iowa near the city limits of Shenandoah, and on willow trees near North Platte, Nebraska. Monarchs with tagged wings have been found more than a thousand miles south of the point of original capture.

The spring return of the monarchs occurs at a more leisurely pace. It is generally believed that they move northward in a series of stages. The first migrants that have overwintered in the south fly northward with tattered wings to milkweeds as they appear in March. They lay their eggs and then the larval, pupal, and adult stages appear. The newly hatched butterflies then move farther northward and repeat the process. Thus several generations appear before the summer journey ends in the grasslands of Canada. In this far northern prairie country autumn return flight usually begins in August. Only one generation is produced at the northern end of the monarch butterfly range.

The migratory insect that has attracted attention since biblical times is the desert locust (*Schistocerca gregaria*) of Arabia and Africa. These locusts plagued the land of Egypt more than three thousand years ago and they still fly in clouds covering hundreds of square miles over the continent of Africa. In 1889, G. T. Carruthers estimated that a cloud of locusts crossing the Red Sea contained enough insects to weigh 43 billion tons.

The history of the North American prairie is too recent to indicate how widespread were its locust plagues before the coming of white men. But grasshoppers have been found in glacial ice in Montana and Wyoming, indicating that swarms of grasshoppers were present in prehistoric times. And, in the nineteenth century, grasshoppers were a dreaded pest in the United States and in Canada. An outbreak of the Rocky Mountain migratory locust (*Melanoplus spretus*) in 1855 extended from the prairies east of the Rockies, south to Mexico, and west to Oregon, Washington, and California. The insects appeared in incredible numbers, filled the air like snow on a winter day, and ate everything green and succulent when they came to earth.

A grasshopper invasion in Kansas came in 1874. They came out of the northwest, covered fields and trees, and destroyed everything green. Ruin and desolation were everywhere. In order to buy supplies for the following winter the settlers and homesteaders collected and sold buffalo bones for $6 to $10 per ton. These were shipped east to be ground into fertilizer. Since then other locust plagues have occurred, but modern control methods have prevented the disasters caused by these insects in the nineteenth century. Locusts and grasshoppers, however, are still present and their population cycles are watched closely by agricultural scientists.

The chief gregarious locust of North America now is *Melanoplus mexicanus* of which *M. spretus* is believed to be the former migratory phase. Specimens of *spretus* have not been seen for more than fifty years, and some authorities believe that it is now extinct. But as long as there is prairie there will be other insects and other creatures that wander over its length and breadth. The prairie, like all other things, is forever changing.

*During the Dust Bowl days of the 1930's, this dust storm tore across the countryside near Springfield, Colorado. The thick, black clouds of dust and whistling winds lasted for half an hour.*

# 11

---

# *Catastrophe and Renewal*

OVER A PERIOD OF TEN YEARS I spent many fascinating days putting together the pieces of a botanical jigsaw puzzle created by the plowing of millions of acres of mixed prairie east of the Rocky Mountains. Plowing of the prairie started when the first settlers moved out of the eastern forests onto the grasslands. The climate of the eastern prairies allowed them to continue their cultivation for generation after generation. But settlers on the western prairies did not foresee the periodic droughts that would come to the plains. When drought came their crops were ruined and thousands of fields were abandoned.

Nature took over with her universal processes of healing the scars and returning the land to a productive cover of native prairie plants. Through plant succession, reversion from bare ground to prairie took place through a series of vegetation stages, each succeeding one being botanically more complex than the one that went before. The process was somewhat orderly, but it was delayed or speeded up here and there by many factors, including grazing, recurring drought, availability of natural seed supplies, and the effects of insects, mammals, and birds. In addition to these influences the farmers did not abandon all of their fields at the same time. Instead, they left a patchwork of vegetation stages on the landscape. Part of my problem in solving this jigsaw puzzle was to arrange the stages of vegetation recovery in the order in which they appeared to have given rise to one another.

This matter of reconstructing the sequence of plant development stages would be simple if one could live in the same place for a lifetime and record the whole process. But even a lifetime might not be long enough to complete the task. In reconstructing the life history of a forest, for example, one might have to live as long as Methuselah, since the whole process might take a thousand years. But the ecologist has a more simple method. He looks at a great many stages of vegetation development on many areas and by inference he attempts to put them in their proper order of appearance. By watching their development for a few years he can see evidence of overlapping—the tail end of one stage in a given area resembles the beginning of another stage in another area.

At first, I believed my study of nature's first aid to the land would be simple. How naïve! I never realized how many personalities, problems, and blind alleys would be encountered. First, I had to know when the prairie had been plowed, or when it had last been cultivated. With this information at hand I could estimate how many years were required to reach a given stage of vegetation recovery. My question "When did you plow the south forty for the last time?" led into many fascinating reminiscences of family history among the farmers on the plains. Memories were not always perfect on these matters. Often, before an answer was acceptable, we had to check the family Bible, or determine the year when neighbor Jones borrowed the cultivator and did not return it until Henry got married and moved to Denver. Sometimes I had to check on such matters as when the county schoolhouse was struck by lightning and Mary Jane had to ride the bus to school in Greeley. But finally we succeeded in recalling the past. Along with much botanical sampling, my puzzle picture cleared and I knew the main plot of the succession story.

The Russian thistles were among the first plants to appear on bare fields. Their tumbling habits, aided by the high winds of winter and early spring, resulted in rapid migration. The scattered plants developed into much-branched tumbleweeds, which in turn broadcast so many seeds that in the second and third years Russian thistles grew in such countless numbers that competition killed most of them before they were eight inches high. This allowed other deeper-rooted plants, which had gained a foothold among the tumbleweeds, to survive the summer. Variations from the Russian-thistle stage occurred. The common sunflower frequently occupied areas which had been temporarily inundated by early spring floods. Other areas supported stands of annuals such as pigweed and goosefoot.

In succeeding years the complexity of the vegetation increased. As many as fifty different forbs were present in a single field five years

*Fire has always been a part of the prairie scene. Since the roots of perennial plants usually are not heated to an intolerable degree, burning does not destroy the grasslands.*

after abandonment of cultivation. Some of these were perennials such as scarlet globe mallow, which would persist through the years until the permanent grassland was once more established. In the meantime, short-lived grasses gained a foothold here and there, and at the end of ten years almost pure stands of tumblegrass or squirreltail were present. Sometimes these occurred in mixture with Indian ricegrass and western wheatgrass. The wheatgrass slowly colonized and held the soil by means of horizontal underground stems and dense root systems. Occasionally a tuft of blue grama or of buffalo grass appeared, portending the ultimate return to prairie. At ten to twenty years the silvery gray of red three-awn dominated the fields. But gradually the main perennial grasses, blue grama, buffalo grass, needle-and-thread, June grass, and a multitude of perennial forbs became firmly established, and the transition to mixed prairie was nearly complete at the end of thirty to fifty years.

The rate of succession was influenced by insects, wind movement, amount and seasonal distribution of rainfall, kangaroo rats, rabbits, mice, livestock, and topography. The numbers of harvester-ant colonies, for example, varied with the stage of vegetation. In the Russian-thistle stage, only an occasional ant mound was present. Then their numbers increased through the forb stage and short-lived-grass stage to as many as fifty-seven per acre in the red-three-awn stage. After that, their colonies diminished until only one or two mounds per acre were found in the final mixed prairie. Their cyclic trend appeared to be associated with food supply, but they also influenced the succession by collecting seeds, which were their principal food.

In the above example of succession we can see some of the processes and some of the reasons for the permanence of the original prairie. In the face of local catastrophe the prairie always tended to renew itself. The healing process did not always go immediately from wounds or scars on the land to complete recovery. The way had to be prepared by ephemeral plants, which gave way to short-lived plants, which ameliorated the soil and held its moisture for longer periods so the long-lived master plants of the grassland could become solidly established. Once established, they then tended to grow in equilibrium with the climate, soil, and animals of the total environment. Succession back to this permanent condition occurred when such disturbances as over-grazing, drought, flooding, wind erosion, buffalo wallowing, grass-hopper denudation, and rodent burrowing had upset the normal balance between competing plants and animals.

It may seem paradoxical that disturbances of the prairie by digging animals, floods, fire, and even local overgrazing were essential to maintenance of the fully developed prairie itself. Close examination of luxuriant grassland will usually show that here and there all the plants that become conspicuous during succession actually persist on the prairie at all times. They are able to sustain themselves in suitable micro-habitats made by gopher mounds, badger diggings, anthills, drifted soil, and abandoned mouse runways. With a little thought we can see that these things must be so. If there had never been disturbance on the prairie, then competition from all the final-stage plants would have killed the annuals, the invaders, and the intermediate-stage plants, leaving nothing to renew the prairie when catastrophe finally happened. When we see harvester ants, ground squirrels, and other disturbers of the soil, we should thank them for cultivating spots where lesser plants can persist in readiness to renew the land in time of need.

In the beginning there was succession on the prairie. When the sea receded from the land there was migration of plants from their refuges on highlands to the whole of the drying mid-continent. When the glacial ice retreated northward there was migration of plant and animal life into new territory. Through thousands of years, then, time, climate, the combinations of species arriving on the scene, and consequent development of soil determined the plant communities that now exist in the varied environments of the prairie. This development ecologists call primary succession, since it started from geological beginnings as contrasted with secondary successions, which are the renewal processes that follow disturbance of flora and fauna that is already there.

Primary successions still occur in the prairie region. The aquatic successions in ponds and lakes left by the glacier are original successions. From the land side, drainage carries in topsoil and nutrients that support submerged communities dominated by pond weeds and other water plants. The reed swamp zones of bullrushes and cattails gradually encroach on open water and in turn are replaced at their outer edges by meadows. At the meadow periphery lies the prairie, which ultimately will occupy the place of the pond as it dries. Overgrazing on the upland may speed the process by adding more silt to the drainage; or fire may slow the succession by burning the vegetable debris around the pond margin in dry seasons. But ultimately the prairie will move in and prevail, or it will be plowed because of the rich agricultural soil accumulated over the centuries in the former pond.

The effects of fire on the prairie have been the subject of speculation from earliest times. Practically all authorities agree that the prairie has been subject to repeated and extensive burning for thousands of years. With good reason it has been suggested that the very existence of the prairie was due to fire. Lightning has always been a prime source of fire on grasslands as well as in forests. And aboriginal man undoubtedly was careless with campfires, signal fires, and hunting fires. On some occasions he may have employed fire in warfare and at other times to combat mosquitoes and insects around his habitations.

When white men first came to the prairie they were the cause of more fires than were aboriginal men. But as their cultivation increased, their plowed fields acted as barriers to prairie fires that formerly ran unchecked for hundreds of miles. As settlement by pioneers increased, forests along the eastern margin of the prairie invaded the adjoining grasslands.

Within the prairie itself, fire was a natural factor in the environment. It affected plants and animals, frequently with cataclysmic results. But

*Drought, the worst menace of the prairie, affects all forms of life.*
*Continued dry spells kill the plant life which is needed to sustain*
*grazing animals, insects, and birds.*

it never completely exterminated all animal life; nor did it completely
kill the vegetation. At times it was even beneficial.

In the lowlands of the prairie, western wheatgrass which had become
sodbound and was dying from self-competition was burned to the
ground without harm to its underground stems. In subsequent years
these rhizomes renewed the stand and lush forage was once more available for the buffalo. On the uplands, blue grama suffered little from
burning since its sod was usually thin and did not produce heat sufficient
to kill the roots. Flower stalk production in stands of prairie dropseed,
big bluestem, and little bluestem was frequently stimulated in the first
year following the burn. This increased vigor tended to speed up the
return to normalcy on the prairie.

Any discussion of the effects of fire on animal numbers on the original prairie must necessarily be somewhat theoretical. The early records

of the explorers contain many accounts of carcasses of buffalo and their bones on the grasslands. The deaths of these animals usually were attributed to winter storms and to scarcity of grass due to severe droughts. But the fires most devastating to forage on the prairie were those that occurred in grass dried by drought or cured on the stalk and left standing in winter. It seems reasonable to assume that buffalo were killed in the fiery blasts that swept across the prairie and that they also died of starvation when no blade of grass remained unburned on areas of thousands of square miles.

In my own experiences with fire on the prairie I can attest that many small animals perish miserably in the mountainous walls of flame and smoke that are pushed forward by seventy-mile-an-hour winds that descend from the western mountains. There is frantic dashing of rabbits when they hear the crackling roar; then they are engulfed by the suffocating breath of heat that precedes the fire itself. When the flames pass by, their bodies quickly lie naked of fur on the blackened earth. Here and there the singed and roasted corpses of sharptail grouse, an

*Wind erosion has exposed many feet of this soil in the mixed prairie.*

unlucky coyote, or a badger that failed to reach its den give testimony to the ruthless power of fire to snuff out life in seconds. And still the carnage is not done. Ignited piles of animal dung smolder on for hours, sending up thousands of little smokes, slowly oxidizing the waste vegetable fiber not used by the grazing animal. This smoldering of the punk-like animal droppings cremates all the dung beetles, fly larvae, and worms that have been working out their life cycles and returning fertilizer to the prairie soil.

Once, in a fire that burned a hundred square miles in eastern Colorado, I saw cows in a grassy swale engulfed in flames that were house high. When the fire passed, the poor animals were devoid of hair. Some stood bawling while others tossed their heads, not comprehending why they could not see through the opaqueness of singed eyeballs. The owner, in his mercy, killed them immediately. Then it occurred to me that the buffalo in similar circumstances in former times had only the prospect of slow, miserable death.

In this same fire, I saw antelope dash for the hills and the thinly vegetated uplands, where the margin of the fire moved slowly and the advancing flames were only inches high. They must have jumped the fire line, for later I saw them wandering over the jet-black earth, nibbling at the leaves and branches of shrubs that stood high enough above the flames not to be scorched and burned. Until green grass appeared a few weeks later the antelope ate these shrubs and the succulent branches of prickly-pear cacti from which all the spines had been singed.

The burrowing animals such as the gophers, kangaroo rats, badgers, coyotes, and prairie dogs avoided the immediate disaster of fire. For some of them a major problem arose when they emerged from their underground retreats in search of food. The insects which were staple items in the coyote's diet were burned and the carcasses of small animals killed by the fire were inedible, or were quickly eaten by scavenger crows, magpies, and buzzards. The coyote's main reliance then was on burrowing animals that had survived the fire. Thus the rodents served as buffers against starvation of the predators that later would again help maintain balance among the wild animals on the normally functioning prairie.

Pocket gophers were not particularly troubled by prairie fires since they could subsist on roots until vegetation became green again. Ground squirrels, mice, and kangaroo rats lived on seeds stored in their caches. Prairie dogs also dug roots of grasses. But, owing to their habit of clipping grass close for better visibility in their towns, fire passed lightly over their territory or did not burn their forage crop at all. Thus the prairie dogs saved not only their own food supply but that of rabbits, mice, and other creatures lucky enough to survive the fire.

Severe and continued drought is the greatest catastrophe that can come to the prairie. When the rains cease, the scorching sun sears the land, the grazing animals deplete the diminishing supply of forage, and the dust blows, then plant life retreats underground and there is universal degeneration of living populations. Droughts are not new to the prairie. Tree-ring studies have shown that moisture-deficient periods have occurred repeatedly in recent centuries. But the drought that came in 1934 was the greatest ever recorded. And in parts of the prairie, especially in western Kansas, it lasted for seven years; in the period 1933–39, precipitation was below normal for every one of these years.

The great drought of 1934 began in spring, following a winter of light snowfall. Dust had already blown over the tall-grass prairies from the plowed and overgrazed plains in the Far West. But there was sufficient moisture in the top layers of soil to permit blooming of the early spring grasses and the vernal forbs. Many plants, however, achieved only short stature, and shallow-rooted species dried in May. Light rains in June temporarily revitalized some of the grasses, but as their roots depleted the deeper moisture their leaves curled and wilted. Then came the summer heat wave with temperatures as high as 111 degrees F. No rain fell for weeks. The leaves of grasses and forbs bleached and dried so they crunched underfoot and fell to dust. Animal life also was greatly depleted. Grasshoppers hastened the depletion by eating shrubs that had survived by virtue of their deep root systems.

The ravages of drought were manifested in various ways. Bare soil was exposed to the heat of the sun. The cover of short grasses on the plains was reduced to two or three percent and buffalo grass disappeared or was greatly thinned by dust burial. Red three-awn and the taller grasses, little bluestem and big bluestem, decreased in abundance and were replaced by western wheatgrass and other drought-resistant plants. Deeply rooted forbs such as scarlet globe mallow persisted against drought, even to the end. But most shallow-rooted plants were destroyed.

In the transition area between tall-grass and short-grass prairie, western wheatgrass thrived where the bluestems had died. Occasional light rains during the latter part of the drought period resulted in great increases in blue grama and buffalo grass, which were relieved of competition with the tall grassés. Six-weeks fescue, which matures in little over a month, grew in dense swards over the bared hilltops and slopes. Native forbs such as many-flowered aster and daisy fleabane became noxious weeds in drought-damaged pastures.

In the seven-year dry cycle the mixed prairie of the plains seemed to migrate eastward and replace the true prairie over a broad one-hundred-mile-wide zone. This was evident in the change in appearance and structure of the true or tall-grass prairie. Where the tall grasses had formerly dominated the landscape the prairie now supported shorter grasses and forbs characteristic of the far western plains. On more favorable sites, such as north slopes, ravines, and river terraces the bluestems survived in patches ten to fifteen yards in diameter. Everywhere, between these patches, side-oats grama and grasses of short stature formed the matrix of the prairie.

With the great catastrophe of drought came the dust storms and the "black blizzards" that blew across the western prairie and made the "Dust Bowl" a matter of national concern. The combination of years of overgrazing, plowing the land for wheat, and extreme drought initiated the dust storms of the 1930's. High winds drifted the exposed fine sandy-loam loess soil far east over the prairie. Dust buried the low-growing grasses and forbs many inches deep. Blue grama and buffalo grass lost heavily but recovered to a degree with spring rains. Then they were covered again. Only the deep-rooted forbs or plants possessed with underground storage organs survived. In localities where intense drought alternated with periods of light rainfall, the mid- and tall grasses died or became dormant and annual weeds, often greatly dwarfed, covered the landscape. Then in the late 1930's, tornadic winds blowing under clear skies brought midnight at high noon to the prairie.

In the summer of 1939, I watched one of these dust storms as it developed many miles west of Springfield, Colorado. At first, it appeared to be a low bank of yellow clouds on the far horizon. My range survey crew and I continued to work as it grew larger and darker over a period of nearly two hours. When it still was several miles away we could see that it was a boiling, moving wall of dust that stretched north and south from horizon to horizon. At its near approach it reminded me of a mountain front moving inexorably across the landscape.

Just before the towering wave of blackness engulfed our car, where we had retreated for safety from the suffocating dust, I heard the melodious whistle of a meadowlark. For a moment there was silence. Then the light dimmed to pale yellow, then to gray, and suddenly to black-

The drought of 1939 killed the grasses in this part of eastern Colorado.
Only annual forbs remain between the clumps of prickly-pear cactus
which flourish during periods of drought.

ness. Instantly our car was buffeted by mighty winds and blasted with abrasive sand that seemed to pour out of the sky and drive horizontally at the same time. Infinitesimal particles of silt seeped into our car and we went into spasms of coughing, even though we breathed through handkerchiefs moistened with water from our canteens. In our closed car the dust was so thick we could not see the dash light, nor any gleam of our headlights.

The sepulchral gloom and the whistling wind persisted for nearly a quarter of an hour. Then by imperceptible stages the light returned, somber at first, then dingy gray, and after an hour a shadowless mauve. When we drove into Springfield that evening, the street lights were on, but they were merely points of light in a turbid rayless atmosphere in which no object was distinct. Our eyes still burned and we still coughed up the stain of the soil that had permeated our lungs. We had lived through one of the dust storms that people of that time blamed on "the plow that broke the plains."

Had I known then what I know now about the history of the prairie I would have accepted this dust storm as a rare opportunity to see one of nature's phenomena that have recurred through thousands of years. I might have thought of it not as a catastrophic thing of the moment but as a reshuffling process that changed the prairie far and near, and that would be followed by renewal of plant and animal life as it always had in the past.

Dust storms and gigantic movements of topsoil have been involved in the making of the prairie from the beginning. The plains east of the Rockies were built by outwash from the western mountains as the processes of geologic erosion chiseled away the uplifted rocks. Then the winds took over the resorting and shifting of western soils exposed by droughts and stirred up by the hoofs of grazing animals, the claws of burrowing mammals, and the vertical transport of silt by ants and other insects digging their homes in the earth.

Massive transportation of western soils began in prehistoric times. The loess soils of Nebraska, Iowa, and Missouri were deposited to depths of hundreds of feet. On eroded bluffs layers of organic matter, sandwiched between other layers of clay and silt, give evidence that prairie repeatedly persisted for centuries and then was covered by more wind-drifted soil. Finally it reached the development known in our own time. Many of the sandhill areas in Nebraska, Oklahoma, and Texas represent the residual of rock particles left after winds of the geological past removed the finer silt and transported it to other places on the prairie.

Evidence of extensive soil blowing during archeological time has been obtained recently from excavation of Indian villages. Periodically these prehistoric villages were abandoned and in the intervals between occupations thick deposits of windblown soil covered the land. The lengths of the soil-blowing periods are unknown but they must have been considerable since modern man has not witnessed equal amounts of soil deposition on the prairie.

Records of dust storms and soil blowing have been extensively recorded during historical time. Isaac McCoy, in recording a boundary survey north of the Kansas River in 1830, mentioned the extensive drought and stated that the ashes from prairie fires and the dust and sand raised by the wind made it impossible to see the trail of the surveyors ahead. The air was darkened and the clouds seemed to be united with the earth. In 1839, J. N. Nicollet, traveling east of the Missouri River in what is now South Dakota, found that the grass was so thin that the incessant winds constantly blew dust and inconvenienced travelers. During the early years of settlement in Kansas, dust storms were extensive and severe. This was the same land which in recent times produced thirty to sixty bushels of two-dollar wheat per acre. Nature in less than one hundred years had repaired the damage of this catastrophe.

The literature on vegetation recovery after degeneration of the prairie is so voluminous it would fill many books. Such a complex of factors affects both the rate and nature of plant succession following injury to the grassland that each area of disturbance shows individual aberrations in trend of renewal. These aberrations and deflections in the path of orderly succession are usually explainable on the basis of differential response to various factors. Some of the important ones are amount and seasonal distribution of rainfall, wind movement, drifting soil, size of the denuded area, grazing pressure during recovery, rodent and insect populations, topography, slope, and type of soil.

In the relatively undisturbed recovery process, the general tendency is toward increased numbers of plant species as healing goes on. Most plant species are retained in niches favorable to their own requirements as optimum development of the new prairie is attained. This means that pioneer plants, such as Russian thistles, pigweeds, and peppergrass, which are the first to invade bare spots or abandoned cultivated fields, still find microhabitats around anthills, on rodent diggings, in trampled areas, and formerly in buffalo wallows. Many plants characteristic of early succession stages also are capable of producing seeds that remain viable in the soil for many years. Thus when disturbance and growing conditions permit, their seeds germinate to produce a new and abundant generation of pioneers capable of starting the renewal process again.

The stages of renewal are never uniform over large areas of the prairie. Usually there is a patchwork pattern which exhibits differences in the variety of plants present from place to place and from year to year. Moderate drought sometimes causes a temporary recession toward more degenerate stages, but in general the overall progress is toward reestablishment of the prairie with all its varied forms of plant and animal life. On denuded soil the process almost invariably starts with a "first weed" stage, characterized by annual forbs. As the soil becomes stabilized the "second weed" stage replaces the first with quickly maturing forbs, many of which are perennials. Short-lived grasses, most of which are unpalatable to grazing animals, also appear. Within ten to twenty years an early grass stage succeeds the weed stages. It includes longer-lived grasses such as red three-awn and sand dropseed. Many of the native prairie forbs enter during this stage, which may exhibit many more showy flowers of goldenweeds (*Haplopappus spinulosus*), prairie coneflower, thistles, and goldenrods than are common in the final prairie mixture. The final stage, of course, is the transition to the dominant prairie plants: blue grama, buffalo grass, wheatgrass, forbs, and shrubs on the western plains; and the bluestems, dropseeds, and the showy forbs and shrubs of the true prairie.

In general, animals are not as important in the recovery of prairie as they are in affecting its variety and productivity in its fully developed state. The earliest stages of recovery from bare soil offer uncongenial habitats for most creatures, although tiger beetles and the sand-loving kangaroo rats put in an appearance soon after the first perennial plants gain a foothold. Insects increase in numbers and varieties as new and different plants appear to offer them leaves for chewing, nectar for their larvae, stems for gall formation and stem mining, and roots or leaves for sap withdrawal and for larval food. The middle stages of vegetation recovery generally show greater variety of insects than the final stabilized prairie.

Meadowlarks usually are abundant in the middle recovery stages because of the large insect populations and because egg-destroying rodents and snakes have not become established in large numbers. The variety of nesting material and the wide choice of grass and forb seeds also make the middle recovery stages acceptable for many other species of ground-dwelling birds and for the harvester ants of the western prairies.

The near-final return of the prairie is accompanied by large populations of rabbits, deer mice, and harvest mice. Ground squirrels thrive in greatest numbers where the grass is of medium or low stature. Moles and shrews are found as the developing vegetation adds organic matter to the soil in sufficient quantity to favor earthworm activity and development of insect larvae in the soil. When vegetation recovery is complete, antelope, badgers, and lesser creatures gradually reoccupy their niches, along with their parasites and predators. The never-ending processes of give and take, invade and compete, live and die, go on in a sort of dynamic equilibrium until the next catastrophe starts the renewal process all over again.

*After the Homestead Act of 1862, settlers migrated to the prairie and built sod houses. Many homes were abandoned when the homesteaders discovered that the 160 acres allowed by the law were not sufficient to produce enough crops or livestock to support a man and his family.*

# 12

---

# *Man and the Prairie*

WHEN I WAS OLD ENOUGH to make my own bows and arrows
of dogwood stems and willow wood I used to visit a large dome-shaped
mound of earth and rock near the western edge of our farm in southeastern Nebraska. This rounded "hill," which had no name, was different from any other topographic feature in Rock Creek Valley. The
mound covered about two acres at the base and was some fifty feet
higher than the stream terrace on which it rested. But, unlike the other
prairie-covered hills and slopes on either side of our valley, this mound
was made of quartzite boulders intermingled with clay and numerous
pieces of flint. Some of these flint rocks had been chipped by Indians.
By searching in the bare areas between the clumps of big and little bluestem grasses I could find arrowheads.

To an expert, I suppose the geological evidence would have indicated
some form of glacial origin for this rock pile. It was not of Indian origin as some of our neighbors asserted. But it did have Indian associations, as the arrowheads and other artifacts suggested, long before the
white settlers came to that part of the prairie.

In my youth I was too dull to be cognizant of all the other former
Indian associations with the prairie around my home or to realize that
many of the familiar names of places and things had come from people
who, through uncounted centuries, had inhabited the land before me.
Now I am amazed at the number of Indian names of places in the coun-
try of my youth. For many years I lived in Nemaha County. Frequently
I visited the place where my father was born in Otoe County. Regularly
I traveled to Nehawka, Weeping Water, Tecumseh, or Omaha without

realizing that these were Indian names. Along with friends and neighbors, I did not know that picturesque Indian villages and cornfields once stood on the banks of the Missouri and Platte rivers or that they were farmed by the Poncas, the Pawnees, and the Otos. And no one of us knew that the Kansas and Osage Indians of northeastern and eastern Kansas, and the Wichitas in central Kansas, were the last in a series of people who lived and migrated back and forth across the prairie in response to the vicissitudes of climate. Nor were we aware that the cultures on the Kansas River were simplified versions of Indian activities that produced the great burial mounds of the Ohio Valley.

Many of us were given the impression in school that the Indians of the prairie were war-whooping, horse-riding raiders and buffalo hunters who slaughtered the white men from ambush and burned the cabins of the settlers. Perhaps we can be excused for our lack of knowledge simply because archeological studies of prehistoric cultures in mid-America have been neglected until recently. Only since 1947, the federal government of the United States has been conducting an "Inter-Agency Archaeological Salvage Program" designed to preserve artifacts and other historical data from the bulldozers and power scoops of the dam builders and resource developers. In the Missouri River basin alone, which includes about one-sixth the area of the nation, 105 dams are projected which will flood much of the area occupied by prehistoric Indian nations. Salvage of archeological materials from reservoir sites is especially urgent since prewhite people, as well as modern men, located their habitations near rivers and streams, but drew upon the bison and other necessities of life that existed in the prairie hinterlands. This archeological salvage, in which the Park Service, the Smithsonian Institution, universities, and other agencies have participated, has in the last two decades amassed an impressive amount of information about prehistoric prairie communities whose existence previously had hardly been suspected.

Nowhere did white men meet the Indians on the western prairie before 1541. In most localities, the initial contacts came a century or more later. By that time the Indian mode of living and adjustment to the grassland environment had been changed through the acquisition of Spanish horses, and later the white man's weapons for war. Subsequent history, based on these contacts, told us little of how prewhite men responded to the fluctuations of climate, the abundance and scarcity of plant and animal life, and the migrations, adjustments, and distributional changes that took place on the prairie in the period extending back into Pleistocene times.

It is now believed that peopling of the New World was from Asia over a former land connection in the Bering Strait locality. Lowering of the ocean level by 180 feet due to water storage in the continental glaciers would have bared a strip of land between Alaska and Siberia as well as a fringe of land along the coasts of both continents. David M. Hopkins has stated: "A reduction in sea level of 300 feet—to the level recorded during early Wisconsin time more than 35,000 years ago—would result in the exposure . . . of an almost featureless plain extending nearly 1000 miles from the north shore of a shrunken Bering Sea to the south shore of the Arctic Ocean." Over this land bridge, which supported treeless tundra, a great assemblage of animals migrated: horses and camels from America to Asia; and elephants, bison, bears, and deer from Asia to America.

*Planted by a homesteader, this tree claim did not withstand the ravages of climate. Drought has killed most of the trees, which also show a "high line" due to browsing by livestock.*

After the animals arrived, men came, perhaps as much as twenty-five thousand years ago, although some archeologists estimate twenty thousand to forty thousand years ago as the time of early human migration. James B. Griffin, however, infers that man finally crossed the Bering land bridge some sixteen thousand to twenty thousand years ago since there are no older sites and complexes known in North America. He states: "There are indeed, dates obtained by the radio-carbon technique for purported archaeological sites from Texas to California which range from 20,000 to more than 40,000 years ago, but so far none of these localities can be regarded as having provided evidence which is the unquestionable result of human activity." Regardless of the exact time of man's arrival, it is now believed there were many waves of people and their coming at different times resulted in dispersal of men to different parts of the continent. Possibly the Eskimos were among the latest to appear in North America.

In the postglacial environment the early hunters gradually developed from a flint-tool culture, which included the use of scrapers, knives, and choppers, to a mixed culture of hunting, trapping, vegetable-food gathering, and the making of ceramic articles. Gradually the Indians made use of many plants for food, magical charms, smoking, dyes, and beverages. Most of the edible animals were eaten. Their skins were used for clothing, their teeth for necklaces, their bones for awls and fish hooks, and the feathers of birds for ornaments. The cultural climax of the prehistoric Indians in the last thousand years was reached in their agricultural achievements in growing maize, beans, and squash, and in their use of a wide variety of native berries, nuts, fish, birds, river mussels, turtles, and game animals for food. The tribal groups on the prairies then adapted themselves to a combination of village life and a nomadic existence intimately connected with the wandering buffalo. Into this culture, with its intercommunication between tribes, its religious symbolism, and its adjustments to varied environments, came European conquest, colonization, and disaster to the Indians.

The history of the Cheyenne Indians illustrates this conquest. The Cheyenne were of western Algonquian stock and their language was related to that of the Mohegans and Delawares of the East. At the coming of the white men they were an agricultural people living at the eastern border of the prairie. Colonization by the Europeans drove them from Minnesota to the Black Hills in South Dakota. Eventually they became part of the nomadic Plains Indians who built their lives around the buffalo with the aid of the white man's horses. Part of the Cheyenne tribe settled on the Arkansas River in Colorado and the remainder, known as the Northern Cheyenne, stayed in northern Wyoming and southern Montana. History vividly records the raids of the Cheyenne upon the settlers, and especially the Custer battle, but the massacres of their women and children and the treaties broken by our government are largely ignored. From a once proud and self-sufficient nation, twenty-five hundred Cheyenne now live on their reservation in southeastern Montana, where the land is semiarid and unsuitable for cultivation or for efficient grazing of cattle.

It was grazing, first by cattle and then by sheep, that started the real conquest of the prairie, a conquest finally completed by the plow. The lines of settlement spread in two directions toward the prairie. The colonists along the East Coast brought with them livestock consisting of horses, pigs, goats, and cows. Importations of livestock arrived at Jamestown in 1611. The Dutch, who settled New Amsterdam in 1625, brought cattle with them. In all the early histories are records of livestock arriving along the East Coast. Apparently the animals thrived. In 1661 in Maryland, for example, permission was granted for the hunting of wild cattle roaming in the woods. By 1775 livestock were common in all the colonies along the Atlantic Coast. From these settlements the livestock industry moved westward and found more congenial grazing conditions in the forest openings and finally on the prairie.

Meanwhile, in 1521, near Vera Cruz on the east coast of Mexico, Gregorio Villalobos, sent to New Spain as governor general, landed troops, supplies, and a number of calves. There is no record that Cortez, the Spanish adventurer, landed cattle in Mexico a few years earlier in 1515. But livestock prospered amazingly in Mexico. By 1538, Mendoza, then Viceroy of New Spain, reported to the Spanish King that his cattle, horses, and Merino sheep were doing well and that the sheep were especially prolific. From these early beginnings, livestock pushed north with other Spanish expeditions. Coronado's expedition, with which he took one thousand horses, five hundred cows, and more than five thousand rams and ewes, unquestionably marks the year 1540 as the date when cattle and sheep first came to the region that ultimately became part of the United States.

Settlements from Mexico spread westward to the Pacific Coast, where many Franciscan missions were founded, with their thousands of cattle. Other settlements spread into what is now Arizona and New Mexico and the coastal plains of Texas. Finally the livestock industry of the

*Crops are now raised where prairie formerly covered the land. Few farmers realize that they are utilizing the fertile soil developed by grasses and other native plants over a period of ten thousand years.*

Southwest moved northward and eastward until it met the expanding tide of livestock coming from the East. Thus the grazing conquest of the prairie was achieved.

The cattle orginally brought from Spain, including those driven northward by Coronado, were the foundation stock of the longhorns of Texas and of the cattle industry in the Southwest. Famed in cowboy song, art, and movie, the longhorn still is part of the romantic West. If we may judge by the stories and legends, a more cantankerous, rangy, hollow-ribbed, horn-armored critter never existed. Long on speed and short on beef, these hungry animals were exceptionally adapted to existence on semiarid prairie left by the vanishing buffalo. Beginning about

1865, some ten million longhorns were driven from Texas up the northward trails. In more ways than one, they left their imprint on the prairie, the culture of the times, and the economy of the nation.

The coming of the longhorns gave further excuse for expulsion of the buffalo and extirpation of the prairie dogs, which were accused of depleting the cattle forage. Overgrazing by cattle killed out the taller grasses and made dust beds of much of the prairie. The wiry longhorns were the best trail-traveling animals ever produced. Their mobility contributed to the rapid expansion of the cattlemen's empire over the vast expanse of grassland where the buffalo herds had supported the Indian economy. As the cattle barons moved northward there was need for markets for their animals, which were worth $4 a head in Texas, $40 in northern and eastern markets, and $150 in California. Thus the great trail drives began.

When the Kansas Pacific Railroad reached Abilene in 1867, a few Texans established shipping facilities at this railhead, and a new era began. Then the trail that Jesse Chisholm, a half-breed Cherokee Indian trader, had used earlier in his expeditions became the route for drovers. Within four years, more than a million head of Texas cattle were shipped from Abilene to Kansas City and Chicago packing houses, or to Iowa, Nebraska, Missouri, and Illinois farms for fattening on corn that grew on fields plowed out of the prairie. Meanwhile, as the buffalo hunters destroyed the sustenance of the western Indians, the way was open for the advancing farmers' frontier and conflicts with the stockmen. New cattle trails were developed and their termini moved westward to Newton, Wichita, and Dodge City, Kansas, to meet the Santa Fe Railway. Farther north, the terminus of the Great Western Trail was Ogallala, Nebraska, served by the Union Pacific Railroad. But soon the trail was extended northward to Montana when stockmen learned that cattle could survive the cold winters. In similar manner the cattle industry spread to Colorado, Wyoming, Idaho, and Oregon, where the cowboys believed the grass would last forever.

The land was free and there for the taking. With a little management skill, and the will to defend himself and his holdings, a man could convert the grass into steers and become rich. The first step was to claim the land around one of the prairie waters: a stretch of live stream, a lake, or a waterhole. If he could defend his water against all comers he could control the use of grass in all the surrounding country. The strong men among them became the cattle kings of the West. But other men came, among them the sheepmen and the homesteaders, and there was violent antagonism on the range. When the farmers came, they "busted" the sod, established towns, built roads, schools, and churches, and established a new civilization. The western frontier was gone.

The "sodbusters" who broke the prairie discovered, when they left the fringing forests and entered the land of tall grass, that their wooden moldboard plows would not scour or stay clean even though they would turn furrows. But the development of the steel plow by John Deere in 1837–40 solved the problem and as many as six yoke of oxen were no longer required to pull the plow.

When my father broke the last of the prairie on our farm he used a "riding plow" pulled by four horses. The tough wirelike roots of the bluestems and prairie clovers twanged with a thousand ringing sounds as each step of the horses pulled the sharp blade forward through the sod of ten thousand years. As the soil was turned, a black ribbon reinforced with the living foundation of the prairie thudded into the trench made by the preceding round of the plow. Bee nests were upturned, mice scurried from their ruined homes, and raucous gulls swarmed behind, picking up worms, insects, and other small creatures evicted from the sanctuary of their grassland homes. This first plowing did not subdue the prairie—some of the grasses took root and grew again. Not for several years were all the cut roots and dried stems rotted and incorporated into the soil. But eventually the land grew corn, and then wheat, and then clover as insect pests increased and the crops had to be rotated.

This land that my father plowed had already been homesteaded according to the Act of 1862, and had passed through several ownerships before he acquired title to his farm. The Homestead Act provided that any citizen or person in the process of becoming naturalized could obtain 160 acres of government land by paying a registration fee, living on the land for five years, and beginning cultivation. Before that, the Land Law of 1820 allowed purchase of 80-acre tracts for $1.25 an acre. But few men could raise the necessary $100 cash, and so they simply "squatted" on the land without benefit of title. Pressure to legalize their rights finally culminated in passage of the Homestead Act.

Settlement in many parts of the prairie proceeded slowly since there was disillusionment caused by droughts, hard winters, and financial collapse of the cattle boom in 1887. The drought of that year in Kansas was the most severe known in the country. Eastern investors in western land wanted their money back from people who were not familiar with

*Man has changed the face of the prairie as he has changed the face of the earth. Most of the prairie is gone forever, but its accumulated productivity now supplies food for the hungry people of the world.*

the soil and the climate. With the opening of Oklahoma in 1889, however, Kansas lost about fifty thousand of her population. At high noon on April 22, at Arkansas City, cavalrymen fired their carbines and the race for land claims was on. In the morning of that day, Oklahoma was an uninhabited prairie. At midday a mass of excited humanity surged forward and by evening it was a land of many people. In a few days the sodbusters began their work and merchants, bankers, saloonkeepers, and adventurers set up their tents and shanties, which would change in future years to towns and cities.

The taking of the public land began, of course, after the conclusion of the Revolutionary War, when, during a series of cessions between 1781 and 1802, the thirteen original states gave the federal government title to 237 million acres extending west to the Mississippi River. Then came the Louisiana Purchase of 530 million acres in 1803; the Florida Purchase from Spain; the addition of Oregon Territory in 1846; the formation of the Republic of Texas in 1836, which held title to lands now in Kansas, Oklahoma, Colorado, and New Mexico; the treaty with Mexico in 1848, which gave us the Southwest; and the Gadsden Purchase from Mexico in 1853. The public domain thus acquired composed three fourths of the continental United States, and the people owned 1.9 billion acres of land.

Much of this land was the last stronghold of the western prairie, a semiarid land, deficient in water and unsuited to agriculture as it had been practiced in the humid East. In such an area of vagaries and extremes of climate it was inevitable that settlement would develop in a pattern different from that in other parts of the nation. Whereas population and manufacturing industries concentrated in the humid eastern and western borders of the country, settlement on the prairie, particularly in the high plains region, centered in localities where irrigation could alleviate the effects of periodic drought and high evaporation. The drought of the 1890's, however, resulted in emigration from many of the settled areas and abandonment of entire towns.

Attempts at dry farming, achieved by allowing plowed land to lie fallow in alternate summers and by maintaining a dust mulch through cultivation after every rainstorm, proved unsuccessful. Soil structure deteriorated, humus content diminished, and wind erosion became a stark reality. On unplowed prairie excessive grazing, based on the erroneous idea that livestock instead of grass was the principal product of the land, resulted in depletion of the range lands. The tall grasses disappeared, the shortgrass sod thinned, and the numbers of unpalatable forbs increased. Then came World War I and a greater demand for grain and livestock products. In the decades that followed, fifty million more acres of grassland were plowed, grazing intensity on the grasslands was increased, and with the great drought of the 1930's came the Dust Bowl.

Newer methods of plowing and terracing the land then were evolved. Irrigation was greatly expanded through impoundment of small streams and by damming the larger rivers until the waters of the prairie hardly ran. Now, where river irrigation water cannot be moved to upland fields, subterranean streams are being pumped by wells. This ground water is of incalculable value to agriculture in the West. But neither river irrigation water nor ground water is universally available throughout the prairie. And already ground water tables are falling as pumping increases and the incessant demand for exploitation of the natural resources continues.

Still, there is a great new boom on the Great Plains. Corn that yields two hundred bushels per acre is being grown where a few years ago a dozen to twenty acres of short-grass prairie were necessary to support a cow for a year. Sugar beets that gross $350 per acre are now growing where grass has been turned into irrigated crop land. Grain sorghum production has doubled under irrigation with the stimulation of hybrid seed, fertilizer, and herbicides. The increased production of all these crops has resulted in the expansion of beef-cattle feeding lots until fed-cattle marketings in the ten Great Plains states now approach nearly half of all United States fed-beef production. This has come about because of increased use of underground water in an area of possibly two million square miles in Nebraska, Oklahoma, Texas, and Colorado.

Thus man believes he has met the challenge of the grasslands after one hundred and fifty years of strenuous attempts at settlement. Will the remaining portions of the prairie disappear if he can achieve the fullest potential of the contribution it can make to mankind? Will he be able to meet the caprices of nature in the artificial habitat he has established where once the earth thundered with the pounding feet of countless bison and the sky rang with the clarion calls of geese and the whooping of the great cranes? Only time will tell.

# Appendix

## *Where to See the Prairie*

IT IS STILL POSSIBLE TO SEE and experience some of the awesomeness and grandeur of the prairie. On the hilltops in Iowa and western Wisconsin, patches of unplowed prairie still remain. Not all of the Minnesota prairies have been plowed nor have all the wetlands been drained. Great stretches of prairie still may be seen in the Dakotas. In the Nebraska sandhill country, some twelve million acres of prairie still exist under different degrees of grazing. In the Flint Hills of eastern Kansas much tall-grass prairie offers opportunity for instructive tours of unplowed grassland. In western Kansas, Oklahoma, and the panhandle of Texas, wide vistas of plains grassland remain where the tourist may travel mile after mile, stopping now and then to examine the cactus and buffalo grass in bloom, listen to the meadowlarks, or watch a tumblebug bury its ball in the prairie soil.

There are no national parks devoted exclusively to prairie, although one has been proposed by the Park Service of the Department of Interior. In the prairie states, however, there are numerous wildlife refuges dedicated to wildlife conservation, administered by the Bureau of Sport Fisheries and Wildlife in the Department of Interior. While intended primarily for waterfowl, these refuges provide excellent habitat for many species of other birds, aquatic animals, and upland wildlife in the grasslands that border the prairie waters. Publications describing the wildlife of individual refuges are available from the Bureau of Sport Fisheries and Wildlife, Washington, D.C., 20240, and at each refuge office.

Within the Great Plains region are seventeen national grasslands, administered by the Forest Service, U.S. Department of Agriculture. These lands of grass, managed on the multiple-use concept, have suffered from past abuse, and now are being restored to productive prairie cover. During the drought and depression of the 1930's these lands were purchased by the federal government, organized into Land Utilization Projects, and finally made a part of the National Forest System. On the national grasslands today, grass is grown as a part of the economy; but they also support wildlife linked with the prairie and the water in ponds and streams. Various stages of vegetation recovery from former catastrophe may be seen on these grasslands, where healthy sod, ponds, livestock, and recreation for people are the ultimate goals of land use. Antelope, grouse, ducks, plovers, curlews, frogs, badgers, and other prairie life may be glimpsed or studied in these areas.

Information on the national grasslands, including maps showing their locations in eleven western states, may be obtained from the Forest Service, U.S. Department of Agriculture, Washington, D.C., 20250. Forest Service Regional Offices also may be contacted for information concerning national grasslands within their administrative areas. For information about national grasslands in North Dakota, write to Regional Forester, Forest Service, Federal Building, Missoula, Montana, 59807. For general information about national grasslands in Wyoming, South Dakota, Nebraska, Kansas, and Colorado, write to Regional Forester, Forest Service, 1117 W. 8th Ave., P.O. Box 25127, Lakewood, Colorado, 80225. Information on national grasslands of Oklahoma, Texas, and New Mexico may be obtained by writing to Regional Forester, Forest Service, 517 Gold Avenue S.W., Albuquerque, New Mexico, 87102. For information about national grasslands in the northwest panhandle of Texas, north central Texas, and western Oklahoma, write to Regional Forester, Forest Service, 1720 Peachtree Rd. N. W., Atlanta, Georgia 30309.

Many outstanding areas for study and observation of prairie wildlife are maintained as parks, refuges, scenic areas, monuments, and recreational grounds by states, counties, and private organizations. Information about these may be obtained by contacting the appropriate agencies within the states. Administration of these areas may be under the Game, Fish and Parks Department, the Publicity and Parks Commission, the State Natural History Survey Division, the State Highway Department, The Nature Conservancy, and many other agencies. Hundreds of these agencies and their addresses are listed in the *Conservation Directory* produced by The National Wildlife Federation, 1412 16th Street N.W., Washington, D.C., 20036. This directory may be consulted in some of the better local libraries. A state-by-state inventory of some 4,800 existing non-urban park and related areas in the fifty states is summarized in *Parks for America*, published by the National Park Service, U.S. Department of the Interior. This tabulation includes many existing and potential prairie park and recreational areas, along with maps showing their locations.

The prairie areas described in the following pages represent only a few of the localities where the interested visitor may go to see grasslands, prairie ponds, lakes, and streams, and the animals that live in these habitats. Some of these areas are outstanding because of their vistas and scenic values, because of their abundant bird and animal life, and because of their attractiveness as wilderness remote from the rush and tension of city living.

## COLORADO

On the Pawnee National Grassland, northeastern Colorado, may be seen original mixed prairie of blue grama, buffalo grass, needle-and-thread, and western wheatgrass. Antelope, badger, coyotes, jackrabbits, and mule deer are present. Many upland birds nest on the grassland. Golden eagles and prairie falcons nest in the Chalk Bluffs near the northern boundary of the grassland. Many stages of vegetation succession can be observed here, since lands purchased by the Resettlement Administration in the 1930's are now grazed moderately by cattle. Buffalo wallows are still visible and many intermittent natural ponds and artificial reservoirs support migratory waterfowl in years of normal rainfall. The Mummy Range, Long's Peak, and Pikes Peak can be seen from the high points on this grassland. Privately owned ranch lands lie within the area. Comanche National Grassland in southeastern Colorado lies in the country of the Dust Bowl of the 1930's. Improved farming practices and management to provide a reliable supply of grazing has resulted in recovery of mixed prairie on thousands of acres. In addition to blue grama and buffalo grass, galleta (a grass of the southern plains) adds interest to the prairie mixture. Yuccas are common, along with sand sagebrush (*Artemisia filifolia*), one of the conspicuous shrubs of sandy prairies. Many thousands of Canada geese rest on Two Buttes reservoir during the fall migration. Mixed prairie in all stages of use and misuse, with associated mammal, bird, and insect life may be seen from any of the major highways crossing the high plains from east to west. Interstate Highway 80 S passes through mixed prairie and follows the South Platte River for many miles. Interstate Highway 70 crosses the high plains where unplowed mixed prairie still exists under various degrees of grazing. Deer and antelope may be seen here along with other wildlife species common to the prairie.

## Iowa

Remnants of tall-grass prairie exist along the western border of the state in the loess hills and on the steep bluffs on the east side of the Missouri River. The dominant grasses are big and little bluestem. These merge with the shrub borders at the upper edges of wooded valleys along the major tributaries that flow into the Missouri River. Natural lakes in the northwestern corner of the state support a variety of fish and bird life typical of prairie waters. Prairie may be seen at Stone State Park and Waubonsie State Park. Nature preserves which include prairie are: Cayler Prairie State Preserve; Hayden Prairie State Preserve; Kalsow Prairie State Preserve; and Preparation Canyon State Park, with biological features in addition to the prairie. Union Slough National Wildlife Refuge, near the Minnesota border, supports several dozen kinds of prairie grasses, numerous birds, and various species of prairie mice and other rodents.

## Kansas

Kansas has a great variety of prairie habitats, varying from the well-managed tall-grass prairies in the Flint Hills section in the east-central part of the state, to the Red Hills section with mesas and buttes along the southern border, to the mixed-prairie and short-grass vegetation in mid-state and on the high western plains. With the exception of the plowed wheat lands, especially in the west, prairie tracts may be seen from almost any highway in the state. All of the major prairie grasses are abundant: these include the bluestems, blue grama, side-oats grama, buffalo grass, June grass, needle-and-thread, sand dropseed, windmill grass, and dozens of other grasses. Sunflowers are the most conspicuous forbs. Waterfowl are numerous in the Flint Hills, Kirwin, and Quivra National Wildlife Refuges. Prairie dogs occur in limited areas in the western part of the state. Ornate box turtles can be seen in abundance in the grasslands south of Manhattan and in the Flint Hills section. Prairie may be seen at numerous state parks and recreation areas. A

Prairie National Park has been proposed to include 57,000 acres of grassland on the east side of Tuttle Creek Reservoir, north of Manhattan, Kansas. This would preserve an important remnant of the once magnificent grassland environment. In the Flint Hills the Konza Prairie is an 8,600 acre protected area used by scientists for grassland research. Permission to visit there may be obtained from Kansas State University. Most tall-grass prairie in other parts of Kansas are grazed by livestock.

## MINNESOTA

Most of the wet prairie west of the wooded area of the state has been drained or plowed. Wildlife, however, still is diversified and the lakes are famous for fish. Five national wildlife refuges support waterfowl typical of the species found on prairie waters in other western states. Sherburne National Wildlife Refuge contains many prairie potholes and other ponds where waterfowl, western bluebirds, green herons, muskrats, mink, beaver, otter, and raccoons are found. Tall grass prairie once occupied much of western and southwestern Minnesota. Now only small relic areas remain in which big bluestem, little bluestem, tall panic grass, and needlegrass grow in company with spiderwort, asters, goldenrods, and other herbs. Minnesota's largest rabbit, the white-tailed jack rabbit is a characteristic animal of the open prairie. Typical prairie rodents are Richardson's ground squirrel, thirteen-lined ground squirrel, and pocket gophers. The Wildlife Management Institute reports that greater prairie chickens are booming again in Minnesota's Lac qui Parle Wildlife Management Area near Milan. Prairie chickens were released there in September 1977. They have survived well and are reproducing. After an absence of 40 years they may again prosper on this restored grassland. In Minnesota, as in Wisconsin and Iowa, the prairie has been reduced to remnants of its former extent. As of September 1979, Mark Heitlinger, Minnesota Chapter, The Nature Conservancy, gave me his impression that, "Most of the prairie remaining is in the inter-beach zones of Glacial Lake Agassiz. There are sizable areas of unplowable prairie on the Prairie Coteau in southwestern Minnesota and along the Minnesota River, but most of it has been grazed beyond recognition. . . . The Park Service owns some degraded prairie in Pipestone National Monument and the Minnesota Historical Society has a nice small prairie at the Petroglyphs Site near Jeffers." The Nature Conservancy, Minnesota Chapter, lists 34 Prairie Preserves acquired between 1961 and 1979. These range in size from 14 acres in Compass Prairie in Nobles County to 1,660 acres in Pembina Trail Preserve in Polk County. Other sizable preserves are: Ordway Prairie, 582 acres in Pope

County; Chippewa Prairie, 769 acres in Chippewa and Swift Counties; Bluestem Prairie, 1,200 acres in Clay County; and Pankratz Prairie, 634 acres in Polk County. Even remnants of the rich, deep-soil prairie are exceedingly rare because of its agricultural value.

## MONTANA

Much of eastern Montana still remains in mixed prairie, where the original grasslands were dominated by blue grama, needlegrass, and western wheatgrass. Antelope and smaller mammals, including thirteen-lined ground squirrels, skunks, rabbits, badgers, and prairie mice are found throughout this section. The Bowdoin National Wildlife Refuge includes about seven thousand acres of mixed prairie, where antelope may be seen. The marshlands in this refuge are populated with a dozen species of ducks. White pelicans, cormorants, great blue herons, rails, grebes, and willets also live here. If you wish to see bison in Montana, go to the National Bison Range north of Missoula. The bison, along with elk, mule deer, whitetail deer, and antelope, graze here on prairie dominated by grasses such as bluebunch wheatgrass, Idaho fescue, and western wheatgrass. The Bureau of Sport Fisheries and Wildlife manages nineteen national refuges in Montana, totaling more than a million acres of land and water. Prairie plants, animals, and birds can be seen, especially in the refuges in the eastern section of the state. In the Medicine Lake National Wildlife Refuge, more than two hundred species of birds have been listed. This area also is of interest because of the ponds and lakes, which are remnants of glacial ponds formed after recession of the great ice sheet. Prairie also is found in and around Custer Battlefield National Monument and in many of the state parks and recreation areas.

## NEBRASKA

For tall-grass prairie as you may have visualized its original appearance, go to the Nebraska National Forest near Halsey. Here on the billowing sandhills are miles and miles of big and little bluestem, bluejoint, prairie sandreed, sand lovegrass, switchgrass, Indian grass, and prairie cordgrass. Wild roses, prairie shoestring, sand cherries, and other prairie shrubs grow luxuriantly. Innumerable showy forbs are everywhere. Sharptail grouse and prairie chickens are found on the uplands. Great blue herons fish in the Dismal River. Kangaroo rats and gophers dig in the sandy soil. If you wish to see bison, visit them at the Fort Niobrara National Wildlife Refuge north of Valentine, Nebraska. Bison, Texas longhorn cattle, and elk are protected here for the benefit of visitors. In this same locality the Valentine National Wildlife Refuge, consisting of 60,000 acres of land and water, provides resting and breeding space for waterfowl of the central flyway. In addition to ducks, more than two hundred other kinds of birds have been recorded. East and west of this area you may see prairie country throughout most of the length of the Niobrara River. Or if you want to follow another prairie river, start at the headwaters of the Republican River near Limon, Colorado, and follow it down through Nebraska as it flows from the short-grass country and then turns southeast into the tall-grass prairie of Kansas near Concordia and Manhattan.

## North and South Dakota

These two states still include great stretches of prairie, although much of the grassland is in poor or only fair condition as a result of heavy grazing. But this is the world of the prairie birds and waterfowl. On the map of the United States in the brochure *National Wildlife Refuges 1967*, the refuges for North Dakota are so numerous the state is shown in a separate diagram. These are the breeding and resting places of innumerable birds, which are the principal attraction for visitors to these areas. More than two hundred species have been recorded on several of these refuges. In North Dakota near the Montana border, the National Park Service administers the Theodore Roosevelt National Memorial Park. Colorful badlands, mixed prairie, bison, and antelope may be seen in this area of 70,374 acres. Prairie plants, mammals, and birds are found in 63 national wildlife and game refuges and in numerous state parks and recreation areas. Prairie lands managed for grazing are included in the Little Missouri, Sheyenne, and Cedar River National Grasslands in North Dakota, and in the Grand River, Fort Pierre, and Buffalo Gap National Grasslands in South Dakota. Wind Cave National Park in the Black Hills has mixed-grass prairie, where bison and antelope graze in the midst of prairie-dog towns. Deer also are plentiful in this area, which is a Mecca for tourists. The great river of the prairie, the Missouri, crosses the center of the state of South Dakota. In the northeast section of the state are many pothole lakes where waterfowl are plentiful.

# OKLAHOMA

Oklahoma has timbered mountains and treeless plains that extend to the high, arid plains of New Mexico. Three great prairie rivers, the Red, Arkansas, and Canadian, drain the prairies. The Wichita Mountains Wildlife Refuge near Fort Sill possesses exceptional geologic and wildlife features. Ancient mountains rise above the plain and are partially covered with oaks and other trees. The bison herd numbers about 1,000 animals. Elk, deer, and Texas longhorn cattle thrive on the native tall- and short-grass prairies. Ornithologists and bird watchers have listed 213 species, including the roadrunner, scissor-tailed flycatcher, painted bunting, bald eagle, and golden eagle. Fifty species of mammals have been listed for the refuge, including opossums, shrews, mice, bats, armadillos, jackrabbits, cottontails, coyotes, red fox, badgers, bobcats, skunks, elk, and whitetail deer. The former prairie-dog colonies have died and attempts to transplant prairie dogs to the refuge have met with failure. Fish are numerous in the lakes and include carp, shiners, minnows, suckers, bullheads, plains killifish, bass, various sunfish, perch, darters, and drum. Many reptiles and amphibians round out the diversified fauna, so that any naturalist or nature observer can find something of interest. The habitat is so varied that mammals of East and West and birds of North and South meet at the Wichita Refuge.

# TEXAS

Grasslands alternate with forests over an area of more than four million acres known as the Western Cross Timbers of Texas. Another belt, the Eastern Cross Timbers, extends southward from Oklahoma about 150 miles as a continuous body of forest or savanna bounded by open prairie. More than a century ago, W. Kennedy described these timbers as a natural curiosity of the country which formed a remarkable feature of its topography. The name "Cross Timbers" possibly alludes to the north and south direction of these timber belts, which cross the east-flowing streams, or to the experiences of the early westward travelers, who left the eastern forests and entered upon open prairie only to find it necessary to cross another body of forest before reaching the continuous grasslands that extended to the Rocky Mountains. These "Timbers" are composed almost entirely of post oak and blackjack oak. Originally the prairie grew beneath the oaks as an understory. Grazing has since reduced the grasses and allowed an undergrowth of shrubs.

The tall grasses are still present and grow luxuriantly in some woodlands as well as in the prairie openings. The area is of geological interest since the existence of the Cross Timbers is largely traceable to "beaches" left by the retreat of the sea in Cretaceous times. The beaches were alternately sandy and clayey and these today are characterized by savanna or forest, and grassland, respectively. The combination of grassland and woodland, with its many miles of grassland-timber border, and the added influence of streams and rivers crossing the vegetation bands, provides a remarkable variety of habitats for plant species and animal life hardly excelled anywhere in the mid-continent prairie. Coastal Prairies occur from the Antonio River on the west to the Louisiana line. Near the coast they are marshlands which merge into tall grass plains that extend inland 50 to 70 miles. Much of this original prairie has been converted to cotton and corn fields. Where grassland remains, cattle grazing is excessive in many areas. The Attwater prairie chickens occur in small numbers. Bobwhite quail are common and long-billed curlews use the prairies and marshes for wintering grounds. The Edwards Plateau until recently was almost a prairie. Extensive burning and livestock grazing have resulted in invasion by cedars, oak, and brush, and an increase of deer, squirrels, and wild turkey. There still is considerable prairie, especially where the soils are shallow and rocky. The Plains of northwest Texas have a diversified agriculture. Extensive grasslands, however, still exist. On higher slopes and hills, short grasses, buffalo and grama grasses, predominate. On lower areas bunchgrasses intermingle with the short grasses. Tall grasses occur on bottomlands, especially along streams. This region of High and Rolling Plains was once the realm of enormous bison herds. Their trails are still evident on some of the remaining pasture lands.

## WISCONSIN

The prairie in Wisconsin has been almost totally destroyed by agricultural usage. John T. Curtis, in THE VEGETATION OF WISCONSIN, wrote in 1959 that probably no more than several thousand acres of the original two million acres now remain with ". . . no single tract of original prairie larger than forty acres known today." As in Minnesota some essentially undisturbed prairie remains along railroad rights of way where boundary fences have prevented the entrance of livestock and destruction by the plow. Even the maintenance of a prairie preserve is difficult owing to outside cultural activities. Curtis wrote, concerning the Faville Prairie

Preserve of the University of Wisconsin, located in Jefferson County, ". . . the prairie has been controlled by burning, but drainage of surrounding lands has greatly changed the water relations on the prairie and has initiated processes of deterioration because no typical dry prairie species are present in the vicinity to take advantage of the new conditions." Artificial prairie communities have been established at the University of Wisconsin Arboretum in Madison.

# Bibliography

ANDERSON, NORMAN L., and JOHN C. WRIGHT. *Grasshopper Investigations on Montana Range Lands*, Montana Agricultural Experiment Station Bulletin No. 486, pp. 1–46 (1952).

ANDERSON, PAUL. *The Reptiles of Missouri*. Columbia: University of Missouri Press, 1965.

BAILEY, ALFRED M., and ROBERT J. NIEDRACH. *Birds of Colorado*. Denver: Denver Museum of Natural History, 1965.

BAILEY, REEVE M., and MARVIN O. ALLUM. *Fishes of South Dakota*. Miscellaneous Publications, Museum of Zoology, University of Michigan, No. 119, June 5, 1962.

BAILEY, VERNON. *Mammals of New Mexico*. North American Fauna No. 53. Washington: Bureau of Biological Survey, 1931.

BAKELESS, JOHN. *The Eyes of Discovery*. New York: Dover Publications, Inc., 1961.

BAKER, MAURICE F. *Prairie Chickens in Kansas*. State Biological Survey of Kansas, Miscellaneous Publication No. 5, pp. 1–68 (1953).

BARKLEY, F. A., and C. C. SMITH. "A Preliminary Study of the Buffalo Wallows in the Vicinity of Norman, Oklahoma." *Proceedings of the Oklahoma Academy of Science*, 14:47–49, 1934.

BERRY, WILLIAM D. *Buffalo Land*. New York: The Macmillan Company, 1961.

BRAGG, ARTHUR N. *Gnomes of the Night: The Spadefoot Toads*. Philadelphia: University of Pennsylvania Press, 1965.

BURT, WILLIAM H., and RICHARD P. GROSSENHEIDER. *A Field Guide to the Mammals*. 2nd ed. Boston: Houghton Mifflin Company, 1964.

BUTLER, J. E. *Interrelations of Autecological Characteristics of Prairie Herbs*. Ph.D. thesis. Madison: University of Wisconsin, 1954.

CAHALANE, VICTOR H. *Mammals of North America*. New York: The Macmillan Company, 1947.

CARPENTER, J. RICHARD. *The Grassland Biome*. Ecological Monographs, 10:617–684, 1940.

CARY, MERRITT. *A Biological Survey of Colorado*. North American Fauna No. 33. Washington: Bureau of Biological Survey, 1911.

———. *Life Zone Investigations in Wyoming*. North American Fauna No. 42. Washington: Bureau of Biological Survey, 1917.

CATLIN, GEORGE. *Letters and Notes on the Manners, Customs, and Condition of the North American Indians*, 2 volumes. Minneapolis: Ross & Haines, Inc., 1965.

CLEMENTS, F. E., and V. E. SHELFORD. *Bio-ecology*. New York: John Wiley & Sons, Inc., 1939.

COCKRUM, E. L. *Mammals of Kansas*. Publications of the Museum of Natural History, University of Kansas, 7:1–303, 1952.

COKER, ROBERT E. *Streams, Lakes, Ponds*. Chapel Hill: University of North Carolina Press, 1954.

CONANT, ROGER. *A Field Guide to Reptiles and Amphibians*. Boston: Houghton Mifflin Company, 1958.

COSTELLO, DAVID F. "Grasslands." In *America's Natural Resources*, edited by Charles H. Callison. New York: Ronald Press, 1967.

COSTELLO, DAVID F. *The World of the Prairie Dog*. Philadelphia and New York: J. B. Lippincott Company, 1970.

COUPLAND, R. T. (ed.) *Grassland Ecosystems of the World: Analysis of Grasslands and Their Uses*. Cambridge, Great Britain; New York; Melbourne: Cambridge University Press, 1979.

CURTIS, JOHN T. *The Vegetation of Wisconsin*. Madison: The University of Wisconsin Press, 1959.

DUNCAN, PATRICIA DuBOSE. *Tallgrass Prairie: The Inland Sea*. Kansas City, Missouri: Lowell Press, 1979.

EIFERT, VIRGINIA S. *River World—Wildlife of the Mississippi*. New York: Dodd, Mead & Company, 1959.

ELLSWORTH, H. L. *Illinois in 1837*. Philadelphia: S. A. Mitchell, 1837.

EVERS, ROBERT A. *Hill Prairies of Illinois*. Illinois Natural History Survey Bulletin, Volume 26, Article 5, 1955.

FASSETT, NORMAN C. *A Manual of Aquatic Plants*. New York: McGraw-Hill, 1940.

FENNEMAN, NEVIN M. *Physiography of Eastern United States*. New York: McGraw-Hill, 1938.

———. *Physiography of Western United States*. New York: McGraw-Hill, 1931.

FERRIS, ROBERT G. (ed.) *Prospector, Cowhand, and Sodbuster*. The National Survey of Historic Sites and Buildings, Volume XI. National Park Service, U.S. Department of the Interior, 1967.

FICHTER, E. "An Ecological Study of Invertebrates of Grassland and Deciduous Shrub Savanna in Eastern Nebraska." *American Midland Naturalist*, 51:321–339, 1954.

FORBES, STEPHEN A. "The Lake as a Microcosm." In *Readings in Ecology*, edited by Edward J. Kormondy. Englewood Cliffs: Prentice-Hall, Inc., 1965.

FRENCH, N. R. (ed.) *Perspectives in Grassland Ecology*. Secaucus, New Jersey: Springer-Verlag New York Inc., 1979.

GARRETSON, MARTEN S. *The American Bison*. New York: New York Zoological Society, 1938.

GERHARD, F. *Illinois As It Is*. Chicago: Keen and Lee, 1857.

GLEASON, HENRY ALLEN. "The Vegetational History of the Middle West." *Annals of the Association of American Geographers*, 12:39–85, 1923.

GRIFFIN, JAMES B. "Eastern North American Archaeology: a Summary." *Science*, 156:175–191, 1967.

GRINNELL, GEORGE BIRD. *The Cheyenne Indians, Their History and Ways of Life*, 2 volumes. New Haven: Yale University Press, 1923.

HALEY, J. E. *Charles Goodnight*. New York: Houghton Mifflin Co., 1936.

HALL, E. R. *Handbook of Mammals of Kansas*. Miscellaneous Publication, Museum of Natural History, University of Kansas, 7:1–303, 1955.

———, and K. R. KELSON. *The Mammals of North America*, 2 volumes. New York: Ronald Press, 1959.

HANSEN, HAROLD C. *The Giant Canada Goose*. Carbondale: Southern Illinois University Press, 1965.

HOOVER, ROBERT L., C. E. TILL, and STANLEY OGILVIE. *The Antelope of Colorado*. State of Colorado, Department of Game and Fish, Technical Bulletin, 4:1–110, 1959.

HOPKINS, ANDREW DELMAR. *Bioclimatics—a Science of Life and Climate Relations*. U.S. Department of Agriculture, Miscellaneous Publication No. 280, 1938.

HOPKINS, DAVID M. "Cenozoic History of the Bering Land Bridge." *Science*, 129:1519–1528, 1959.

HORNADAY, W. T. "The Extermination of the American Bison." *Report of the U.S. National Museum*, 1886–7:369–548, 1889.

HUDSON, GEORGE E. *The Amphibians and Reptiles of Nebraska*. University of Nebraska, Nebraska Conservation Bulletin No. 24, 1942.

JEWELL, M. R. "Aquatic Biology of the Prairie." *Ecology*, 8:289–298, 1927.

JONES, J. KNOX, JR. *Distribution and Taxonomy of Mammals of Nebraska*. University of Kansas Publications, Museum of Natural History, Volume 16, No. 1, 1964.

KING, JOHN A. "Social Behavior, Social Organization, and Population Dynamics in a Black-tailed Prairiedog Town in the Black Hills of South Dakota." Contributions from the Laboratory of Vertebrate Biology, University of Michigan, 67:1–123, 1955.

KLOTS, ALEXANDER B. *A Field Guide to the Butterflies of North America, East of the Great Plains*. Boston: Houghton Mifflin Company, 1951.

KLOTS, ELSIE B. *The New Field Book of Freshwater Life*. New York: G. P. Putnam's Sons, 1966.

LARSON, FLOYD. "The Role of the Bison in Maintaining the Short Grass Plains." *Ecology*, 21:113–121, 1940.

LEGLER, J. M. "Natural History of the Ornate Box Turtle, *Terrapene ornata ornata*." University of Kansas, Museum of Natural History Publication, 11:527–669, 1960.

LEHMANN, VALGENE W. *Attwater's Prairie Chicken: Its Life History and Management*. North American Fauna No. 57. Washington: U.S. Department of the Interior, 1941.

LEONHARDY, F. C. (ed.) *Domebo, a Paleo-Indian Mammoth Kill in the Prairie-Plains*. Contribution No. 1 of the Museum of the Great Plains, Great Plains Historical Association, Lawton, Oklahoma, 1966.

LINCOLN, FREDERICK C. *Migration of Birds*. U.S. Department of the Interior, Fish and Wildlife Service Circular 16, 1950.

MALIN, JAMES C. *The Grassland of North America. Prolegomena to Its History*. 5th printing, with postscript. Gloucester, Mass.: Peter Smith, 1967.

MALONE, CHARLES R. "Killdeer (*Charadrius vociferus* Linnaeus) as a Means of Dispersal for Aquatic Gastropods." *Ecology*, 46:551–552, 1965.

McARDLE, RICHARD E., and DAVID F. COSTELLO. "The Virgin Range" in *The Western Range*. Senate Document 199, 74th Congress, 2nd session. Washington, D.C., 1936.

McCOOK, HENRY CHRISTOPHER. *The Agricultural Ant of Texas*. Philadelphia: Academy of Natural Sciences, 1879.

――――. *The Honey Ants of the Garden of the Gods and the Occident Ants of the American Plains*. Philadelphia: J. B. Lippincott Company, 1882.

McHUGH, TOM. "Social Behavior of the American Buffalo." *Zoologica*, 43: 1–40, 1958.

MOSS, E. H. "The Vegetation of Alberta." *Botanical Review*, 21:493–567, 1955.

PAYNE, JERRY A. "A Summer Carrion Study of the Baby Pig *Sus scrofa* Linnaeus." *Ecology*, 46:592–602, 1965.

PECK, J. M. *A Gazetteer of Illinois*. Jacksonville: R. Goudy, 1834.

PENNAK, ROBERT W. *Fresh-water Invertebrates of the United States*. New York: Ronald Press, 1953.

PETERSON, ROGER TORY. *A Field Guide to Western Birds*. Boston: Houghton Mifflin Company, 1961.

PETTINGILL, OLIN SEWALL, JR. (ed.) *The Bird Watcher's America*. New York: McGraw-Hill Book Company, 1965.

PROCTOR, VERNON W., CHARLES R. MALONE, and VICTOR L. DeVLAMING. "Dispersal of Aquatic Organisms: Viability of Disseminules Recovered from the Intestinal Tract of Captive Killdeer." *Ecology*, 48:672–676, 1967.

RILEY, LAURA and WILLIAM RILEY. *Guide to the National Wildlife Refuges*. Garden City, New York: Anchor Press/Doubleday, 1979.

RISSER, P. G., E. C. BIRNEY, H. D. BLOCKER, S. W. MAY, W. J. PARTON, and J. A. WIENS. (eds.) *The True Prairie Ecosystem*. Stroudsburg, Pennsylvania: Dowden, Hutchinson and Ross, Inc. (In press).

ROE, FRANK GILBERT. *The North American Buffalo*. Toronto: University of Toronto Press, 1951.

SCHWARTZ, CHARLES W. *The Prairie Chicken in Missouri*. Conservation Commission, State of Missouri, 1944.

――――, and ELIZABETH R. SCHWARTZ. *The Wild Mammals of Missouri*. University of Missouri Press and Missouri Conservation Commission, 1959.

SHACKLEFORD, M. W. "Animal Communities of an Illinois Prairie." *Ecology*, 10:126–154, 1929.

SHANTZ, H. L. "The Natural Vegetation of the Great Plains Area." *Annals of the Association of American Geographers*, 13:81–107, 1923.

————, and R. L. PIEMEISEL. "Fungus Fairy Rings in Eastern Colorado and Their Effect on Vegetation." *Journal of Agricultural Research*, 11:191–246, 1917.

SHEA, J. G. *Discovery and Exploration of the Mississippi Valley with the Original Narratives of Marquette, Allouez, Membre, Hennepin and Anastase Douay*. New York, 1853.

SHELFORD, VICTOR E. *The Ecology of North America*. Urbana: University of Illinois Press, 1963.

SHORT, C. W. "Observations on the Botany of Illinois, More Especially in Reference to Autumnal Flora of the Prairies." *Western Journal of Medicine and Surgery*, n.s., 3:185–198, 1845.

SMITH, HOBART M. *Handbook of Amphibians and Reptiles of Kansas*. University of Kansas Publications, Museum of Natural History, Miscellaneous Publication No. 2, 1950.

SMYTH, H. RUCKER. *Amphibians and Their Ways*. New York: The Macmillan Company, 1962.

THOMSON, FRANK. "Last Buffalo of the Black Hills." Privately printed. Spearfish, S.D.

TRANSEAU, EDGAR NELSON. "The Prairie Peninsula." *Ecology*, 16:423–437, 1935.

WALKINSHAW, LAWRENCE H. *The Sandhill Cranes*. Bloomfield Hills, Michigan: Cranbrook Institute of Science, Bulletin 29, 1949.

WEAVER, J. E. *North American Prairie*. Lincoln, Nebr.: Johnsen Publishing Co., 1954.

————, and F. W. ALBERTSON. *Grasslands of the Great Plains*. Lincoln, Nebr.: Johnsen Publishing Company, 1956.

————, and ELLEN ZINK. "Length of Life of Roots of Ten Species of Perennial Range and Pasture Grasses." *Plant Physiology*, 21:201–217, 1946.

WEBB, WALTER PRESCOTT. *The Great Plains*. New York: Grosset & Dunlap, 1931.

WEDEL, W. R. *Prehistoric Man on the Great Plains*. Norman: University of Oklahoma Press, 1961.

WELLS, PHILIP V. "Scarp Woodlands, Transported Grassland Soils, and Concept of Grassland Climate in the Great Plains Region." *Science*, 148:246–249, 1965.

WILDING, L. P. "Radiocarbon Dating of Biogenetic Opal." *Science*, 156:66–67, 1967.

# *Index*

Exhibit Themes

Prairie Pot Hole — Ecotone   Water to Prairie
                Amphibs & Reptiles
                Birds / Insects + other Inverts

A Prairie River

Grass